The
MAN WHO
WROTE
the
PERFECT
NOVEL

Jess and Betty Jo Hay Series

The
MAN WHO
WROTE
the
PERFECT
NOVEL

John Williams, *Stoner,*
and the Writing Life

CHARLES J. SHIELDS

University of Texas Press ❦ Austin

Published by University of Texas Press under license from Lebowski
Publishers/Overamstel Uitgevers B.V.
First English-language edition, 2018
First paperback printing, 2020

Requests for permission to reproduce material from this work should
be sent to:

Permissions
University of Texas Press
P.O. Box 7819
Austin, TX 78713–7819
utpress.utexas.edu/rp-form

∞ The paper used in this book meets the minimum requirements of
ANSI/NISO Z39.48–1992 (R1997) (Permanence of Paper).

LIBRARY OF CONGRESS CATALOGING-IN-PUBLICATION DATA

Names: Shields, Charles J., 1951–, author.
Title: The man who wrote the perfect novel : John Williams, Stoner,
    and the writing life / Charles J. Shields.
Description: First English-language edition. | Austin : University of
    Texas Press, 2018. | Includes bibliographical references and index.
Identifiers: LCCN 2018012653
    ISBN 978-1-4773-2010-5 (pbk : alk. paper)
    ISBN 978-1-4773-1737-2 (library e-book)
    ISBN 978-1-4773-1738-9 (nonlibrary e-book)
Subjects: LCSH: Williams, John, 1922-1994. | Authors, American—
20th century—Biography. | Williams, John, 1922–1994. Stoner.
Classification: LCC PS3545.I5286 Z86 2018 | DDC 813/.54 [B] —dc23
LC record available at https://lccn.loc.gov/2018012653

doi:10.7560/317365

To my wife

Contents

Introduction   ix

PART I. *Nothing But the Night*

Chapter One. He Comes from Texas   3
Chapter Two. "Ho, Ho! Wasn't I the Character Then?"   15
Chapter Three. Rough Draft   28
Chapter Four. Key West   39
Chapter Five. Alan Swallow   47
Chapter Six. Love   58

PART II. *Butcher's Crossing*

Chapter Seven. The Winters Circle   73
Chapter Eight. "Natural Liars Are the Best Writers"   85
Chapter Nine. *Butcher's Crossing*   100
Chapter Ten. Fiasco   112

PART III. *Stoner*

Chapter Eleven. "It Was That Kind of World"   137
Chapter Twelve. "The Williams Affair"   153
Chapter Thirteen. *Stoner*   163

PART IV. *Augustus*

Chapter Fourteen. Bread Loaf and "Up on the Hill"   183
Chapter Fifteen. The Good Guys   192
Chapter Sixteen. "Long Life to the Emperor!"   208

PART V. *The Sleep of Reason*

Poem. "An Old Actor to His Audience"   221
Chapter Seventeen. "How Can Such a Son of a Bitch
    Have Such Talent?"   223
Chapter Eighteen. In Extremis   233

Epilogue. John Williams Redux   249

Acknowledgments   256
Notes   259
Works Consulted   286
A John Williams Bibliography   289
Index   297

Introduction

D riving slowly down North Woolsey Avenue in Fayetteville, Arkansas, hunting for an address, Anne Marie Candido had no idea what kind of house she was looking for. John Williams, she had been given to understand, was a novelist and former professor at the University of Denver. He'd moved to Fayetteville for his health—the lower altitude was easier on his breathing. A friendship between him and John Harrison, dean of the libraries at the University of Arkansas, had led to Williams agreeing to donate his papers to the university's special collections.

But that had been a year ago, in 1987, and all of Williams' materials were still awaiting disposition in cardboard boxes at the library. When Candido, a PhD in literature, heard there was grant money available to hire someone to organize the collection, she applied for the position—anything to do with books and manuscripts sounded interesting.

She hadn't read any of Williams' novels, though. She wondered whether she should have before coming over to his house. Maybe it was presumptuous or discourteous to arrive without having done her homework. Her husband, a professor of English, was a fan of Williams', and he had been glad to praise him: Williams' novels were outstanding—especially *Stoner*, about a Missouri farm boy who becomes a professor. Williams was from Texas during the Depression, so it could be autobiographical. He won the National Book Award for *Augustus*, a fictional life of the Roman emperor. But the committee split the fiction award between him and John Barth that year—the first time it had ever happened in that category. Some said Williams got half as a kind of consolation prize for the committee having ignored *Stoner* ten years earlier. And there was one other novel, too, which was about buffalo hunting—*Butcher's Crossing*, published early in his career. Too bad his books were out of print, but they had just never caught on for some reason.

Candido slowed down to see the house numbers on North Woolsey, a humble street like an afterthought without curbs or streetlights. She expected some kind of rambling old place, fit for a professor in retirement, an author whose career had peaked some time ago. And then there it was—number 1450. Set back in the bare January trees, a small house with a large, steeply pitched roof like a building on a farm that had been remodeled. It looked rural, somehow.

For the next three months, she arrived at John Williams' home every other week with her special file folder of mysteries. Items in his papers, such as letters without dates, handwritten drafts of correspondence, photos of unidentified people—oddments from his life that might be important. She wanted to be thorough. So she sat at the dining room table, observing him as he read from the folder.

He was a small man, petite, in his late sixties with thick hair that was still resolutely dark. Could he be part Native American? He was cordial, almost courtly. He took care to be presentable for their sessions. House slippers, green slacks, and tangerine shirt with socks to match on one occasion. His voice was deep, a baritone with a trained, musical quality. He chuckled at his own droll comments. Most striking, though, were his eyes: very large, light blue, and owlish, behind a pair of heavy, black-framed glasses that she never saw him without.

Now and then while they were working together, Nancy, his wife, would pause during her comings and goings to check on them. She was tall and much younger than he was. As a couple, they seemed comfortable around each other, Nancy making the point that the mystery file was "John's thing."

It was curious how uninterested he was about dates and the details of his life. Often he would just smile and say, "I don't remember—I can't recall," as if some kind of story had already been told, and these typewritten carbons and penciled notes were like wood shavings from a completed cabinet, or lint from the office he'd occupied for thirty years in the English Department at Denver. Sometimes, as they talked, he took a mist inhaler from his pants pocket and pumped a puff of vapor into his mouth. He was a chain-smoker, never quit. If he wanted to fetch something from his second-floor study, she waited. She heard him struggling to breathe between his slow footfalls on the stairs.

She grew to like him. His fields of study had been Elizabethan poetry and creative writing. By coincidence, her father had attended the University of Denver and majored in English, and he was an English Renaissance scholar too. She invited John and Nancy to her house for dinner the next time he was visiting.

The two men did have much in common, and she and her husband enjoyed hearing a pair of older heads reminisce about their careers in academe. Both World War II veterans, they'd been in graduate school in the 1950s. And they'd both known many of the same people—names that had kept appearing in Williams' papers—the literary critic Yvor Winters and his wife, the novelist Janet Lewis; the poets Wallace Stegner, John Ciardi, and J. V. Cunningham; and Alan Swallow, the owner of a small press in Denver. So many names from long ago that the room, illuminated by the candlelight, seemed inhabited by listening ghosts, eager to hear themselves mentioned.

She found it hard to reconcile the English Department talk with a photograph of John she'd come across in his papers. It was a black-and-white studio portrait from the 1940s, the kind you'd have to make an appointment for. He was in his early twenties then. In the picture, he was wearing a lightweight sports jacket with a small-checkered pattern, over a button-down white shirt with a dark, regimental-stripe tie. His face was turned slightly to the side, his smooth cheek reflecting some of the light that fell favorably on his narrow lip mustache, parted in two artistic brushstrokes, left and right—the image of a young man who wants to give the impression of sophistication. She hadn't seen it on the book jacket on any of his novels, so maybe it was taken before he'd been published.

Now he was across the table, half a century later. She caught herself thinking how lined his face had become since that photograph. Proof once again of her belief that sometimes you can tell just by looking at people how interesting their lives must have been.

The
MAN WHO
WROTE
the
PERFECT
NOVEL

PART I

Nothing But the Night

CHAPTER ONE

He Comes from Texas

Don't read so much, you'll make your brain tired.

—JOHN WILLIAMS' GRANDFATHER, 1930S

To the jobless men killing time in Wichita Falls, Texas, in 1939, John Ed Williams—the son of the janitor at the post office—invited a second look as he passed by after school to his job assisting customers at the Lovelace Bookstore.

Students like the Williams boy were becoming a fairly common sight downtown, ever since Hardin Junior College had opened just a few years earlier. In the early 1920s, college classes of about seventy-five students had met on the third floor of the high school at the intersection of Avenue H and Coyote Boulevard. But after oil tycoon John G. Hardin plowed close to a million dollars into a whole new campus on forty acres of former pastureland in the city's south end, going to college had become a possibility for almost two thousand students. Wichita Falls, formerly just a railhead in northern Texas for cattle drives, now had a two-year college for the grandchildren of pioneers—a point of pride among the residents—and it had been built, it needed to be said, right in the middle of the worst economic depression in the nation's history. The banks had gone bust; the Great Plains were ripped up from overfarming; and during the long, ruinous droughts, mountainous dust storms the color of dirty snow blew across northern Texas.

But here was a flamboyant young man who apparently expected better times. John Ed wore a blazer and pleated trousers. Instead of a tie, he wore a silk scarf, as if he were imitating some kind of English country squire or poet. He acted as if he were from another time and place. And indeed, in his mind at least, he was.

––––––––––

John Edward Williams' grandparents, Elbert G. Walker, from Virginia, and his wife, née Laura Belle Lee, from Tennessee, were southerners. Elbert was twenty-five, and Laura Belle only sixteen, when they married in 1886. Within a few years they headed west, drawn by the Oklahoma Land Rush of 1889, which opened for settlement two million acres of the best free public land in the United States. The Walkers' two daughters, Emma and her younger sister, Amelia—John Ed's mother—were born in 1896 and 1898, respectively, in Oklahoma's Choctaw Indian Territory.

Elbert Walker's line of work was market gardening—raising vegetables for local sale. But he seemed convinced that there was always a better situation to be had elsewhere. For the next twenty years, the Walkers circled the lower Great Plains, picking up and starting over each time. By 1910, they had left Oklahoma and settled on a farm in Texas outside of Young, a prosperous hamlet of cotton farmers and cattle ranchers. Then, ten years on, they could be found dirt farming in Logan, Arkansas, in the Arkansas River Valley, where many of their neighbors had come from Kentucky and Tennessee. Amelia and Emma—both young ladies now in their early twenties—lived at home, although Emma taught at the school. But Elbert was still not satisfied with his lot, and he decided, in his early fifties, that things would work out better if they went down to Clarksville in northeast Texas, where his mother had settled until her death in 1908, and they moved there.

He had reason to believe he might be right, because Clarksville was doing well in the 1920s. Its 3,500 residents enjoyed the services of two banks, two newspapers, two flourmills, and an electric power plant that illuminated homes and businesses. The biggest employer in town was a factory that crushed cottonseed for its light golden oil, filling the air with an aroma that was sweet and nutty. On Saturdays, farmers sold watermelons, livestock, and vegetables in the town square from trucks and wagons. In the center, above them, a statue of a Confederate soldier stood high on a twenty-foot pedestal facing north—its face and uniform eroded smooth like a pillar of salt from the weather—perpetually ready to repulse another Yankee invasion. Sunday mornings, the ministers of seven churches, five white and two black, delivered sermons to their congregations.

It was in Clarksville that Amelia Walker, twenty-five, met J. E. Jewell, a gentleman a few years older than she. They married on January 21, 1921. Nineteen months later, she gave birth to a son, John Edward, named after his father.

Like the Walkers, J. E. Jewell was comfortable with impermanence. He shared his father-in-law's yearning to find El Dorado along the way to somewhere else. Together, the two men led their families to their next destination, Wichita Falls—250 miles north— the scene of the first memories of the little boy who would become John Ed Williams.

————

In the early 1920s, Wichita Falls was infected with oil fever. Ever since the Lucas No. 1 Well near the town of Beaumont on the Gulf Coast had struck "black gold" in 1901, oil fever had been boiling over in Texas. Fresh water that smelled like rotten eggs meant there was a pocket of oil below somewhere—maybe a whole sea of it—trapped inside a salt dome. Giant drill bits, centered by A-frame derricks, twisted down deeper and deeper into the earth like iron hypodermic needles. At Sour Lake Springs, where the water stank like burning sulfur, a black sticky plume of petroleum flared a hundred feet high. The oil reservoir was so huge that before long, derricks sprouted everywhere, like rows of wooden Eiffel Towers, hundreds of them, serviced by thousands of roustabouts who rinsed the dust and grit from their throats in fifty-two saloons.

In 1918, "Texas tea" erupted near the edge of the Wichita Falls city limits. Fortune-seekers stampeded the boardinghouses, willing to pay ridiculous rates. If no rooms were available, newcomers slept in shacks, in tents, and in cars and trucks, deluging the local schools with bewildered children. Bank deposits increased by 400 percent. Street corners became outdoor exchanges where buyers and sellers wrangled over real estate, water permits, and deeds to mines. Companies that existed on paper only advertised themselves with "come-and-get-it" names like Over the Top, Sam's Clover Leaf, Bit Hit, and O Boy!

The Walkers and the Jewells followed the flood. J. E. found an apartment for his wife and infant son, and a job selling animal feed and agricultural supplies at Miracle Coal & Feed Store. The Walkers, now without their elder daughter, Emma, who had stayed behind to teach in Clarksville, rented a farm a few miles outside the city on Walnut Road. But at least everyone was in the proximity of riches.

————

The work at the feed store was steady, but J. E. wanted a better life. The *Wichita Falls Times* carried classified advertisements hinting that a clever man could climb higher—like the one promising "An opportunity to make some real money. Quick action, too. If you have a few hundred dollars in cash, see Mr. McKinney at the Morgan Bldg." The nature of the opportunity for "real money" didn't need explaining. You'd have to be living on the moon not to know it had to do with oil.

With opportunities for "quick action" also came frauds, double-talk, and the old switcheroo, however. The get-rich-quick game was not for the credulous. One of the biggest scams in memory had turned the Wichita Fall city fathers into a laughingstock in 1919. A property title researcher named J. D. McMahon offered to answer the demand for office space by building the first skyscraper in Texas at the corner of Seventh and La Salle Streets. Local investors envisioned a business beehive, a tower of ringing phones and ticker-tape machines opposite the prestigious St. James Hotel. After eagerly inspecting the blueprints, they raised the equivalent of $2.7 million to build it. But the completed Newby-McMahon Building, though handsomely appointed, was only 40 feet high, 10 feet wide, and 18 feet deep. The staircase took up a quarter of the interior. Outraged, the investors sued McMahon, only to have the judge rule against them when it was pointed out that the blueprints clearly stated that the wonder of Wichita Falls would be 480 *inches* high, not feet.

According to a story told in the family, J. E. made his move as an investor one day at an open-air exchange downtown where transactions consisted of handshakes, wads of cash, and contracts signed on the spot. He purchased some land located outside the city, intending to turn it around for profit by selling it to another speculator. He found a prospective buyer, showed him the property, and got paid in cash. On the way home, he stopped at a gas station to fill up. It's said that he mentioned his good luck. If he did, it marked him as a tinhorn who talked too much, like the hapless Swede in Stephen Crane's "The Blue Hotel," who literally bragged himself to death. A hitchhiker approached and asked for a lift into town; Jewell, maybe feeling magnanimous, told him to get in. At some point during the ride, the stranger stuck a gun in Jewell's ribs, forced him to pull over, and killed him. A roll of bills that had already changed hands once that day ended up in still another man's pocket. The murderer continued off into the wilderness on foot.[1]

However, the real casualty might have been the truth. An examination of newspapers both in Clarksville, where the Jewells were married, and in Wichita Falls, where they lived, turns up nothing about the murder of a John Edward Jewell. Court records make no mention of it in either location. Furthermore, the robbery scenario is problematic. Why would the killer abandon a car with a fresh tankful of gas and a dead driver?

Perhaps the last glimpse of J. E. Jewell, alive and heading for the red horizon, appears at the bottom of the front page of the August 12, 1924, edition of the *Vernon Record*, published fifty miles from Wichita Falls: "Cupid is taking a vacation according to officials of the County Clerk's office. Only two marriage licenses have been issued—one for a Miss Rose Lee Owen and her fiancé, J. W. Todd; the second for a Mrs. L. L. Moreland and J. E. Jewell."

Very little has been recorded about John Williams' father, and much less was remembered. Many years later, when Williams was filling out his own marriage license, on the line asking for his father's birthplace he wrote "Unknown."[2] "Unknown" will have to stand for Mr. Jewell's final disposition in the world, too.

Without a husband, Amelia listed herself in the Wichita Falls phone directory with "(wid)" after her name, indicating she was a widow. The suffix "(wid)" served to safeguard the reputation of an unmarried woman with a child. On the other hand, since the abbreviation was voluntary, it could also be interpreted as a kind of plea from a young woman possessing just a year of high school, and raising a small child alone. A studio photograph taken of her about that time shows Mrs. Jewell, quite lovely and dark-haired, gently balancing John Ed, a blond toddler, who is demonstrating, with a slightly surprised look, that he can stand on his mother's lap.

Not long after that, Amelia received a gentleman caller—George Clinton Williams.

———

Ten years older than Amelia, George Williams hailed from Tyler, Texas. During World War I he had served in the National Guard, claiming an exemption from the draft as the sole supporter of a wife and a daughter in Dallas. His people were in banking, but he had shunned the family's expectations, preferring instead to get paid on Fridays for shift work. He had driven a city bus, toted bricks in construction, and picked crops. He was squat, with a broad back and large hands.

George proposed and Amelia accepted. For a woman not quite thirty, marriage meant a husband, a wage earner, and a father for her boy. It was another fresh beginning, the sort her migrant parents had counted on so many times in their lives. Romance may have played a part too, but the reality is that Amelia's options were few.

But George, a heavy drinker, couldn't make a go of it, not even with an oil boom all around. Several times, he and Amelia jumped the rent in the middle of the night before the landlord arrived with the sheriff in the morning.[3] Six months after they had moved into Wichita Falls proper, George and Amelia, with John Ed in tow, arrived with their belongings back at Grandfather Walker's farm just as he was putting in the spring vegetables. By then, another hard-luck relative had joined the Walker household as well: an elderly aunt who rocked all day in the parlor except to announce, now and then, "Well, I believe I'll go to the bathroom!"[4] In May 1925, Amelia gave birth to John Ed's sister, who was given a boy's name, George Rae, because her father would have preferred a son.[5]

Defeat seemed to follow Amelia. When John was four, a terrible and touching image of his mother impressed itself on his memory. He heard a sound coming from the closet in the hallway. Opening the door, he saw his mother kneeling behind a curtain of swaying coats and jackets, hiding like a child, her face in her hands, sobbing.[6]

———

Because they were poor, and the work they did was manual labor, silence was like a physical presence for the Walkers and Jewells. Williams later wrote, of the farm family in *Stoner*, "In the evenings, the three of them sat in the small kitchen lighted by a single kerosene lamp, staring into the yellow flame; often during the hour or so between supper and bed, the only sound that could be heard was weary movement of a body in a straight chair and the soft creak of a timber giving a little beneath the age of the house."[7] Fortunately, there was a radio, and John Ed was allowed to listen to it with the adults, "watching it," he remembered, as if voices became faces in the yellow glow of the dial.[8]

Also, there were a few magazines to read. For the price of ten cents, his mother could escape into the pages of some of her favorites. She doted on *Ranch Romances*, *Clues*, *Love Romances*, and *Sweetheart Stories*. Rather than allow her son to become too interested in swooning and kisses, however, Amelia introduced him to *Flying Stories*, a monthly magazine featuring the Skywaymen—leather-helmeted, square-jawed pilots—who crossed the Arctic, flew low over thrashing waves in hurricanes, and rescued fellow aviators from their tattered biplanes in midair. In *The Blue Book of Fiction and Adventure*, there were better stories, by contributors such as Sax Rohmer, Agatha Christie, and Edgar Rice Burroughs. From the school library, he borrowed every western by Zane Grey he could get his hands on, including the most famous, *Riders of the Purple Sage*.[9] Grey, a midwestern dentist who had suffered under his father's authority (and beatings), found an outlet for his passions writing novels about an imagined American West with a wildness almost untouched by formal law and order, and governed instead by an unwritten code of loyalty, generosity, fair play, and integrity. Grey's idealized frontier restored men and women to natural grace, as if they had returned to Eden:

> Venters turned out of the gorge, and suddenly paused stock-still, astounded at the scene before him. The curve of the great stone bridge had caught the sunrise, and through the magnificent arch burst a glorious stream of gold that shone with a long slant down into the center of Surprise Valley. Only through the arch did any sunlight pass, so that all the rest of the valley lay still asleep, dark green, mysterious, shadowy, merging its level into walls as misty and soft as morning clouds.[10]

Williams would one day challenge the paradise myth of the Old West in *Butcher's Crossing*, especially Emerson's belief that living close to nature imparts virtue to human souls. But during his boyhood, John and his mother shared a wholesale love of stories—the more melodramatic and more vivid the better—for their power to spirit them away from the humdrumness of rural life.

———

Perhaps that's why Amelia Walker waited until John Ed was nine years old to tell him the most important story of his life. Her decision to give away the secret of his birth might have been an act of love, because there are indications that John was unhappy around George Williams, who was often described as "a difficult man." Revealing the truth might have been a mother's attempt at reassurance.

Given her love of romance, it's likely she presented it as a tale that her reader-son would appreciate. The setting and plot weren't uncommon in the West—the Walkers were humble people, farmers, who had worked hard all their lives. But a mysterious stranger and a tragedy had changed everything. John's last name wasn't Williams—not legally, because George hadn't adopted him—it was Jewell. George was his stepfather; and his little sister, George Rae, who had just turned five, was his half-sister. His father, J. E. Jewell, had been murdered when John was still an infant, ambushed and killed while he was on his way home to his family, years ago, and the killer had never been caught.

Williams later claimed this revelation about his identity—a thunderclap from his mother's lips—didn't affect him, because George felt "unfamiliar" to him.[11] But it's hard to believe that a nine-year-old boy could have been so philosophical. Personal identity is fundamental. Immediately after the creation of the world, God gives Adam the responsibility of assigning names to things to distinguish himself from other creatures. And the psychological work of constructing self-identity is repeated every time one child asks another, "What's your name?" In fairy tales, the unveiling of a secret, *hidden* identity can be momentous—the ugly duckling who becomes a swan, the despised stepdaughter who fits the glass slipper, or, more recently, the boy who learns he's a "wizard, and a thumpin' good one"—because it cracks open self-perception, usually revealing fantastic, unrealized potential.

But in John Williams' case, news that he was not the person he thought he was called into question the importance of telling the truth. Until the moment of his mother's confession, the adults in his family had been deliberately lying to him. They had all been complicit in perpetuating a fiction about him. Whether they did so out of love or shame, the gist was the same: they had known all along, but he didn't. The lesson was that if everyone believes something is true then it might as well be. Lies, fictions, whoppers, and fibs could create meaning, and the best ones were the most convincing. Hadn't teachers called out "John Williams?" for the roll every morning, and hadn't he answered, "Here!"? For John Ed, the future novelist, the experience was profound, if terribly painful.

————

About this time, Grandfather Walker decided his grandson needed some toughening-up. Although the boy spent time outdoors doing his chores before and after school, he spent a lot of time in the house reading. When he talked, he stammered, as if he was fearful.[12] "Don't read so much," Walker cautioned him. "You'll make your brain tired."[13]

So when John was ten, come the first cold day of winter, Walker got down his .22 rifle and escorted his grandson across the yard over to the pig pen. "If you're going to eat pork, you should know where it comes from." They discussed which one was the healthiest-looking pig, then the old man climbed into the pen, took a couple of short boards, and used them to swat the animal on the rump and sides, steering it toward the fence. It ambled up to John, sticking out its muddy snout to snuffle at him. Walker leashed the pig to the fence post so it would stay there.

"Shoot it," he said. The old man tapped at a spot right between his eyes.

John Ed raised the barrel of the rifle, aimed through the fence boards, and pulled the trigger. The rifle jumped and the report sent the other pigs scampering away. The old man knelt, reached with a butcher knife through the fence, and sliced the pig's jowl, releasing a splash of blood on its front feet. It collapsed butt first on the dirt then lolled halfway to one side, bleeding out through the gash. They got the truck, tied the rope around the pig's hind trotters, and dragged it over to the barn.

They filled an oil barrel standing on bricks with buckets of water from the pump, set fire to kindling underneath, and waited until it turned into a scalding bath. When Walker judged the water was hot enough, he looped the free end of a rope through a pulley overhead on a barn joist. Then they hauled the pig up into the air by its hind legs, swung it into place, and lowered it like it was diving into the boiling water. After a few minutes, they pulled it out again, steaming and clean. John Ed helped scrape the bristles off the hide until the flesh was white. With a smaller knife, Walker cored the rectum, pulled it out, went around to the front, split the crotch, and tied off the pizzle so there wouldn't be pee everywhere.[14]

In *Butcher's Crossing*, Williams' description of an experienced buffalo hunter skinning a carcass carries the same precision and matter-of-factness:

The hide parted neatly with a faint ripping sound. With a stubbier knife, he cut around the bag that held the testicles, cut through the cords that held them and the limp penis to the flesh; he separated the testicles, which were the size of small crab-apples, from the other parts of the bag, and tossed them to one side; then he slit the few remaining inches of hide to the anal opening.

"I always save the balls," he said. "They make mighty good eating, and they put starch in your pecker."[15]

Then Walker took a hacksaw, held the pig's head steady by one ear, so the carcass wouldn't swing, and sawed through the neck. It separated and fell heavily to the floor of the barn. He shoved it away with his boot. He inserted the butcher knife into the neck hole and flayed upward through the chest, stopping to pull the rib cage apart, and stepped back out of the way. The gut sack leaned out and tumbled through, landing wetly at his feet.

It was hog butchering, a routine task on a farm, but Williams, observing it with a writer's eye, noted a procedure that had a beginning, middle, and end. How a beast falls from a gunshot and surrenders to the knife; how its flesh comes off like rind on a fruit; how slaughtering an animal was done rapidly and clinically.

––––––––

As John Ed was leaving childhood and beginning adolescence in the early 1930s, his family was swept into a new life. In 1932, the third year of the Great Depression, Franklin Delano Roosevelt's confidence about the future—his campaign song was "Happy Days Are Here Again"—carried him into the White House. During his first one hundred days in office, billions of dollars rolled out from Washington across the nation through the New Deal federal recovery and reform programs.

The Williamses were among the beneficiaries. In Wichita Falls, at the corner of Tenth and Lamar Streets, built where a decrepit Methodist Church had been, an enormous new post office advertised for custodians. George Williams applied and landed a civil service job at a pay rate equal to an entry-level accountant. He and Amelia rented a house on Lee Street. In 1938, John Ed's grandparents, Elbert and Laura Walker, left their hardscrabble farm and joined them. For over fifty years, Grandmother Walker had followed her husband from one place to another: from Tennessee in the 1880s, to Oklahoma Indian Territory, to Texas, to Arkansas, and then back to Texas again. But now, at sixty-eight, she was dying from cancer, and she passed away soon after moving from the farm into town.

Not long after her death, George purchased a good-sized house on Broad Street for Amelia, the children, and their grandfather. It was their first residence not owned by someone else.

CHAPTER TWO

"Ho, Ho! Wasn't I the Character Then?"

*We linger for an instant in a morass of stupidity and
conceit and then we graduate from high school.*
—JOHN WILLIAMS, AGE SEVENTEEN, 1939

The subject of a biography should be the person's search for identity. Answering the question "Who am I?" is the great work of life, and all of a person's efforts are, in some way, responses to that unvoiced question, which begins to be heard in childhood as soon as children perceive themselves as different and apart from everyone else. The amount of freedom to spend creating the opus of the self isn't the same for everyone, but at least a basic sense of "Who am I?" belongs to any child who knows where he lives, who his parents are, who loves him, who doesn't, and so on.

John Williams' discovery at age nine that he was someone else— not his father's son, not a Williams, and not related to his little sister, George Rae, in the way he had been led to believe—upended his world. The narrative of who he was, the one he had been telling himself all along, was actually a story about another boy who was like him, but not him. He had the skin of John Williams on him, and the adults in his family—his mother, stepfather, and grandparents—had agreed to present him that way to everyone, including himself. It would be hard to imagine a more convincing early lesson for a future writer about the power of words to suspend disbelief.

In the meantime, the question "Who am I?" was reopened just when he was entering adolescence, a period when young people try out various faces on the world to see how they're received. Because of what he'd found out, he was more susceptible than most to choosing a radically new appearance, one that would compensate for how he had been fooled, one that would give others the impression of competence and self-possession. Ideally, too, it would be in sync with his love of books and stories, and his fascination with the heroism of airmen and frontiersmen.

One afternoon when he was thirteen, in the spring of 1936, he saw such a character—a persona, really—at the movies in Wichita Falls. The experience enchanted him.

———

John was invited by an aunt to bring a friend to see the film *A Tale of Two Cities*, starring Ronald Colman as Sidney Carton. Before buying their tickets, they stopped for lunch, and the boys ordered glasses of cold buttermilk, waiting to drink it until their lady chaperone excused herself to use the restroom. Once the coast was clear, John produced a cough syrup bottle filled with whiskey—probably from his stepfather's stash—and sociably poured half of the contents into his friend's glass and the rest into his. By the time his aunt returned from freshening up, the boys were wiping off buttermilk mustaches and grinning.[1]

As a prank, it was a good one for a pair of adolescent boys. And the spiked buttermilk gave Williams his first real glow from liquor in public, besides adding to the excitement of watching a splendid Hollywood version of Dickens' nineteenth-century novel. Westerns were the usual matinee fare, and audiences were delighted by cowboy idols on the screen and their cold "violence without rage," as Williams later called it.[2] But Ronald Colman's performance thrilled him in ways no gunfighter ever had.[3]

In *A Tale of Two Cities*, Sidney Carton is an eighteenth-century English barrister wasting his talent with drinking and self-pity. But then he takes the case of French aristocrat Charles Darnay, arrested on charges of spying for the French. During the proceedings, Carton meets Darnay's love interest, Lucie Manette. Carton falls in love with her and wishes he were a better man, someone worthy of a woman like her. Ironically, Carton and Darnay resemble each other enough to be brothers, an allusion to the type of person Carton might have been. For Lucie's sake, Carton makes the case for Darnay's innocence brilliantly and brings in a verdict of not guilty, after which Darnay and Lucie marry and return to Paris.

But sometime later, Darnay is arrested again, this time caught in the net of the Reign of Terror, and he's sentenced to die. Carton sees a chance to atone for his failed life and ensure that he will live honorably in Lucie's memory. Because they look so much alike, he can impersonate Darnay and take his place on the guillotine.

As he waits to be called at the foot of the guillotine—an innocent man exchanging his life for another's—Carton, the former cynic, is at peace. "It is a far, far better thing that I do, than I have ever done; it is a far, far better rest I go to than I have ever known." As he ascends the steps, the heavens above the rooftops of Paris come into view, underlining his redemption.[4]

Williams was smitten—he thought he'd seen a parable unfold with a message just for him. On the one hand, *A Tale of Two Cities* is a story about injustice, oppression, and one man's Christ-like sacrifice for another, but it appealed to him because it is also a fable about two identities, like the prince and the pauper story.

Carton and Darnay are two halves, dark and light. One embodies lost chances and bad luck; the other, his double, represents goodness, rectitude, and success. Ronald Colman delivered the character of Carton with a combination of grace, sex appeal, and vulnerability. His insouciant response to heartbreak is a jaunty tip of the hat. Inwardly, he suffers, but outwardly he appears cavalier, a little mad, the poet with a cloven hoof. But by bearing the worst of things with dignity, right up until the moment of his death, he turns misfortune into a moral triumph.

Here was a message, a view of life that Williams—a smallish boy who felt different from others—could take to heart. Maybe it was possible to will yourself to be the kind of person you wanted to be. Practicing that person, performing him, despite other people's skepticism, might bring off a new invention, which would be you, the hero of your own life.

A week later, his eighth-grade English teacher at Reagan Junior High, a Miss Annie Laurie Smith, assigned an essay on a topic of the students' choosing. John Ed pounced on Colman's performance as the subject of his. Miss Smith, head of the English Department, was his favorite teacher, and he tried hard to impress her.

A few days later, he listened abashed and proud as she read his paper aloud to the class. She finished by saying that his analysis of Colman as Sidney Carton was "the work of a college student."[5] Not only did she praise it, she honored it by placing it in her special display case in the hallway reserved for outstanding work.

He never forgot that moment. "It was one of the first compliments I had received about anything I'd done," he later said. In the stroke of a day, he had been elevated from ordinary to, as one of his classmates put it, "someone special among us."[6]

————

Moving into town as a result of his stepfather getting a job at the post office put John Ed within the boundaries of Wichita Falls Senior High School. With Miss Smith's praise still ringing in his ears, he began his freshman year in 1936.

From then on, he counted himself as writing with "serious purpose and intent." He joined the school newspaper and submitted poems to the literary magazine. Writing, he said, was "something I could do, and I felt some confidence in it."[7] From the school and public library he borrowed armloads of titles by Willa Cather, John Steinbeck, and William Faulkner, fastening on Thomas Wolfe as his favorite author. Reading *Look Homeward Angel* introduced him to the journey of the young artist-hero Eugene Gant, who rises above circumstances in many ways similar to Williams' own. It felt like a "religious experience," he said, realizing that his upbringing didn't disqualify him from becoming a writer, which he thought would be a romantic life.[8]

He fell upon the school library with such ferociousness, in fact, that the *Wichita Times Record* ran a feature about the student "poet-critic" who was reading "four to five novels, poetry collections, or biographies a week." The reporter posed the young dynamo beside a table stacked high with books, contrasting Williams' size with his appetite for reading. "You, reader, are the victim of an optical illusion. Those books aren't over John Ed Williams' head. He has read them all and a great many more." The high school librarian spoke proudly of him, confirming that John Ed was "the heaviest and most constant reader of the entire student body. No other student even approaches him in the number of books read."[9]

The joke comparing his size to the height of the books behind him was an on-the-spot inspiration of the photographer, probably, but it called attention to Williams' height. In vain he waited for the growth spurt that teenagers usually get. But by the time he could drive it was plain that he would not be a "tall lank boy" like Wolfe's Eugene Gant. He was leveling off in the mid-five-foot range and possessed of a stubbornly small frame that resisted the effects of exercise that might add to his shoulders and chest. Aware that tall men get a kind of built-in respect that is not available to others, he worked at ratcheting up his presence and masculinity instead.[10]

He was careful about his appearance and laid out his clothes as ensembles, a habit that never left him. His cinematic hero Ronald Colman appeared in movie adaptations of James Hilton's novel *Lost Horizon* and Anthony Hope's *Prisoner of Zenda,* modeling the kind of sophistication that Williams wished to have. In the breast pocket of his sports jacket, he tucked a folded handkerchief. He let his hair grow long like Eugene Gant's, combing it carefully before the mirror every morning. To conquer his stammer, he enrolled in drama courses, learning elocution and how to produce a baritone voice that came from his midsection. He discovered from school productions that he was a good actor, and wrote a one-man "imaginary sketch of Abraham Lincoln's musings some troubled afternoon in the White House," which he performed at a school assembly. It's a sign of his willpower that he would write and perform an original piece before the student body, believing that he had every right to seek their attention because he was talented.

In the high school yearbook, the *Coyote,* he listed the two things he liked: first, "Me," and, as would befit a Byronic young man like himself, the color "Black." (One afternoon cleaning his .22 rifle at home, he shot himself in the shoulder and was taken by ambulance to the hospital. After that episode, he strolled around the downtown jauntily smoking a cigarette, his other arm in a sling. Who could doubt that he was mad, bad, and dangerous to know?)[11]

Sex raised its tumid head, of course. At the Lovelace Bookstore on Ninth Street where he worked after school, an older boy, T. G. Willis, manager of the stamp-collecting department, loaned him a censored edition of D. H. Lawrence's *Lady Chatterley's Lover*, which had been rinsed for American readers of "fuck," "orgasm," and "penis." But it was still instructive: "And he took the leaves from her hair, kissing her damp hair, and the flowers from her breasts, and kissed her breasts, and kissed her navel, and kissed her maiden-hair, where he left the flowers threaded."

For rougher stuff, there were drugstore magazines, such as *Spicy Adventure*, *Spicy Mystery*, or *Spicy Detective*, copies of which he sometimes picked up on his way home. *Spicy Detective* carried a comic strip starring "Sally Sleuth," a maverick crime fighter. The point of the comic was to have her clothes come off just a few panels into the story. In one episode, crooks tied her by her wrists to a chair back; she was wearing nothing except panties, and they whipped her.

By his senior year, he had acquired a reputation as a kind of finer soul among his classmates. He was editor of the school paper, and the previous year, he had been awarded first place in the state poetry contest. "Hail and farewell!" he wrote in an essay for the 1939 yearbook. "We linger for an instant in a morass of stupidity and conceit and then we graduate from high school." He had finished in three years instead of four. ("Ho, ho!" he laughed when that was read aloud to him many years later. "Wasn't I the character then?")[12]

In August, he enrolled at Hardin Junior College. A young man now, and a college student, he adapted the attire of an artist, wearing a knotted scarf above his open shirt—an outfit that gave the broken-down farmers and unemployed businessmen on the street corners of Wichita Falls reason to believe that the younger generation was going to hell.

———

Despite the hard times of the 1930s, Hardin Junior College offered students a wide range of academic choices. But Williams fed his imagination and career ambitions mainly from the buffet of extra-curricular clubs and activities. By the end of his first semester, he was so involved in things that he was flunking freshman English. His excuse was, "I had already read most of what we were studying. And I had read a lot of it in high school."[13]

He preferred putting his energies into things that showcased his talents. He added his name to the roster of every organization dedicated to self-expression: the literary club, the student senate, the student newspaper, and the Blue Curtain drama group. He made friends with two students who were serious about becoming actors—Marjorie Coleman and Jack Newsom. On Thanksgiving, they performed for broadcast on KWFT, a new radio station in Wichita Falls, an original drama by Williams called *Dr. Cooper Speaking*, about an English headmaster. It went so well that he wrote and directed one every week for KWFT after that, for which he would "kind of produce it, play a part myself and get local actors around to play the others."[14] George Rae, his half-sister and a teen-ager now, basked in the afterglow of her brother's prominence in the local arts scene. She began telling her high schools friends that she, too, planned to act, commencing an affectionate rivalry with her brother.

But come September 1939, he didn't reenroll at Hardin. The reason was money, he said, which is surprising, because he had a part-time job at a bookstore, and his stepfather, George, was a civil service employee who, according to the 1940 census, was one of the better-paid workers on Broad Street.

Williams later said too many people in Wichita Falls cared about money. It was "absolutely pervasive. . . . They were conscious of the lack of money and the possession of money . . . a kind of consciousness about the *existence* of money that seemed involved with identity."[15] It could be that despite his stylish clothes—paid for with his own money—and his accomplishments in school, some of his peers kept in mind that he was the son of the post office janitor. It wasn't lack of money that kept him from reenrolling in college, perhaps, but the social side of student life.

In any case, he spent what would have been the fall semester of his sophomore year preparing to stage a piece of theater for the public—Thornton Wilder's *Our Town*, the winner of the 1938 Pulitzer Prize for drama. With his friend Jack Newsom as codirector, the two young men held open auditions. To play the townspeople in crowd scenes, John prevailed on twenty-four members of his family's church, First Presbyterian, to take the parts. For the role of Emily Webb, the female lead, they cast their friend Marjorie Coleman, who had been acting in summer stock in upstate New York.[16]

Our Town was so innovative for its time that the *Wichita Daily Times* gently primed readers about what to expect: "Instead of a rising curtain to open the show, there will be the stage manager— Jack Newsom in this production. The stage manager starts it off by making the audience acquainted with Grovers Corners, New Hampshire, right there on the stage behind him. Then the natives begin to stir about in the morning air, and the play is on." Because the "entire play is of such disarming simplicity," there would be no sets, and actors would mime the props. All that was necessary was the audience's imagination, the newspaper guaranteed.[17]

Three weeks after staging *Our Town*, Williams presented a costumed biblical pageant for Christmas at First Presbyterian and narrated the Nativity story, with his deep, mellifluous voice filling the sanctuary.

For a young man of nineteen, he was off to a quick start in the arts. He thought he saw his way ahead, although optimism among Americans was scarce in the spring of 1941. Conservatives in Congress had buried Roosevelt's New Deal under counter-legislation; newspaper headlines predicted war in Europe; and rainfall in dusty northern Texas was just half the yearly average. A crash in farm prices would trigger another financial quake and further depress the job market. But to young Williams—budding actor, writer, poet, he wasn't sure which yet—the stars were aligning for him, at least. He had a sense of knowing what he was about.

His reading kept pace with his ambitions, too. He upgraded from boys' magazines to *Liberty* magazine and the *Saturday Evening Post*. He also discovered the "little magazines," as they are still called, such as the *Partisan Review*, where writers talked about the craft of writing and the book reviews suggested to him what to read next. Wolfe, his favorite author, was replaced by Conrad Aiken. Aiken introduced him to psychological fiction, which led on to Proust. He grazed in the public library and purchased books at a discount at the Lovelace Bookstore, reading whatever he liked. "It wasn't anything I had to study. It seemed like kind of a fraud, it was so much fun." He read for enjoyment—"And I think that finally, when I began to read so-called more 'serious' things . . . they became a great deal more authentic than if I had gone to them thinking they were supposed to be terribly good."[18]

Likely his sister, George Rae, would be the only one interested in talking about books at the dinner table on Broad Street in the spring of 1941. Their mother, Amelia, listening to them, had only completed the eighth grade; Grandfather Walker, who had fallen back on the kindness of his daughter and son-in-law, was a simple man. And George Williams, of course, would be tired from finishing a ten-hour day cleaning the post office.

It's interesting to speculate what George Williams might have thought as he listened to his stepson hold forth about another extravaganza he was involved in. George had turned his back on his banking family and everything that tribe had stood for. How did he regard John Ed's slightly raffish clothes and his talk about poetry, novels, and his actor friends? His stepson, just like the stage-struck teenager in Willa Cather's short story "Paul's Case," had "high, cramped shoulders and a narrow chest," and large blue eyes that he used "in a conscious, theatrical sort of way." George, a stocky man with a broad back from years of labor, may well have regarded Amelia's boy as a kid who needed to concern himself less with putting on make-up for plays or striking arty poses, and more with finding a steady job to support himself. Williams never mentioned his stepfather, an indication, perhaps, that the relationship was unpleasant.

In the spring of 1941, John Ed struck out on his own. Beckoning him was radio—and more experiences like performing *Dr. Cooper Speaking*. National broadcasting had become a kingdom of the air, featuring soap operas, symphony concerts, news commentary, variety shows, and eyewitness reporting. Such was the popularity of radio that the problem of overlapping programs created wild cacophonies of voices and screeching music on the dial. By order of the federal government, over seven hundred broadcast stations shifted their frequencies to untangle the airwaves.

Williams' voice and timing were perfect for the medium, and he had already demonstrated that he could write dramatic scripts. In April he appeared on stage a final time in the Wichita Players' production of Henrik Ibsen's *Pillars of Society*, and then he was gone, to add his voice to those competing to be heard, and not returning to Wichita Falls, as it would turn out, until after World War II.

———

The summer of 1941, listeners to station KRRV, "The Voice of the Red River Valley," broadcasting from Sherman, Texas, were introduced to a new morning announcer—"Jon Williams," the on-air handle for John Ed Williams.

The format of KRRV was folksy but proper. The small staff of women running the station, some of them volunteers, worked to make radio an uplifting instrument of the home. On Sundays, "Jon Williams" set up the equipment for live broadcasts from area churches. During the week, he interviewed local politicians and civic leaders who wanted to say a few words to KRRV's listeners about a wholesome topic, anything from religious freedom to the firemen's annual bake sale. September found him broadcasting live from the county fair. From a booth beside the pickle display, he queried farmers about their crops, and asked homemakers for tips about how to make a dollar stretch in the kitchen. Listeners could hear the cheers and whistles of ranchers and farmers in the background who were watching Negro football teams play on a field of mown hay.

In KRRV's family-oriented broadcast day, there was no room for Williams' original sketches or news commentary. But in Denton, Texas, just north of Dallas, Harwell V. "Shep" Shepard, the owner of KDNT, could use an extra hand.

These were the wildcatting days of radio, and entrepreneurs hurried to sink broadcast towers into the ground ahead of the competition. "Shep" Shepard, born and raised in Denton, had tried his hand at other things before the radio business, including running a funeral home. But broadcasting appealed to him as a better business idea, because Dallas, a big market for advertising, would be within range of a low-power station in Denton. With a borrowed investment of $6,000, Shepard hand-wired the cottage adjacent to his home at 400 Ross Street. Above it, local plumbers constructed a 160-foot broadcast tower. It fell over, then rose again. On June 1, 1938, KDNT-AM went live. To pay the station's bills, Shepard called on advertisers in a 1932 Plymouth sedan with the station's call letters and thunderbolts painted in gold on the doors. His wife, "Red," handled the bookkeeping.[19]

When Williams arrived to interview for a job as a newsman, Shepard showed him the new United Press International Teletype machine clattering away in a corner of the studio, generating enough bulletins from around the world for news broadcasts throughout the day. Williams was impressed and wanted the job. But Shepard also needed someone who could write advertising copy for merchants purchasing airtime. If Williams was interested in that—on commission—then they had a deal. They shook on it.

A week later, "Jon Williams" was the station's main announcer and engineer. He reported the news, wrote advertising copy, played records, and ran the instrument board for his own broadcasts. Some Saturday nights, he stayed late at the station to set up the studio like a barn dance, adding hay bales for atmosphere. Those nights, traveling western swing bands took their turns at the standing microphone, singing and telling corny jokes until midnight for the listeners of KDNT.

The job had an unexpected bonus, though. The station also carried the *Saturday Night Variety Show* from the campus of North Texas State College in Granbury, southwest of Dallas. Williams' official reason for making the two-hour drive down to Granbury was to set up the equipment in the auditorium before the show. But for socializing and meeting smart girls, there wasn't anything like North Texas State College for miles around. Over 90 percent of the student body was female. During one of his trips to campus, he met Alyeene Rosida Bryan, a junior majoring in music and drama.

Alyeene's father was a lumberman in Granbury, her mother a housewife. There was something a little exotic in her Mexican-Irish features—dark eyes and tight ringlets of hair that fell to her shoulders. She acted, sang, and performed as a soloist at recitals and weddings. Like John, she had been editor of her high school newspaper, and she wrote poetry, too, which she showed him, knowing he had won prizes for his. She was said to be a little melodramatic, and abided by a rarefied southern code of behavior common to the better class of young ladies. If John hadn't given her proper warning that he was coming to campus, she let it be known, through her roommate answering the door, that she "was not accepting callers" that evening—could he call again?[20]

They married six months after their first date, on Easter Sunday, April 5, 1942, in the Granbury Methodist Church. Both families went to lengths to see that it was a traditional ceremony, despite the demands of the war. The church altar was decorated with irises and lilacs in tall baskets. Jack Newsom, Williams' actor friend, was best man. The bride wore an afternoon dress of taffeta instead of a bridal gown, and carried a white Bible. Her bridesmaids wore pins: a pink enamel heart pierced by a wooden match with the words "It's a Match—Alyeene and Jon, April 5."[21]

In addition to changing his name, Williams had also burnished his educational achievements. The *Hood County Tablet* printed on its "Weddings" page that the bridegroom had earned a bachelor's degree from the University of New Mexico and done "graduate work in Chicago."[22] These credentials were later amended to "attended the University of New Mexico" in the wedding announcement appearing in the *North Texas State* campus newspaper, which was read by many of Alyeene's friends who knew Jon.

CHAPTER THREE

Rough Draft

"Take any man," I said, reaching across the table and lighting your cigarette, "study him carefully. . . . Take him, season with a little imagination and sympathy—and you'll have a novel."

—JOHN WILLIAMS, DRAFT FOR A STORY, MARCH 1944

Scanning the newspapers in September 1942 for items he might use for broadcast, Williams noticed repeated calls for men to enlist in the Army Air Corps. Since the bombing of Pearl Harbor ten months earlier, recruiting officers were advertising for volunteers to join up before they were drafted, especially ones with certain skills. The drumbeat on page two of the *Lubbock Morning Avalanche* was typical:

If you're between the ages of 18 and 50 and physically able to pursue any kind of mechanical trade in civilian life, and if you're interested in enlisting directly into the United States Army Air Corps, you're urged to drop in at the recruiting station and airplane engine exhibit at 1012 Main Street today. . . . Men with any mechanical or radio technical experience may be qualified.[1]

In this instance, specialists were needed for crew duty in bombers and transport planes. During World War I, air combat had been fought between the pilots of single-engine biplanes made of canvas

28

and plywood. They fired at each other, raked the mud trenches below with machine-gun fire, and hand-dropped bombs the size of footballs. But now, heavy aluminum and steel bombers required crews of six to ten, including a radio man, for high-altitude, long-distance missions over Europe, Asia, and the South Pacific. An officer quoted in the article still had one foot in the previous war when he said that radiomen contributed as much as pilots to "helping the Doughboys."

For John, military service would defer his career just as opportunity seemed to be opening up. His boss, Harwell Shepard, had a request in at the federal level to boost KDNT's broadcast output from 100 to 250 watts. A stronger signal would carry Williams' newscasts down past Dallas all the way west to San Antonio and east to Beaumont, doubling the listening area. If a national network like CBS heard him, it might syndicate his public affairs reporting. Shepard was nevertheless resigned to going the duration of the war with no increase of signal, given the emergency state of things and the bureaucracy in Washington.

Williams decided there was no point in delaying his military service. If he waited until he was drafted, he might be assigned to the infantry. But if he enlisted in the Army Air Corps, he could take the exam for radio technician, which he knew something about.

———

Married only five months, Williams enlisted "somewhat reluctantly" in the Army Air Corps at the recruiting station in Dallas on October 6, 1942, quite possibly the same place where his stepfather had registered for World War I in 1917. No patriotic surge of feeling swept Williams into the armed services, however. "We had to get into the goddamn war" was his attitude.[2] And the majority of Americans felt the same way. As one historian wrote of lack of choice in the matter, "If there was no practical alternative, there was certainly no moral one either. Britain and the Commonwealth were carrying the battle for all civilization, and the overwhelming majority of Americans, led in the late election by their president, wished to help them."[3]

John's young wife, Alyeene, would have to finish her teaching degree at North Texas State without him. A week after he enlisted, she saw him off at the bus depot as he departed for basic training. She had hoped he would be able to attend her solo performance coming up at Granbury Methodist Church, but recruits were never granted leave during the two months of basic training. Three hours later, he arrived at Sheppard Field, still under construction on three hundred acres of former pastureland outside Wichita Falls.

He was a twenty-year-old bantamweight, and boot camp was fierce. His pack and rifle tugged against his 104-pound frame during ten-mile marches, but he passed the radio technician examination. Alyeene came by bus from Denton in mid-November to say goodbye before he transferred to the Air Corps Technical Training Command in Greensboro, North Carolina.[4] Then, on the morning of Christmas Eve, she set out from Dallas by train to visit him, arriving exhausted in Greensboro on Friday, Christmas night, after thirty hours of traveling, with only two days remaining on John's three-day pass.[5]

Saturday was warm for December but rainy, and they spent most of it alone. The movie theaters, restaurants, taverns, and stores were open on Sunday, which the strict religious "blue laws" normally would have prohibited. But it was wartime and restrictions had been lifted. Come very early Monday morning, they parted at the Southern Railway train station while it was still dark. By the time he reported for roll call, she had already begun the two-day trip back to Texas.

His orders, when they came through in mid-January 1943, assigned him to the 10th Air Force, 443rd Troop Carrier Group, 1st Troop Carrier Squadron. From San Francisco he would leave aboard a troopship bound on a fifty-day voyage to Bombay, the port city on the Arabian Sea. A train would take him to Calcutta, followed by truck transport to Sookerating Airfield on India's border with Tibet in the Assam Valley.

Sookerating was the Allies' closest airbase for supplying General Chiang Kai-shek, who was directing the Chinese National Army

fighting the Japanese. Allied transport planes flew the five-hun-
dred-mile resupply route every day, sometimes twice, soaring over
the highest mountain range in the world, the thirty-thousand-foot
wall of the Himalayas, nicknamed "the Hump" by pilots. The only
overland route, the Burma Road, was in the hands of the enemy.
Journalist Eric Sevareid visited the airfield at Chabua in the Assam
Valley and found it "a dread and dismal place. . . . They were trying
to do too much with far too little. Pilots were overworked, and when
they had made the perilous flight to China and back the same day,
having fought storm and fog and ice, they simply fell into their
cots as they were, unshaved and unwashed, to catch a few hours of
unrefreshing sleep before repeating the venture the next day."[6]

In March, Williams debarked in the port of Bombay to begin a
train journey of eight hundred miles across mountains, plains, and
desert toward Eastern India and the thickly jungled province of
Bengal. For five days and nights, he passed through "small, inde-
scribably filthy villages," so described by an army engineer who also
traveled the same route.[7] Using his duffel bag for a pillow, radioman
Williams tried to sleep on his wooden bench in the drowsy heat, but
was awakened whenever the one-note locomotive whistle shrieked
at people or animals on the tracks. Each time the train stopped,
villagers rushed forward selling trinkets, or begging for food or a
little *baksheesh*, money.[8]

In Sookerating, Williams got to work supervising "tea parties"
of local laborers who loaded C-47 Skytrains—"Gooney Birds,"
the crews called them—using blocks and tackles, and sometimes
elephants sleepy with opium to keep them calm. Jeeps, trucks,
grenades, coffee, gasoline, bombs, spare parts, and ambulances—
anything useful to the Chinese army, including generals—went
over the Hump. Once the aircraft had been closed up and made
ready, Williams set aside his clipboard and changed into his role as
radioman. First, he tested the beacon box, which beamed a secret
signal identifying the airplane as friendly, and installed it in the tail
section. Then he took his seat behind the cockpit and checked the
communications equipment to his left and in front of him. Over
the next three and a half hours, his job would be to communicate

with ground operators using the daily code, take time checks, make entries in his log, and provide position reports to the navigator plotting the course.

The airbase was so near the foot of the Himalayas that, to climb fast enough for takeoff, pilots locked the brakes, waiting for the twin Pratt & Whitney 1,200-horsepower engines to roar to a thunderous, whining pitch—until everything on board was shaking. The instant the brakes were released, the plane leaped forward and rushed down the runway, gathering speed and lifting its two-ton cargo into the sky. Even so, C-47s had a ceiling altitude of only twenty-three thousand feet, and if the pilot or navigator lost his way, some of the Himalayan peaks were still half a mile higher.

As the plane rose out of Assam Valley, and above the steam bath of the jungle, the men pulled on fleece-lined leather jackets. Temperatures inside the plane slowly dropped to below freezing. There were no heaters, because they weighed too much. From the Upper Assam Valley to the Yunnanese plateau, they first crossed the Mishmis Hills, which are between two and three miles high.[9] At this point, Williams flipped on his oxygen and began using a mask. He was a chain-smoker, so he pushed the mask off-center, allowing enough oxygen to spill out the side to keep a cigarette lit in the corner of his mouth.[10] Through his headset he sometimes heard the voice of a Japanese disc jockey the men nicknamed "Hanoi Hannah." In between playing American songs and big band music, she delivered personal messages. "To the boys on N99131—turn back, fellas. Lt. Jim Kelley, turn that plane around. Because if you don't, you're all going to die on this flight."[11] Williams and the rest of the crew were more concerned about the weather. From June to October, the monsoon season brought anvil-headed thunderclouds with violent updrafts that could flip a plane on its back. During night thunderstorms, the propellers sometimes became wrapped in the blue orbs of St. Elmo's fire. Spidery filaments of electricity crackled around the windows of the cockpit like miniature lightning. Occasionally, when a pent-up charge arced with the airplane's steel frame, an explosive blue fireball knocked out Williams' radio equipment and stopped communication with the ground.

Winter storms brought another kind of terror. The C-47 was a workhorse, but when the wings were glazed with ice, it waddled drunkenly. At those times, Williams came forward and grabbed the retraction lever between the pilots, running the landing gear up and down to help reduce the plane's tipsiness. The wheels partly down acted like a keel, but they also created an additional drag that might cause the plane to stall. A sudden drop in altitude sent loose objects slamming against the cabin roof. If the plane crashed in the jungle, tribes of headhunters—the tattooed Naga people—were down there to meet them.[12]

In a novel left uncompleted at his death, *The Sleep of Reason*, Williams included a scene of an Army Air Corps desk officer, Capt. Parker, hitching a ride on a C-47 with an enlisted man named Matthews:

They sat apart from each other, wedged tightly between lashed crates that nearly filled the interior of the plane's long body, and when the C-47 began its long, shuddering takeoff down the runway, [Matthews] was glad that Parker could not see his hands clutching the slats of the crates on either side of him.

But when they were airborne and Matthews became more used to the odd, unsteady floating sensation, which he found not altogether unpleasant, he looked across the aisle and was astonished by Capt. Parker's face. It was a pale, yellow contortion with staring eyes and open mouth. Beads of sweat glistened on his forehead, and he breathed in heavy gasps that could be heard above the roar of the airplane.

For a moment, Matthews thought that he was ill and he started to speak to him, but he realized in the instant before he spoke that what he saw was a terror as pure as he had ever imagined.[13]

After the Mishmis Hills, Williams' plane traversed the Hukawng Valley and the muddy meadows of the Upper Irrawaddy River. Next came the Kaolikung range, which hid the cavernous gorge of the Salween River below, walled on the other side by the four-mile-high Hump itself. When at last the silvery Tali Lake came into view, the crew was ten minutes from a plate of eggs and a cup of coffee on the Yunnanese plateau. A sign over the mess hall sounded slightly incredulous: "You Made It Again."

He said he was shot down once. A shell from a spring-loaded Japanese knee mortar struck the plane on its final approach. He found himself on the ground with his back up against a tree, a pain in his side from broken ribs. Pieces of the plane were hanging in the jungle canopy. The pilot and copilot survived, but the five men in the rear were killed.[14] Williams and the pilots found their way through the underbrush until they hit a safe stretch of the Burma Road. Once back, he volunteered to join a party to retrieve the dead men's dog tags. On the way, they ran out of rations, so they skinned a monkey and roasted it. He remembered it "looked like a baby on a spit." A Japanese patrol passed by so close that their white puttees could be seen flashing through the jungle foliage.[15]

But the Japanese didn't wear white puttees in the jungle: they wore khaki leggings, wrapped to their knees. And among the names of men flying out of Sookerating who crashed—over a hundred were killed—"John Edward Williams" doesn't appear.[16] Also, if he suffered broken ribs, he would have received a Purple Heart. But his name is not among the list of recipients. What, then, to make of Williams' account of being shot down by the enemy?

His bravery is unquestionable, of course. The flight over the highest mountain range in the world was the graveyard of the air. He "almost got used to people being killed."[17] He came down with malaria, the effects of which plagued him for the rest of his life, and a touch of scrub typhus near his eye, a marshland disease that produces skin lesions and high fever. He endured a lot, and his superiors thought well enough of him to promote him to sergeant.[18]

But to come home without a few good stories would have been unthinkable to Williams. Crafting a tale—embellishing it, adding surprises—becomes an opportunity to get a little better at the art. And the best stories, the memorable ones, hardly ever fall into the teller's lap fully formed. "Remember Charlie," Ernest Hemingway wrote to his friend Charles Poore in 1953, "in the first war all I did mostly was hear guys talk; especially in hospital and convalescing.

Their experiences get to be more vivid than your own. You invent from your own and from all of theirs."[19] Call it lying, but writers call it creating fiction.

The round scar on his shoulder, for instance, was left from shooting himself by accident at age seventeen. When one of his daughters asked him years later, pointing to the mark, "What's that?" he said, "I got that when I was a co-pilot in the jungle and the Japs shot us down."[20]

"Dear John ..."

Sometime in the early spring of 1944, Alyeene wrote him to say she wanted a divorce. There was somebody else—that's what he claimed she said, although she wouldn't remarry for ten years. Or maybe she chose a reason that was irrevocable but short, one that would fit on a couple pages of overseas V-mail. In any case, they would have to wait until he returned to make the divorce official, because that was the law.

What could he do about it, and how should he respond from the faraway edge of eastern India? For the rest of his life, he took a sporting attitude about his first marriage. "Oh, I don't even count that one," or, "That one was my fault." He said he grieved about it for about two weeks.[21]

But the failure with Alyeene was one in a series of attempts at respectability. He had dropped out of junior college and tried his hand at radio plays and stage direction. Next, he had started a career in broadcasting, which turned out to be a disappointing job of covering county fairs and selling advertising. To compensate, he bestowed on himself a nonexistent degree from the University of New Mexico.

About the time of her letter, Williams had a studio portrait taken in Calcutta. Like a movie star, he is looking up and off to his left, the light falling on his face, accentuating his large eyes and close-cropped mustache. Most men and women in uniform preferred a straight-ahead shot like a yearbook photo, but Williams went for effect. He's dressed in a sharply pressed airman's tunic, his right shoulder thrusting forward with the China-Burma-India campaign patch, a striped shield on whose blue field rests the Kuomintang Sun of China and the Star of India. There's a bid for transcendence about the way he looks up into the light. It isn't accidental. It's part performance, part personal narrative—he means to say that he's different, and he's artistic. A romantic. He's still Ronald Colman in spirit, the gentleman swashbuckler. But the facts of Williams' young life so far did not shine favorably on him becoming successful.

While he was in Calcutta, Williams purchased half a dozen composition booklets, like the kind he'd used for school: red covers, blue-lined pages with a vertical red line for the margins. Writers tend to be particular about their materials, and by reaching back for the tools he first used for essays and poems, he was indicating a wish to reconnect.

He spent some of his off-hours in the tent he shared with two other airmen, lying on his cot writing. If it was getting dark, he had to reach up and light the kerosene lantern hanging from the ridgepole. The gray mongoose they let hang around to kill snakes appeared at sunset begging for scraps.[22] In his attempts at fiction, at first he emulated his favorite authors. He wanted to invoke Conrad Aiken's psychological language that had impressed him so much, and the interiority of Proust. He hoped to sound both literary and sophisticated to the reader, and show his characters' thoughts. From a page in one of his composition notebooks, dated March 4, 1944:

> "Take any man," I said, reaching across the table and lighting
> your cigarette, "study him carefully, know him so well that you
> premeditate his basic reactions. Understand his likes and dislikes,
> his prejudices and convictions; know a little about his background,
> his environment. Take him, season with a little imagination and
> sympathy—and you'll have a novel."
>
> You leaned back in your chair and sipped slowly at your drink.
> You didn't say anything. You put your drink back on the table and
> drug [*sic*] heavily on your cigarette and let the smoke dribble out
> of your lazy, skeptical mouth.
>
> "I'll go even further," I insisted. "Take any man—fat or lean,
> wise or foolish, good or bad—take one day, or one night of that

man's life. Know what he does during that appointed time, understand why he does it—and you'll have a novel."[23]

He kept revising, adding, starting again. "I didn't know what I
was doing," he later said.[24]
The best passages he copied out and mailed home to his family.
What they thought about such missives from the edge of the jungle
is anyone's guess.

––––––––

He would be returning to the United States in six months or so—at
the end of the year, or in early 1945, at least. His marriage was
over and he would be single again. The GI Bill would give him the
financial wherewithal to attend college, but he didn't know where
someone with ambitions should enroll. Through a friend, he wrote
to a college instructor, Satyavati C. Jordan at Thoburn College in
Lucknow, India, hoping for some advice. Mrs. Jordan was a woman
in her forties who had been educated at Baker University in Kansas
and Northwestern University near Chicago. Her father was the first
Indian bishop elected to the Methodist Episcopal Church.
    She replied that she would be "very glad indeed" to meet Ser-
geant Williams, and extended an invitation to the Sunday evening
service at the Victorian-style Lal Bagh English Methodist Church,
where she was the organist. "I think you would like our service. . . .
I can take you around the Isabella Thoburn College and we can have
a visit."[25]
    Williams was nearing the end of his military service and on the
cusp of deciding about the direction of his life. Perhaps during his
walk with Mrs. Jordan through the gardens on campus, he mentioned that his mother was ill with tuberculosis. His family had
moved while he was away from Wichita Falls to Pasadena, California, to be near his sister, who was performing at the Pasadena
Playhouse. When he returned, everything would be different.
    Mrs. Jordan responded with another invitation to dinner to meet
her family, and followed up by letter with the names of two friends—
a journalist in Tennessee, and a poet in Kansas—who might help

him think through his choices. "Remember, when you come this way again," she told him, "you have friends here—we'll be looking for you."[26]

Back in his tent at the airfield, he had kept a letter from his actor friend Jack Newsom. He liked to reread it because Newsom was back home and preparing big plans for the future. Jack was in advertising, selling radio airtime in Florida, and he'd gotten a tip that the worldwide Mutual Broadcasting System was going to tie in with a brand new station, WKWF, in tropical Key West:

> Williams, at present I have things lined up so that the minute you step foot back into this country we can at once pack up and head for the most wonderful [radio] station in Florida you ever laid eyes on. . . . I really got going and met the right people and as a result have things lined up like we used to dream about. Now here's the deal. You have been fucking around over there long enough. . . . [Y]ou are a big boy now and must settle down. If you will just get a move on, we shall take up where we left off.[27]

CHAPTER FOUR

Key West

I knew I could make a living as a writer for radio, but it meant you just hacked it out. I grew up a little bit, and realized this was a crappy way to live your life—to be a radio announcer and hawk products or whatever.

—JOHN WILLIAMS, 1981 INTERVIEW

Arriving stateside again in the spring of 1945, he was in a hurry. Life was precious, and yet paradoxically, not very important in the scheme of things. Sometimes, when the big C-47 cargo plane put down in China, its rubber wheels smoking on impact, he would feel an extra bump as they taxied, followed by a disgusted shout from the cockpit—"Aw *shit*! We hit another one!" A Chinese civilian had rushed in front of the plane because he believed that the blurred, chopping blades would destroy his evil spirits. Instead, he disappeared into the slipstream of nothingness and left gore on the runway.

The former "Jon" Williams, the smooth-faced boy of twenty, had disappeared over the Himalayas with the sound of Hanoi Hannah crooning in his headset. In his place a veteran had returned home, sporting a mustache, sometimes plagued by bad dreams or periods of cold sweats from the effects of malaria. And who relied on drinking—alone, if no one was handy—to take his mind off things.[1]

His resources for civilian life were slim—one year of junior college; a year of professional broadcasting; sixty days of Army Air

Corps radio school; sergeant's stripes, and a dozen composition notebooks filled with drafts of a novel. He wasn't in a position to do whatever he wanted; he would have to take what looked promising.

As soon as his ship dropped anchor in New York Harbor, he began wrapping up what still remained of his prewar life. From New York, he headed southwest to Wichita Falls to finalize his divorce from Alyeene. In the three years since he'd seen her, she had changed from a teenager into a young woman supporting herself as a bank teller. Then he continued on to Pasadena, California, northeast of Los Angeles near Hollywood, to visit his family in their new home on North Summit Avenue. He also wanted to collect the sum of his poker winnings, and the bet he'd won at the Royal Calcutta Turf Club. His parents were supposed to put the money aside for him, but it turned out they hadn't. It had gone instead into the down payment on their new house.[2] He didn't begrudge what they had done—the climate was better for his mother, and George Rae was performing at the Pasadena Playhouse, which benefited her acting career. But he left again quickly, explaining that he didn't care for California, and there might be a job in radio waiting for him in Florida.

By June, he was seated at the control board of "the most wonderful station in Florida you ever laid eyes on," as Jack Newsom had described it: WKWF, "the nation's southernmost radio station," in Key West, Florida. Actually, it was still a small operation in a bungalow, and owned by a local businessman with political aspirations, but John Williams was more knowledgeable than anyone in the studio.

Key West, an island four miles long and a mile wide, suited him well—it hit the median somehow. The sleepy, sea-level island, hanging from a string of sandbars at the tip of Florida, provided a good transition to civilian life. Key West is almost precisely the same latitude as Calcutta, and he was accustomed to the languor and sultriness. There was an air of exoticism about the town, too. Sailors, pilots, and technicians from the Naval Air Station and the Fleet Sonar School consorted with the population of bohemians, sidewalk strollers, and sun-worshippers. Few other places in the United States had Key West's admixture of ordinary and strange, but it was palpable here at the endpoint of an archipelago jutting into the Caribbean where tropical sunlight shone down on the old romance of an eastern bazaar.

And some of Key West's residents were writers, including the poets Elizabeth Bishop, Wallace Stevens, and Robert Frost, the playwright Tennessee Williams, and the novelist Ernest Hemingway. John Williams collected local anecdotes about "Papa" Hemingway, which he repeated over the years. If he had to make a living as a broadcaster in order to write, then Key West was a good loose fit, until he got his bearings.

Sometime that fall, he finished the novel he'd begun fitfully in Sookerating, titling it *Nothing But the Night*. It had gone through six rewrites on the way to completion, and he hated revising. To avoid it as much as possible, he rehearsed passages in his mind before committing words to paper, a method he used for the rest of his life.[3] Unlike his author-hero Thomas Wolfe, who could write thousands of words at a single sitting, a good day for Williams was a paragraph he liked.

Nothing But the Night is an ambitious novel, steeped in psychological realism—illuminating characters' interior lives by reaching into their subconscious.[4] Having read and admired Proust and Conrad Aiken, Williams hoped to reach even further by adding daubs of psychoanalytic theory: pretty formidable stuff for a new writer. *Nothing But the Night*, which plays out in one Joycean day and night, explores a disturbing, perhaps abnormal relationship between a young man and his mother, opening the doors to related pathologies such as masochism, sadism, and a desire to subjugate women.

It begins with a dream unfolding. The unnamed dreamer is observing a party going on. Among the guests is a pale, flaccid young man. He makes the others uncomfortable, and they try to ignore him: "To these people he was a noise without meaning, an explosion with disruption." Gradually, to his shock, the dreamer realizes that he's the detestable young man everyone dislikes. They surround him, menacingly. Then, as a kind of biblical stoning, they beat him into senselessness.[5]

The dream over, Arthur Maxley, a young man of leisure, begins waking up. He's expecting the maid to arrive soon to clean his disordered room, but before she arrives he decides he should go out for a walk. He distracts himself by repeating the beginning of the Lord's Prayer, like a chant, until he pares it down to "Father, Father, Father . . ." "What an ugly word," he says to himself.

Stopping into a diner for breakfast, Maxley comes across as neurotically aesthetic. Smells and images affront him. "He wiped a fleck of breadcrumb from the soiled cover of a chair and sat down at a table near the front. . . . The menu was one of those typewritten affairs, and this must have been a fourth or fifth carbon, well used and smudged by previous customers. He sniffed delicately and dropped it on the table." He primly but silently scolds his waitress, telling her to please "try to hide the remnants of last night's debauch." On all sides, the world looks like an ugly place to him, full of gross behavior.

Returning to his apartment, he plays a tantalizing game of keep-away with the maid. "He raised his free hand and let the back brush negligently across her breasts." Behind her back, she's hiding a letter for him. It's from Arthur's wealthy father, Hollis Maxley, who's in town and wants to meet him for dinner. In a flashback, Arthur remembers a scene of seeing his mother and father in a room, and "that terrible thing which he could never purge from the darkest reaches of his mind," and how he had screamed, "*Mother Mother Mother* until he was in a hoarse stupor." Their bond seems faintly Oedipal:

> Sometimes she would fling her arms about him, lie beside him, tousle his hair, and whisper to him. At other times she would seem distracted, absent, not really there beside him at all. Then she would hold him to her briefly, talk to him in short stops and starts. But the rarest moments of all—and to him, the startlingly

beautiful—were the times when she floated into his room like a white angel, sat beside him, held him softly, saying little, gazing at his eager moon-bathed face with great tenderness and calm . . .

But there was always the goodnight kiss.

They would linger over that. And when her lips had left his face, he would remain so, his eyes closed, an unconscious smile hovering over his mouth.

After receiving his father's invitation for dinner, about which he isn't happy, he meets a gay friend for drinks. This is an edgy scene for the 1940s. (The bartender throws them both out. "What kind of place do you think this is?") Williams seems intent on salting the manuscript with passing references to characters' psychological states. Arthur continues on his way after drinks to meet his father, Hollis, at a posh hotel.

The elder Maxley, it turns out, wants to make amends, to heal a rift with his son. Something has happened which neither of them wants to revisit, so they only allude to it. Just as Arthur begins to feel sorry for his father, a beautiful woman stops by the table. Awkwardly, it becomes apparent that she and Arthur's father are having an affair. She apologizes for interrupting and leaves. Arthur feels nauseated because the woman reminds him of his mother. He refuses to accept his father's explanation that "they all look like *her*. I try to make myself believe that . . ." Angered by what he perceives as his father's betrayal—or, his realization that his father has a sexual connection to his mother that he can never overcome—Arthur leaves and goes out into the night.

He wanders into a nightclub, where a young woman, abandoned by her date, plops down drunkenly beside him. Arthur's unhappiness is triggered again unexpectedly when on the nightclub's stage, a female dancer performs a highly erotic number. "The smooth muscles of her belly turned and twisted; her body throbbed uncontrollably in effortless spasms." Her face turns into the face of Arthur's mother and he rises to his feet, crying out in pain. He recalls in a dreamlike sequence what he witnessed as a child: his mother shooting his cringing father, a repressed wish to kill his father acted out.

But then "she inserted the still-smoking barrel into her mouth. He heard the muffled report and saw the head jerk backward."

Arthur whisks the girl away from the nightclub in a taxi. Upstairs in her room, some kind of urge for revenge, or maybe just disgust, compels Arthur to lash out and strike her. She falls to the floor, naked, blood coming from the corner of her mouth. The bedroom door bursts open and in comes a large, rough man who pushes Arthur out of the room and downstairs into the darkness.

For the first time we find out that Arthur is "little," like Williams. "You know what's going to happen, don't you?" says the man, who calls him "sonny." Mutely, without protest—like a guilty son at the hands of his violent father—Arthur submits to a beating. His passivity suggests he's aware of having broken a taboo, because "his hands were leaden weights that hung at his side." When it's over, he crawls along the sidewalk and finds his glasses, then gets to his feet unsteadily. Without a word, he walks away, "toward where the darkness converged and there was no light, where the night pressed in upon him, where nothing waited for him, where he was, at last, alone." The novel ends with a sense that Arthur got what he came for—or what he deserved—and that the violence associated with his punishment was ordained.

———

Now that *Nothing But the Night* was finished, Williams needed a reader whose opinion he trusted—someone who knew about fiction and literature and not just an obliging friend. By chance, just such a person appeared at the radio station: a vacationing professor from the University of Alabama who chatted on-air once a week about books, writers, and summer reading. Williams, listening behind the glass in the control room, heard a language he was hungry for.

George K. Smart—"Ken" to his friends, held a doctorate in American literature from the University of Alabama. An outgoing gentleman, Smart resembled a balding southern salesman with a preference for bow ties and light-colored suits. Beneath his friendliness, however, was a serious scholar whose specialty was William Faulkner. Ten years older than Williams, Smart had a tendency to attract or seek out young people in need of advice.[6] He and Williams arranged to meet at the La Conga Bar on Duval Street in the oldest part of Key West.[7]

What Smart gleaned from listening to Williams was that here was a bright, thoughtful, ex-GI who was sincere about his desire to write, but who did not have much of an idea about how to proceed. Smart had been an assistant professor at Harvard, but his instincts told him that his younger friend probably wouldn't enjoy it—it was too much of a leap. He recommended the University of Alabama, and for several reasons. First, he was in the English Department there. Also, he and his wife, Virginia, had an extra room that Williams was welcome to use. Smart could put a word in with the admissions office, too. But most important for Williams' benefit, Alabama offered one of the few creative writing seminars in the country. It was taught by Hudson Strode, who had been successful bringing several of his students' novels to market. Williams could get the kind of guidance he needed. "Alabama is a friendly, easy-come-easy-go place," Smart assured him. "It's big, rambly [*sic*], and extroverted."[8]

But for the present, at least, Williams wasn't sure he wanted to commit to more schooling. A little magazine of contemporary art and literature in New York, *The Tiger's Eye*, had accepted one of his poems. He had also completed a one-hour radio play; and there was the manuscript Smart had just read, *Nothing But the Night*. If there was any way he could write for a living, maybe he owed it to himself to try. Smart agreed that the novel was ready to send out, and gave Williams the name of an acquaintance, a senior editor at Harper and Brothers, Edward Aswell—who had also been Thomas Wolfe's editor, by an auspicious coincidence.[9]

The decision over whether to reenroll in college or continue writing independently was temporarily delayed, however, when Williams received word in December that his mother was seriously ill with tuberculosis. She was forty-seven and had been in and out of sanitariums since he was in high school, the first time for a minor operation in Paris, Texas.[10] The owner of WKWF replied to Williams' resignation with a letter praising his talents, which, it was understood, Williams could use as a recommendation to find another position in radio.[11]

But he never used it, or looked for another opening in broadcasting. Despite his friend Jack Newsom's cheery letter about making good on their adolescent plans, he realized now that he didn't want to pick up where he'd left off in 1942, before he'd enlisted. "I knew I could make a living as a writer for radio, but it meant you just hacked it out," he told an interviewer. "I grew up a little bit, and realized this was a crappy way to live your life—to be a radio announcer and hawk products or whatever."[12]

He headed to California to see about his mother.

CHAPTER FIVE

Alan Swallow

I think Denver is a good idea. This guy Swallow
sounds like a very good Joe.
—GEORGE K. SMART TO JOHN WILLIAMS, 1947

In the spring of 1946, residents of Pasadena became accustomed to seeing a slight, dark-haired young man in a biscuit-colored uniform and black bow tie wearing a peaked cap with a badge. He would be walking quickly between houses to peer at the meters and take a reading for the Southern California Gas Company. Williams kept up a good pace, covering about four hundred properties a day. He followed a different route each week to complete his territory, averaging about four miles of walking daily before clambering into the truck to head back to the central office.

He was living with his stepfather; his sister, George Rae; and his grandfather, Elbert Walker, who was almost ninety, at 363 North Summit.[1] George Williams had retired from the Wichita Falls Post Office on a civil service pension and was taking care of Amelia, whose tuberculosis kept her resting in bed most days. The first antibiotic for the disease, streptomycin, was introduced that year. But it was too late for Amelia; in July, she died.

With her death, John was the last member of the evanescent Jewell family of Clarksville, Texas. His nature was to be reserved about personal matters, and later he preferred not to reminisce about his mother. When asked about her, his embarrassed silence gave the impression that "he loved his mother too much to talk about her." Ten years after her death, he wrote "Memories: Texas, 1932," which begins with the poet recalling how he had needed his mother when he was nine years old, the age, probably not coincidentally, at which she told him the secret of his birth:

> They are gone now, but I remember
> The narrow room and the nine-year-old boy
> Who lay at night on a bed so wide
> That hands and feet could find no falling
> From softness into the dark around him.
>
> Deep in the drowse of childhood, he heard
> His mother's voice in the next room,
> Unmeaning, soft as his first comfort;
> And thought of what he could not know—
>
> And his room
> shifted in its darkness, a presence
> Gathered where he could not see,
> His arms flailed at the blackness; and he called
> From his terror, "Mother!"—and called
> Again.[2]

The summer his mother died, a rejection letter arrived from Edward Aswell, the editor at Harper and Brothers whom Smart had recommended. Aswell believed *Nothing But the Night* was irretrievable. "Your central character is presented in such a way that the reader is unsympathetic toward him. Thus it is difficult to care very deeply about what happens to him." Smart tried to humor his young friend out of his disappointment. "I know you have good sense enough not to pay any attention to his twaddle about 'sympathetic.' You might write him back that he, Aswell, is an unsympathetic character."[3] The poems Williams circulated didn't meet with any better luck. Editors pointed to insufficiencies, such as a lack of "development," or language that was too "anonymous." In August, yet another rejection of a different sort occurred. Taking Smart's advice, Williams had applied to the University of Alabama. A letter from the admissions office informed him that he had not been accepted for the fall semester. Thus, there was nothing to look forward to, no good news. For the time being, then, his suddenly diminished world would consist of being a gas meter reader, divorced, sleeping on the couch in his stepfather's house and writing at the kitchen table.

Months passed until a bright spot appeared. Williams had heard that Swallow Press in Denver, Colorado, was on the lookout for manuscripts that had been overlooked by eastern publishers. He thought he'd give it a try and sent *Nothing But the Night* to publisher Alan Swallow. Judging from the letterhead on his reply in November, apparently Swallow was a member of the English Department at the University of Denver. And apparently, he didn't have a secretary. Every capital letter jumped higher than the rest of the sentence. But there was sincerity in the warm tone. "I was glad to see your novel come in yesterday. I look forward eagerly to reading it, and you may be sure I will do all I can for it. Manuscripts have piled up on me more than I anticipated, so that I am running about three weeks for consideration. However, I shall try to handle yours in two weeks or less."

The promise to "do all I can for it" was unexpected—there was no suggestion that Swallow Press might consider other work, if he cared to submit it.[4] Williams put the letter aside and waited.

In the meantime, George Rae was trying to get her brother to stay in California. The University of Alabama didn't have to be his only choice. There was no lack of colleges in the area, for one thing. Also, he'd done some acting and directing, and the big film studios in Culver City, Burbank, and Hollywood were minutes away. She was proud of John and supplied him with reasons to stay, including fixing him up with one of her friends from the Pasadena Playhouse, a nineteen-year-old brunette in junior college with freckles and a beaming smile, Yvonne Elyce Stone.

Yvonne was on the lookout for adventure—some kind of change. She had been born in Los Angeles and never lived very far from it, spending her childhood in Beverly Hills, then her teenage years in Salinas, after which she returned to Los Angeles.[5] Yvonne's mother, who was divorced from her father, was a bit of a crackpot. After being introduced to Yvonne's new boyfriend, Mr. Williams, and listening to his conversation, she decided he was a communist.

It was Williams' way to always have a woman in his life—sometimes more than one, never going for long without a female in the background, supporting his efforts.

"Don't work too hard, baby, and be sure to write me," Yvonne wrote on a postcard after they had been dating for several months. It was postmarked Pacific Groves, where she was enjoying the beaches near San Francisco—four hundred miles up the California coast from Los Angeles. She dropped him another postcard the next day from Carmel, telling him coquettishly, "I finally got my suitcase and am wearing clothes again."[6]

———

Swallow followed up his initial response to *Nothing But the Night* with two typewritten, single-spaced pages of criticism for Williams, going beyond what an editor-publisher would normally do. "It starts out with a scene that I call surrealist, continues with a long stretch of minute emotional writing—all torturous—and then, approximately the last third, comes a solid psychological writing that one grasps, understands, and finds exciting." What concerned him was that "the novel lacks a certain consistency or observable direction of development. . . . [I]t seems to prey a good bit on rather deliberate obscurantism in the early parts, and then, toward the end, becomes rather simple in comparison, a good ending, but not tied together thematically and stylistically as well."

He suggested that Williams "may well be a writer who needs to throw away about two or three novels before the thing starts clicking." In other words, perhaps he hadn't served his apprentice-

ship yet, and Swallow added that although his press "sponsor[ed]
early work, unusual and experimental work," he had to be careful
with his money. His advice—"if you care to hear it"—was "that you
try the novel many other places" and benefit from the experience of
having a number of editors read it.[7]

Swallow's letter was at once generous, instructive, and respectful of a new writer's hopes, but ultimately he confessed that he
couldn't do it justice at present and wouldn't stand in Williams'
way. It was a remarkable response, but then, Alan Swallow was an
unusual person.

———

A glimpse of him as a boy in Wyoming captures his personality
and, as his friend Yvor Winters once said, Swallow's "curious inner
violence that contributed to his success and to his death."[8] In 1927,
he was twelve years old and speeding down a road on an Indian
motorcycle that he had repaired himself. As he leaned into a curve,
he thrust out his arms, threw back his head to the sun, and let the
wind take its chances with him.

He had been born in Powell, Wyoming, in 1915, within sight
of the eastern slope of the Rocky Mountains. His parents raised
beets and sheep three miles outside of town on formerly Shoshone
wetlands that had been drained by the federal government. The
farm belonged to his grandmother; she had been working the land
since her husband, a railroad detective, had died from an accidental
gunshot wound to the stomach. Swallow's sister Vera recalled "the
gasoline lamps, the kerosene lights . . . the house so cold in the
mornings, the wood burning stoves, the wonderful scent of fresh
bread and cinnamon rolls, the baby chicks behind the stove in the
spring."[9] Alan was a stout boy with reddish-blond hair and a habit
of standing with his hands in his pockets. He was quiet, a loner, and
liked working on junked cars and tractors, thinking that he might
want to go to college to become a mechanical engineer. And then at
sixteen, he had an experience that—in an overused, but necessary
phrase—changed his life.

He was working at a gas station in Gardiner, Montana—the

north entrance to Yellowstone National Park—and passing the time by reading titles in the Little Blue Books series. The publisher was the Jewish American socialist, atheist, and social reformer Emanuel Haldeman-Julius, whose low-priced paperbacks were intended for working men and women. Printed with slate blue covers and priced at ten cents apiece, the Little Blue Books offered thought-provoking, self-improving subject matter intended to elevate readers, and perhaps lift them out of poverty, such as Thomas Paine's *The Age of Reason*, Boccaccio's *Tales from the Decameron*, *Hints on Writing Poetry* by Clement Wood, Margaret Sanger's *What Every Girl Should Know*, *A Guide to Emerson* by H. M Tichenor, *Do We Need Religion?* by Joseph McCabe, and *How to Be an Orator* by the socialist governor of Illinois, John Peter Altgeld. Ultimately, there were over a thousand titles in the series.

Swallow purchased a boxful of used copies and read them all.[10] As interesting to him as the subject matter was the concept of selling high-quality literature for the price of pocket change. If he had a press, he could publish uncopyrighted classics for his list, then advertise for submissions, review them, and grow larger. His stock could be printed on a hand press in small runs to save money. The post office would take care of the rest.

In April 1932 he received a scholarship to the University of Wyoming, but by then engineering as a major had fallen by the wayside in favor of English literature. By his sophomore year, he was mimeographing and distributing his own literary magazine, *Sage*. He married his sister's friend Mae Elder, a Powell girl, in 1936, the year he graduated from Wyoming. For graduate school, and ultimately a doctorate, Alan enrolled at Louisiana State University, where Robert Penn Warren, Allen Tate, and Cleanth Brooks were leaders in the New Criticism movement—which stressed close reading to see how a work, particularly poetry, functioned as a self-contained piece of art.[11] Mae worked in the office of the New Critics' literary quarterly, the *Southern Review*, proofreading manuscripts, keeping the accounts, collating the printed pages, and preparing magazines for mailing—experiences which brought nearer the reality of Alan becoming a publisher one day.

In 1939, he borrowed $100 from his father and purchased a used electric Kelsey Excelsior Press, which ran like a miniature locomotive. A coupling rod drove the main wheel, making all the parts move and clank, including the platen that pressed the paper against the bed of type. In fact, Alan was as enamored of the craft-mechanical side of publishing as he was of books. "I don't object to setting the type," he wrote to a friend. "In fact I rather like it," he later said. He enjoyed printing, collating, and stapling in a "workmanlike fashion some of the things I would be wanting to publish."[12] In 1940, in a garage in Baton Rouge, he published *Signets: An Anthology of Beginnings*, featuring poems, stories, and artwork by student contributors. It was the first to bear the imprint "Alan Swallow, Publisher."

After accepting a position teaching at the University of New Mexico, he expanded his publishing fivefold, still relying heavily on Mae, though the marriage lopsidedly favored what was important to Alan. "Although she has no particular interest in literature," he admitted, "she helped me with the publishing work, and she has suffered by being left to her own devices, while I worked night after night at the press or the typewriter."[13] From his noisy Kelsey Excelsior came chapbooks and quarterlies of poetry under various short-lived imprints—Big Mountain Press, Sage Books, Modern Verse, Swallow Pamphlets—typical of his tendency to leap from one project to the next. As someone said of him, just having "an idea was always a call to action."[14]

He ran Swallow Press according to his principles: first, he used his own judgment to choose what to publish, instead of being driven by what was popular. He was proud of being a maverick.[15] Second, he would keep a lookout for writers from the West. The eastern literary establishment tended to have a double standard: writers who lived in the West were treated as regionalists. Nebraska-native Mari Sandoz's novel *Old Jules*, set in the Sand Hills of the Plains, had been rejected by every major New York publisher before it won a fiction contest and became a best seller in 1935. It seemed that an author was taken seriously only if he had the fairy dust of eastern cosmopolitanism on him—such as Owen Wister, author of *The*

Virginian, a groundbreaking western. Swallow was out to prove that literature originating in the West deserved to be honored.

In addition to being a small-press publisher, Swallow was indeed an English professor at the University of Denver, as Williams had surmised when he received Swallow's reply about *Nothing But the Night,* typed on English Department stationery. The overlap was a result of the university administration urging him to create a university press. Excited, but unwilling to abandon his own imprints, he had decided he could do both. By 1946, he was simultaneously running the University of Denver Press and negotiating with William Morrow and Company in New York to distribute Swallow Press books. At his brick, split-level suburban home at 2679 South York Street, which he shared with Mae and their infant daughter, Karen, he happily anticipated how he would need a bigger garage to accommodate all the business and inventory that would be coming his way.

————

In the meantime, Williams had revised *Nothing But the Night* several times and shopped it around to other publishers, as Swallow had recommended, but the responses all harped on one thing: it just wasn't strong enough. "We think you have writing talent," said an editor at Harcourt, Brace and Company, "and we think it would be a mistake to start off with this book as your first long work. It is an excellent exercise."[16] Ken Smart, at Alabama, urged him not to give up, writing, "There are still a lot of people rooting hard for you to break down the barriers, and for Christ's sake don't get too discouraged."[17] And in fact, a "second-look" letter had arrived from Swallow in April 1947, justifying Smart's faith in Williams.

"My lateness may have destroyed any opportunity I had to see what you have done with the re-worked novel," Swallow wrote rather breathlessly. "But I am eager and interested." He said he was creating a category of titles in his catalog called The Short Fiction Club. "Selections for the club will come in part from other publishers, but primarily I will publish for it under my private imprint. I don't care a damn about making money on it."[18] He thought Williams' novel would fit nicely among his titles. And he had something even better to offer: if Williams would consider enrolling at the University of Denver to complete his undergraduate degree, he promised to help him in any way he could. "I'd be damned glad if you could come to Denver next fall. . . . The writing program would interest you, particularly, I think; and especially if you plan to stay for the MA, too, for which we have a good program."[19] The English Department was actually quite small, with fewer than a dozen full- and part-time instructors. But Swallow had a hunch that a personal invitation to an undecided young man with an unpublished novel might just do the trick.

Williams replied that he and Yvonne were marrying in August and things were up in the air until then, but he would have his credits transferred from Hardin Junior College, just in case. A snag occurred when the University of Denver admissions office refused to accept his unofficial transcript, but Swallow rushed in. "The transcript matter has probably been cleared up by now. And I imagine you have received admission," he wrote. "That leaves the most troublesome problem, of course—housing." But "we are certain to be able to get [you] a pretty pleasant sleeping and study room, very likely with [the] privilege of getting your own breakfast, so that the two of you would have to eat out two meals a day at our cafeteria or elsewhere. So if you are willing, both you and your wife, to put up with the inconvenience . . ."[20]

Yvonne, twenty, and John, twenty-four, were married on August 28 in Pasadena by a Methodist minister. Less than a week later, they left on a combination honeymoon and road trip, heading to Denver and a new life, like millions of other postwar couples just starting out.

"I think Denver is a good idea," Smart wrote when he heard the news. "This guy Swallow sounds like a very good Joe."[21]

———

Denver sits twelve miles east of the foothills of the Rocky Mountains, where Cherry Creek runs into the South Platte River. Its story has the romance of the Old West. Prospectors arrived on the banks of the South Platte panning for gold when it was still Kansas Territory. The Pike's Peak Gold Rush in 1858—a decade after the California Gold Rush—brought saloon operators, blacksmiths, carpenters, developers, and speculators swarming like bees to the mining camp on the Platte named for James Denver, the Kansas territorial governor. Within a few years, Denver was a town with streets laid out on a grid aligned with the four points of the compass. In 1870 the transcontinental railroad came through, ensuring that the location would become one of the commercial hubs of the Pike's Peak region. It became the state capital in 1876.

The region had such an abundance of agricultural and mineral resources—the Colorado Silver Boom occurred in 1879—that by the early part of the twentieth century, four thousand boxcars of goods and raw materials left Denver annually. Yet the city remained the "reluctant capital" of the Rocky Mountains West. It was "Colorado's cow town," worried about losing its frontier independence, "contentedly disinterested in its own continuing growth, abhorrent of risk-taking, chary of progress," according to historians writing in 1949. After World War II, the old-timers looked on unhappily as thousands of ex-servicemen, like Williams, enrolled at "GI Tech," as the university was called. When a reporter asked Denver's seventy-two-year-old mayor, Benjamin F. Stapleton, how he planned to address the housing shortage, he replied, "Oh, well, if all these people would only go back where they came from, we wouldn't have a housing shortage."[22]

But they had come to stay. Enrollment at the university shot up to ten thousand, its highest ever. When the poet Alan Stephens, who later became one of Williams' friends, enrolled in 1949, he found his classes dominated by "some exceptionally able and resolute people. Being amongst them was like being in an electrical storm—the air seemed charged with dangerous intelligence. Exciting days."[23] The dormitories overflowed and students resorted to living in Quonset huts, old hotels, basements, and converted garages. Williams applied for a $90 per month subsistence grant available to veterans, enough to rent the one-room apartment that Swallow located for him and Yvonne at 1000 South Clarkson Street.

Williams took a stroll not long after arriving to take the measure of his new life. Everywhere the university was scrambling to expand. Nineteen new buildings were under construction for the liberal arts and the sciences, physical science, engineering, and physical education. In *Stoner*, Williams describes young William Stoner, until recently a farmer, exploring the campus of the University of Missouri for the first time:

> For several minutes after the man had driven off, Stoner stood unmoving, staring at the complex of buildings. He had never before seen anything so imposing. The red brick buildings stretched upward from a broad field of green that was broken by stone walks and small patches of garden. Beneath his awe, he had a sudden sense of security and serenity he had never felt before. Though it was late, he walked for many minutes about the edges of the campus, only looking, as if he had no right to enter.[24]

The same sense of strangeness and exhilaration also fell upon Williams at the University of Denver. None of his people had ever attended a university. He had grown up poor, and had received mediocre grades in junior college because he had been too busy with his own plans to care. He thought of himself as "the most unlikely person possible to enter an academic setting."[25]

CHAPTER SIX

Love

All of my belongings had been moved into a locked closet and there were some items that belonged to another female all over the apartment.

—YVONNE WILLIAMS, UNPUBLISHED MEMOIR

"We are settled in a little four room apartment near the center of town," Yvonne wrote to friends at the end of their first academic year in the spring of 1948. "The first two months we were here we lived in a stinking room. But with the right connections and a small amount of capital we were able to get this apartment and also buy the furniture that is in it. John has a study to himself and we have a front room, bedroom, kitchen and bathroom. It's on the fourth floor and not too bad."

Their new apartment, at 2058 California Street, was convenient for Yvonne, because she worked in the offices of an oil company that was within walking distance. She hated the job. John was "doing pretty good in his studies," she wrote. "I think it was the right choice of schools. The main reason being that Alan Swallow is here. He and John get along magnificently; you couldn't ask for a better set up. Throughout the past months they have become very good friends. Alan has bestowed upon John many of the duties of a publisher and has just recently asked him to be Associate Editor of the Swallow Press. Which shows that Alan must admire John's work and ideas."[1]

The two men were indeed getting along well. On afternoons when Williams didn't have class, he walked the four blocks from campus to South York Street and let himself into Alan's combination garage and publishing house. Business was good, and fortunately for Alan, the English Department had reduced his teaching load in return for his work managing the fledgling University of Denver Press.

With the radio playing, the two men—and whomever else Alan had enlisted, usually graduate students—spent the hours arranging metal type in trays, running the hand press, collating pages, distributing the type back into its proper cases, and boxing finished books for shipping.

Among the students pitching in was twenty-two-year-old Avalon "Lonnie" Smith, from Silverton, Colorado, who had recently graduated from Stephens College, an all-women's college in Columbia, Missouri. She knew John in another capacity outside of Swallow Press, too, as the poetry editor of *Foothills*, the campus literary magazine, to which she contributed verses. She took note of the up-and-coming writer. His essay on the poetry of J. V. Cunningham was slated for the summer 1950 issue of *Arizona Quarterly*. Not only that, but Swallow's smartly dressed associate editor also had a novel in the book catalog they were assembling, *Nothing But the Night*, dedicated to Ken Smart.[2] They were mailing dozens of review copies; Alan rarely took out advertisements, convinced that in the great scriptorium where good books were cherished, good literature eventually would meet its reward.

"Holy Jesus Christ, man!" Smart wrote, when he received his copy. "Multiple congratulations to you. I hope your wife realizes she has a talented husband whose chief accomplishment is knowing how to dedicate books. I am touched and overcome. . . . You have my permission to dedicate anything you like to me, including three or four thousand-dollar bills."[3]

Sales of the book were "not too good and not too bad," Yvonne reported. "It feels swell to be old married folks but it doesn't seem like six months it seems more like six years. But it's wonderful. Wouldn't trade it for anything."[4] The downside was that John wasn't home very often, and she worked downtown during the week, nine-to-five. He went to school and stayed out most evenings. When he was home weekends, she couldn't get him to go out and have fun.[5]

———

Back in Los Angeles, George Rae, who was twenty-two now and working as a keypunch clerk in the US Office of Price Administration, was having fun, too. She was in love.

Her boyfriend, Willard "Butch" Marsh, was only a month older than John—about the same size but stockier, with black hair and black-framed glasses. They looked enough alike to be brothers. Also, both men had been Army Air Corps sergeants during the war; both had been married once; and both wrote fiction, although Butch also needed "plenty of time to blow jazz, man." Before he was drafted, he had put himself through three years of school at Chico State College north of Sacramento, California, performing on trumpet and trombone with Will Marsh and the Four Collegians. The GI Bill had paid for a senior year at San Francisco State, but he had dropped out because he wanted to write full-time—an ambition still subsidized by playing gigs in nightclubs.[6]

George Rae and Butch were living together in his three-bedroom, white stucco house in West Hollywood on North Gardner Street. "We can't get married until August, because his divorce isn't final until then. . . . Daddy doesn't know anything about it—not even where I live," she wrote to John. Should John object to this subterfuge, his sister put him on notice: "I've never been so happy in my whole life as I have been in the two weeks we have lived here, and, of course, Butch is the most wonderful person I have ever known. I never really thought I could care about anyone as much as I do him. He's a really fine person. I know you will like him, you better!"[7]

John sent her paramour a copy of *Nothing But the Night* at George Rae's insistence, she thinking, probably, that it would give the two men something to talk about. Marsh replied to Williams' gift with a seven-page, single-spaced typewritten critique, establishing his credentials as a writer who was every bit as serious (and talented, presumably) as his girlfriend's brother was.

He started off by listing the small magazines for poetry and stories he had submitted to, such as the *Southwest Review*, *Matrix*, *Sibylline*, and *Narrative*. Helpfully, he provided summaries of the editorial needs of other magazines, in case Williams might want to try them. Finally, he got into the meat of his letter on page three: "I was only a little way into [*Nothing But the Night*] when I wondered why it had been turned down by a couple of major publishers. . . . [A]t the same time I simultaneously respected, envied and was amused by your complete violation of the only real taboo in novel writing. . . . One simply does not have a yen to fuck Mother, unless one is Poppa." He gave his opinion on Williams' tone, his word choices, his sentences, and whether the ending was satisfactory.

Then he warned Williams about publishing with Swallow Press: "I don't think it is going to do you any good as a writer, and may hurt you a hell of a lot." Marsh had never heard of Alan Swallow and couldn't find any of his titles in bookstores. But then, perhaps that was because Swallow Press mainly only published writers who were eggheads—the kind that the average reader wouldn't appreciate—the phonies and aesthetes. Butch thought he knew the type: "Lucinda Longhaire has been writing some of the most provocative and stimulating prose of the past decade, and is author of *Duet for Trombone and Tombstone* and *Years Like Turds*. These challenging novels may be obtained by sending $1.75 to Watercloset Publications, or from Miss Longhaire, 69 Finger Blvd., Greenwich Village, NY. Miss Longhaire's previous appearance in *Thunderjug* was with an essay on Gertrude Stein's use of the split infinitive."

Speaking for himself, Butch said he would be a dumb "son-of-a-bitch" if, like John, he busted his "ass writing a novel and then, after one or two rejections by major publishers, gave it away to a well-meaning amateur with utterly no means of promoting it." He had twenty-eight stories and eight poems finished; and when he had fifty stories, he would blitz the publishing world, warning editors that he was not about to sit around for three months waiting for form letters. If they liked what they saw, they had better say so, and then he would send them his novel (as yet unwritten). He concluded, "Jealously Yours, Butch."[8]

Williams wasn't upset by Marsh's gratuitous critique of his novel, or his career. He could have pointed out that he'd just had a poem, "Drouth"—about the regenerative power of tilling the earth— accepted by *The American Scholar*, which trumped any of the little off-set magazines Marsh was courting. But he replied in a friendly way, thanking him for taking the time to read his work so carefully, though disagreeing with him on a few points, too. For his sister's sake, he would withhold judgment on her bellicose boyfriend, who seemed so cocksure of himself.

———

Cooped up in the apartment in the evenings by herself, Yvonne was getting fed up with how much time John spent working. If he was at home, he was either studying or writing; or if he was away during the day, she left the door unlocked after she'd already gone to bed. She lay awake nights, thinking about this state of affairs. "John and I never did anything together and that wasn't enough for this twenty-one-year-old. I had belonged to a little theater group in Pasadena, California as well as attending a radio school. Alone in a strange new place wasn't enough for me." The reluctance to socialize wasn't coming from her: She enjoyed meeting her husband's friends—artists and writers mainly.[9] Fortunately, invitations to dinner parties at the Swallows' home came regularly. In April 1948, as the school year was drawing to a close, Alan invited them over to meet a young friend of his from New England who was on his way to the Southwest, Douglas Woolf.

Woolf was guaranteed to be interesting. He was a cousin of Leonard Woolf, Virginia Woolf's husband, and shared with him the same long, thin face, wide forehead, and strong nose. Born in New York City in 1922, he had been raised in Larchmont, a wealthy enclave outside the city, and in Connecticut. He came from a rather eccentric family of some means, achievement, and social standing. His father was a world-renowned expert on Persian rugs; his stepmother was Thomas Edison's granddaughter. During World War II, Woolf had served as an American Field Service ambulance driver in North Africa as well as in the Army Air Corps, experiences he later used in his 1962 novel, *Wall to Wall.*[10] He was also an early Beat poet, rejecting literary tradition and writing Zen-like verse:

Memory
isn't just of the past
I went there
I saw that
Memory is of the future too
I'll go there
I'll do that
Perhaps I'll see you,
too[11]

The poet Robert Creeley was struck by how Woolf seemed to let the world come to him, without expectations. "Douglas Woolf was an uncannily reflective person," Creeley wrote, "as though he chose to take his color and shape from the surrounding world rather than to force upon it his own determinations and judgment. However, what he did exercise, unremittingly, was an acute perception, *his* witness, *his* recognition, *his* fact in being there, wherever there was or might be."[12]

At the Swallows' dinner with Woolf in attendance, conversation-starved Yvonne enjoyed listening to him. "Where does your accent come from?" she asked.

"Harvard." ("Har-*var*-dians," Williams sarcastically called them.) "Oh." She thought she should have known that, for some reason.[13]

As everyone was saying their goodbyes later, Woolf mentioned that he didn't have a car; neither did the Williamses. But he was staying in a hotel near their apartment, so the three of them caught a streetcar. Yvonne slid over on the seat to make room for Douglas to sit beside her, "and we talked about the various entertainments in Denver. He told me of an upcoming concert at the park and we decided to go the following Sunday. John was going to be busy that day so Doug and I made arrangements to go."

They stayed most of the afternoon at the concert, walking around the park afterward. Yvonne was pleased that Douglas was "interested in what I said and did." She arranged a double date with a friend of hers from work, but John paid more attention to her friend than Doug did. A few days later, Woolf phoned her at the oil company office and suggested they grab a bite during her lunch hour. John's reaction when Yvonne suggested they invite Woolf over for dinner was a shrug of the shoulders. "When Doug arrived John wasn't home yet," she said. "We waited for quite a while, even went for a walk to the Platt River." By the time they came back, the meat loaf was burned and there was still no sign of John. She didn't know what to make of it. She always assumed he was working at Swallow Press, or perhaps he had "his own social life which didn't include me. I didn't know for sure. I just knew that for a relatively new bride, very naïve, I needed more attention than I was getting from John and I enjoyed Doug's company."

The lunch dates continued, sometimes over martinis; other times, after Yvonne had finished work, they met at a drugstore counter for chocolate mint Cokes, their favorite treat. At some point, the friendship turned serious; when Doug told her he was heading to Tucson, Arizona, in June, she told him she would meet him there on her way back from a trip to California to see her parents.[14] In Douglas Woolf's novel *Wall to Wall*, Yvonne is the barely fictionalized Vivien; the narrator, Claude, runs away with her to the deserts of the Southwest. Vivien pleads, "'Twenty-one is too old to go anywhere alone, you know that. I want to go with someone. I don't mean as a bride, I'm not so gauche as that, but as a mistress or paramour or concubine or companion or friend or pal or anything else. I just don't want to be left alone! I want to get out of here!' She said it again for all the wide-faced flowers to hear: 'I want to get out of here!'"[15]

———

That summer, too, the Swallows were away from Denver for three months. Alan had accepted an eight-week lectureship at the University of California, Berkley. But he had perfect confidence in John, and temporarily handed him the reins of the press as if it were his own. From Berkeley, Swallow redirected a submission to him. "John Williams, my associate editor, has taken a great interest in these poems of yours. I am returning the manuscript to Williams in Denver, and you will hear from him next."[16]

As associate editor, into Williams' hands came submissions of poetry and fiction from both established writers and those who were on their way to making a reputation. In the former category were Louise Brogan, Caroline Gordon, Thomas McGrath, Archibald MacLeish, Henry Miller, Wallace Stevens, Allen Tate, and Mark Van Doren. In the category of new and notable writers were Herbert Gold, Weldon Kees, Janet Lewis, and Anaïs Nin. When it was literally hot off the press, Williams read a collection of critical essays by Yvor Winters published by Swallow Press—*In Defense of Reason*, a reply to the Romantic poet Shelley's *In Defense of Poetry*. Winters argued for a moral versus a romantic theory of literature, and for practicing rationality in art over feeling. He attacked Walt Whitman's "loose and sprawling poetry to 'express' the loose and sprawling American continent," adding, "In fact, all feeling, if one gives oneself (that is, one's form) up to it, is a way of disintegration; poetic form is by definition a means to arrest the disintegration and order the feeling."[17] Winters' perspective so impressed Williams that he left behind his romantic, scarf-wearing persona in Wichita Falls forever. He counted himself as a Winterian from then on, and took a special interest, as Winters did, in English Renaissance poetry and rationalism.

Thus, Williams, the "most unlikely person possible to enter an academic setting," was finding himself quite at home in university life. He enjoyed his coursework. And by temporarily taking over Swallow's chair as editor and publisher of the press, he was being schooled in the freshest contemporary literature.

But his fiction, still a bit overwrought with psychology and exquisite language, hadn't changed. *Mademoiselle* magazine rejected his first-person short story "The Summer" with an unusual amount of scorn, saying, "It offered more poetically than fiction-wise. The theme, for example, is developed so cynically that the piece takes on the nature of a philosophical treatise. Similarly, the characters are bloodless, paper-people. . . . Our whole feeling is that the story could, and should have, generated power within itself, but even its natural pace has been slowed by [a] too stylish treatment."[18]

"The Summer" is largely an interior monologue by an unnamed narrator who recalls spending a vacation, when he was sixteen years old, with friends of his family at their cottage on a "foam-tipped cobalt lake." It's a coming-of-age story. "For I was doubly in love that summer, first with Tom and then with Doris; or first with Doris, then with Tom," says the narrator. "It was impossible to determine which was more important." He is infatuated with Romantic poetry, reporting: "I imagined myself sinking into the blue cold lake behind our cabin, a poem on my lips." The style is breathless and word-drunk, which smothers the quieter story about the boy's first love. But Williams' early penchant for big words and abstractions reveals something important. In his later fiction, too, there tends to be a lag between a character's thought and emotion—overthinking gets in the way of feeling. Later, in Williams' first major novel, *Butcher's Crossing*, the young buffalo hunter Will Andrews runs from the room rather than let a young woman seduce him:

> "What is it?" Francine said sleepily. "Come back." "No!" he said hoarsely, and flung himself across the room, stumbling on the edge of the rug. "My God! . . . No. I'm sorry." He looked up. Francine stood dumbly in the center of the room; her arms were held out as if to describe a shape to him; there was a look of bewilderment in her eyes. "I can't," he said to her, as if he were explaining something. "I can't."[19]

In *Stoner*, Williams' second major novel, middle-aged Professor Stoner struggles to express himself to Katherine, his graduate student, with whom he's falling in love. Stoner's presentation of himself as a suitor is sadly funny as he uses his classroom approach to discuss their "problem":

> "I was perhaps selfish. I felt that nothing could come of this except awkwardness for you and unhappiness for me. You know

my—circumstances. It seemed to me impossible that you could— that you could feel for me anything but—"

"Shut up," she said softly, fiercely. "Oh, my dear, shut up and come over here."[20]

In the final scene of "The Summer," the story kicked to the curb by *Mademoiselle*, it's nighttime, and the narrator is sitting in the front seat of the car beside his friend Tom. The vacation is ending, and Tom's sister never did return his love, or sexual desire, because he didn't let her know how he felt:

"Well, it was a good summer?" [Tom's] face was placid, calm, unconcerned, the composed eyes staring straight into the darkness. I did not speak. He looked at me. "Wasn't it a good summer?"

"Yes," I said bitterly, too agonized to think. "Oh, yes." Then I turned away [. . .] to look back up into the impenetrable past darkness, searching always, vainly, fruitlessly, without hope, another face somewhere lost, somewhere shrouded, somewhere dead and half-forgotten in the dim irretrievable past.[21]

Williams could build his fiction around thought warring with feeling, which creates tension, and to suggest that emotions are ineffable, beyond characters' reach. But he was also writing poetry, and the intellectual distance, the control, he wielded in fiction did not serve him well as a poet, which will be addressed later.

———

In July, George Rae received a phone call from Yvonne, who was back in Pasadena, visiting her parents, and wanted to meet for lunch. Had her courage not failed her, she intended to tell her sister-in-law that she was falling out of love with John, and there was another man in her life. What George Rae heard instead was that Yvonne was more mature now. "I hope you and Yvonne get your difficulties straightened out," she wrote to her brother the day after seeing Yvonne. "She seems to have developed into quite a nice kid—no longer the bobby-soxer type. . . . And she was missing you like the devil already." By then, Yvonne had called John to say she needed time "to think about our strange marriage."[22]

From Pasadena, Yvonne went by train to Tucson, and Doug met her at the station. For a few weeks, they lived the kind of life Yvonne had been expecting to have with John. They enrolled in courses for the second half of the summer term at the University of Arizona and did their homework together. Earlier, Doug had renounced his family's wealth in favor of art, and Yvonne was willing to join him in that. Lugging a suitcase full of sample wares in the summer heat, they sold plastic household items door-to-door: tablecloths, shower curtains, plates, knives and forks. She loved the adventures they were having. "We would work the same neighborhood and meet in a little mom and pop grocery store to cool off with a cold soft drink. When we weren't going to school or walking the streets selling, we would often go for nighttime swims at El Conquistador Hotel. We took buses and at times even hitchhiked to town. Doug and I had lots of fun together."[23]

In August, John phoned. He was having second thoughts about their break-up, and he wanted to give the marriage another try. George Rae and Butch were getting married in Los Angeles, and he wanted Yvonne to attend the ceremony with him. Although he didn't say so, perhaps the reason he wanted her to go with him was that he didn't want to face a lot of questions about why she was not there. Gallantly, Doug paid for Yvonne's bus ticket home to Denver and saw her off.

John wasn't in the apartment when she arrived, so she let herself in. But as she entered, she had a sense of being in the wrong place. "All of my belongings had been moved into a locked closet and there were some items that belonged to another female all over the apartment." Putting her suitcase on the bed, she noticed a crumpled piece of paper in the wastebasket. It was a note in John's handwriting: "Better get your stuff out of the apartment today. My wife is coming back from the insane asylum."[24]

She called Doug and he wired her money for airfare to Tucson. She filed for a quick divorce in Florida—which was available only to state residents, but she met the requirement by signing a lease for a rented room in Miami. She was not someone who was starry-eyed about the institution of marriage and the courts; she suspected "all they ever wanted was money, anyway."[25] The divorce became final in February 1949.

———

George Rae loyally took her brother's side. "It's a tough stinking deal about Yvonne, but it is slightly understandable with the bitch-mother she had. I guess early training sooner or later shows." Butch added a postscript, figuratively throwing his arm around John's shoulder as a comrade-in-arms, saying, "I don't suppose it would be quite safe for me to express a wistful envy for your status as a bachelor; not unless I intend to start getting my own breakfasts— a prospect which I am too cowardly to face." He recommended Williams go to a free legal aid clinic and explain that he was an ex-GI enrolled in college, broke, and needing help with a divorce.[26]

Without Yvonne, though, John didn't want to attend their wedding, news his sister was not pleased to hear. "You've got to—we have everything planned and you must! Besides, I want to see you, and I want you to meet my boy. So, you see, you can't get out of coming."[27] But he demurred, saying he had too much work. "Damn! Damn! Damn!" his sister replied, disappointed and hurt. "You don't have enough time between semesters to make the trip, do you? This is very upsetting—we had planned so on you coming."[28] When she asked for a postcard update—"Write to us, you stinker, and let us know what goes"—he sent her one with a paragraph of typed gibberish that ended, "Nyet, nyet, klumph."

Butch, bothered that George Rae was upset, picked a fight with John by bad-mouthing Swallow Press again. "I will have to risk stirring your hackles by pointing out what seems to me to be an embarrassing inconsistency in your stand: your own book has been the only publication of Swallow's that I've read that I would trouble to wipe my ass on. . . . All of the selections of The Short Fiction Group I've seen . . . have been so consistently pitiful."[29]

George Rae feared a permanent break and tried making peace

before it was too late: "I hope by this time you have stopped bristling with anger at our last letter. Butch really isn't a violently commercial boy. . . . It is true that he hasn't liked the recent Short Fiction selections. But you can't completely condemn him for that. He feels that Swallow is giving you a bad deal, etc. Well, enough of this—but I wish you two could meet—then you would stop fighting—I know you would, because you would find that you were pretty much in agreement."[30]

Williams, as a peace offering, sent a signed copy of his poetry collection, just published by Swallow Press, *The Broken Landscape*, which included the poem "The Lovers":

> *This cluttered room knows form tonight. Before*
> *My window, casual and tense you stand,*
> *While to the north an erosive moon explores*
> *The freezing sky, and crumbles on your hand.*
>
> *Now we, though silent in our rafted room,*
> *May meet, although we do not speak, or brush*
> *As unique petals on earth's blackened rim:*
> *Here distance is made finite in time's hush,*
>
> *And here the shrinking dark conspires with space.*
> *But you must turn and shatter me, invite*
> *Dispersion through your body's aching space.*
> *—Thus all is huge again, and depthless night.*[31]

Acknowledging its receipt, Butch replied, "We were both surprised to learn, from the dust jacket, that you are 'Currently attending the graduate school of the University of Denver.' Why didn't you tell us you had graduated?"[32] Butch didn't remark on, or perhaps he didn't notice, that the volume was dedicated to "Lonnie"—Avalon Smith, who worked at Swallow Press.

In March 1949, a month after Yvonne's divorce was final, John and Lonnie married in Provo, Utah, where her parents lived, in a private ceremony, again at a Methodist minister's home.

PART II

Butcher's Crossing

CHAPTER SEVEN

The Winters Circle

Yvor Winters cut a giant's figure. . . . [N]o one whom Winters touched as a poet, critic, colleague or teacher could remain indifferent to his passionate convictions about poetry.

—KENNETH FIELDS, WINTERS' COLLEAGUE, *STANFORD MAGAZINE*, 2000

s John Williams' marital problems waxed and waned, quarterly statements began indicating that Swallow Press was in real trouble. It wasn't because of anything Williams did or failed to do; it was because Swallow had his fingers in half a dozen pies—teaching classes on creative writing, directing the university's creative writing program, and managing both his own and the university press. He was overwhelmed, and his business showed it.

On the positive side, he had a keen eye for spotting worthy submissions, which time alone would prove. Swallow Press carried a few strong titles, such as Janet Lewis' *The Wife of Martin Guerre*, which Williams admired tremendously; and Allen Tate's *On the Limits of Poetry*. But Swallow's business acumen was almost nonexistent. And in his haste to publish what he liked, Swallow Press books were riddled with typographical errors.[1] Mark Harris, one of Williams' fellow students at Denver, and later the author of *Bang the Drum Slowly*, wondered how Swallow could carry on. "His publishing struck me as crazy," he later said. "He published poetry and criticism by people I had never heard of, assumed financial losses, and was constantly in search of warehouse space for thousands of books he never sold."[2]

Nevertheless, Swallow tended to operate from a happy frame of mind. All would be well as long as he was moving in literary circles and his Swallow Press books were going out the door. He wrote to Williams, in fine spirits, "Glad everything is going so well there." He was in San Francisco now, after his summer teaching stint at Berkeley. There was "a poet on every block, and about every tenth poet has written some rather decent poems," he said. "And the influences and crosscurrents are remarkable and almost impossible to straighten out, I'm afraid. . . . The wonderful thing about it is that they all, on the surface, get along well and help each other create the atmosphere of much activity going on; privately, they scratch each other like cats."[3]

———

Nearly at the top of the intellectual heap of cats who were into poetry was Williams' hero, the poet Yvor Winters and husband of the novelist Janet Lewis. Winters was the "sage of Palo Alto," Swallow called him, and Winters would not have minded the appellation. From his high place at Stanford University forty-five miles south of San Francisco, "Yvor Winters cut a giant's figure," said Kenneth Fields, a student of his who later became a colleague. "He stood out from the crowd and was often viewed with awe—or, occasionally, near-loathing. Whatever the reaction, seemingly no one whom Winters touched as a poet, critic, colleague or teacher could remain indifferent to his passionate convictions about poetry."[4] His reputation was at its peak in the late 1940s, and there was nothing he liked better than defending it with a good intellectual spat. Critic Stanley Edgar Hyman said Winters' "heart and mind seem firmly back in the London of 1700," where "violent oracular tradition" ruled.[5] Winters warned his adversaries, "I have spent my entire life in the remote west, where men are civilized but never get within gunshot of each other."

Some of it was bravado. He had not always been such an Augustan; or even a Californian, for that matter, much as he loved the West. His roots were in Chicago, where his father had been a well-to-do stock and grain broker on the Chicago Stock Exchange. As an undergraduate at the University of Chicago during World War I, where he met his future wife, Janet Lewis, he had cofounded the Chicago Poetry Club to redress the lack of modern poetry in the university's English courses. He was writing experimental verse then and would have counted himself an imagist. Had he stayed connected to the university somehow, he might have become a Chicago poet, instructor, and literary critic, a contemporary of Carl Sandburg's.

But during his junior year at Chicago, Winters was diagnosed with tuberculosis and sent by his family to St. Vincent's Sanatorium in Santa Fe, New Mexico, for a dry-climate treatment. Writers of his generation, including Lewis, went to Paris if they could, but due to Winters' health—and perhaps a break with his family—he supported himself for three years by teaching poor children in Raton, New Mexico, an experience that turned him into an advocate for social causes. He published the first of two collections of mainly free verse during those years, *The Immobile Wind* (1921) and *The Magpie's Shadow* (1922), both of which were well received. He was completely at home in modernism at that time, considering poetry as escapist and druggy, "a permanent gateway to walking oblivion."[6] His early poems were moody, concrete as opposed to abstract, and not overly concerned with ideas.

From Paris, Lewis wrote him to say that she, too, had been diagnosed with tuberculosis: What did he think she should do? He found her a position as a tutor at the Sunmount Sanatorium in Santa Fe. A passionate correspondence between them followed, and they married in 1926. From New Mexico, they went to the University of Colorado, Boulder, where he earned degrees in Romance languages and Latin. He disowned his youthful work, which had followed in the tradition of the Romantic poets. To Harriet Munroe, founder of *Poetry* magazine, he expressed his views humorously, but succinctly:

May hell wipe out divinities
And a-cerebral infinities
And other asininities,
Praise hell, praise hell, praise hell.[7]

Now he was writing poetry with the aims of the English Renaissance poets, to go "from oblivion to definition"—without vagaries, or Romantic flights. Winters now had a "rage for order."[8] Poetry should reflect certainty and clear moral choice, he argued, arrived at by thought, not by an "impulse from a vernal wood," as Wordsworth would have it. The venerated English poet Thomas Gray had waxed sentimental on nature and death in "Elegy Written in a Country Churchyard" (1751). But Winters, a New Critic, wanted nothing hovering outside the text itself—no ghosts, no Thanatos, no nostalgia, no fearful impulses. In one of his best poems, "On a View of Pasadena from the Hills" (1931), he gazes with satisfaction on his tidy garden, the product of thoughtful planning, carefully maintained and hemmed in by "seeping concrete walls / Such are the bastions of our pastorals!"

A poem, he insisted, should reveal meanings in human experience that were expressed in precise terms. The problem distorting modern poetry was extravagant and obscure language. He called for replacing it with a return to the classical or plain style—sometimes called the Native style in English Renaissance poetry—which uses concrete words rather than abstract ones, and native words rather than borrowed ones. Plain style called for modulating emotion versus abandoning oneself to mystery, obscurity, or the supernatural. As was said of the Greek historian Herodotus, his writing was, "clear, rapid, euphonious, marvelously varied according to variations of his subject matter; he can write in a plain and simple manner, with short sentences loosely strung together, but he can also build up elaborate periodic structures making effective use of many poetical words."[9]

For teaching to students his approach to poetry, Winters assembled a new canon of poems from the 1500s through the 1950s. Dashing expectations, he largely excluded the poets of the English

Petrarchan School—their language was too rich, he claimed, and most of their substance was clever rhetoric—though he did include two of its most famous representatives, Sir Philip Sidney and Edmund Spenser. Instead he elevated plain-style poets of the period, including George Gascoigne, who "deserves to be ranked," he said, "among the six or seven greatest lyric poets of the century, and perhaps higher." Other members of his pantheon included Sir Walter Raleigh, Ben Jonson, Thomas Nashe, Thomas Wyatt, and John Donne. And then, reaching down into the realms of obscurity, Winters pulled up Barnabe Googe, George Turberville, and Fulke Greville and set them among the best, too, where he believed they belonged.[10]

It was a bold project, examining four hundred years of poetry, and his methods were hard to understand. "He gives only his conclusions," complained Hyman, "almost never with any evidence approaching adequacy, and in a form in which it is not possible to argue with him or even understand what he is trying to say." The poet Kenneth Rexroth was more blunt: Winters was "responsible for some of the most wrong-headed and eccentric criticism ever written."[11]

But Williams accepted Winters' *In Defense of Reason* as a manifesto. It was fresh, yet old school and reactionary, and it was anarchic, but held in place by Winters' uncompromising doctrine:

> The Romantic theory assumes that literature is mainly or even purely an emotional experience, that man is naturally good, that man's impulses are trustworthy, that the rational faculty is unreliable to the point of being dangerous or possibly evil. The Romantic theory of human nature teaches that if man will rely upon his impulses, he will achieve the good life. When this notion is combined, as it frequently is, with a pantheistic philosophy or religion, it commonly teaches that through surrender to impulse man will not only achieve the good life but will achieve also a kind of mystical union with the Divinity: this, for example, is the doctrine of Emerson. Literature thus becomes a form of what is known popularly as self-expression.[12]

Williams was not being dogmatic by taking sides during exchanges of robust, provocative criticism like this. Some of the sharpest minds on American university campuses were attracted to English and American literature after World War II. Criticism by I. A. Richards, William Empson, T. S. Eliot, D. H. Lawrence, Lionel Trilling, Allen Tate, and F. R. Leavis swept away the older nineteenth-century approaches of philology and literary history. "You waited for their essays," said the poet Robert Lowell, "and when a good critical essay came out it had the excitement of a new imaginative work."[13] By allying himself with the Winters Circle, Williams sought to join a school of poets that included Edgar Bowers, Thom Gunn, Helen Pinkerton, Philip Levine, Margaret Peterson, Donald Hall, J. V. Cunningham, Catherine Davis, Donald Justice, Alan Stephens, and Robert Pinsky.[14]

Williams also heard in Winters' summons to return to a restrained, classical style of writing a call to stoicism—thinking one's way to clarity and understanding; practicing rational acceptance of what is. Life promises nothing and will never yield, especially not to those who attempt to please or mollify it by losing their integrity. Ecstasy was self-indulgent; giving over to feeling meant renouncing self-possession; and every line of poetry or sentence should reflect, Williams came to believe, the writer's will, rather than awe.

––––––

"How is it really all working out?" Ken Smart wrote from the University of Miami in early 1949. "How do you feel about the future— I mean would you ever seriously like to do any teaching, do you plan to stay writing as a major undertaking, or are you like so many people, content to make plans for the next ten hours only?"[15]

Williams, newly married, was juggling his time between writing fiction and poetry; working as an editor at a small press; and, if he continued in graduate school, possibly laying the groundwork for a career in academia. Of the three, teaching at the university level would provide a stable base, one that would also allow him time to write. He didn't anticipate that writing and teaching would interfere with each other. "My God, since when is working for a living

selling out?" he asked. "Writing isn't something you do in the mind
of God, or in some abstraction; you write in the world, in a room,
on a table, with a typewriter or a pencil. You've got to eat in order
to live; and if it distracts you less from your writing to eat well than
to eat badly, then you ought to eat well."[16] Besides, teaching would
strengthen him as a man of letters who understood texts, historical
periods of authorship, and so on, unlike Butch, who believed that
talent, inspiration, and time were enough for a writer. "You boys in
Denver are missing a great opportunity in not providing me with a
crate of muscatel and a tape-recorder," Butch, the jazzman/writer,
exalted. "I could turn out pages of fantasy in the joyous mode: you
could sell it, not in thin pamphlets, but by the laundry-basket full,
and make a fortune."[17]

Williams ignored the taunt; he was convinced that a writer needed
to be better read than any scholar. Earning a PhD and teaching
would provide what he needed and was what he sought to accom-
plish, working "in a room, on a table, with a typewriter . . ." He'd like
to be an author-academic. Alan Swallow had introduced him at a
party to someone in that category, who happened to be a member of
the Winters Circle, besides—poet and essayist J. V. Cunningham.

Cocktail parties for the literary-minded were one of the perks of
being friends with Alan Swallow. He invited students and colleagues
over to meet Swallow Press authors. Sometimes the gathering was
an autograph party; other times, just a Friday afternoon shindig
after work. Williams attended regularly; like his fellow graduate
students, he appreciated the chance to feel a "sense of connection
with the world of achievement."[18]

It was generous of Swallow and Mae to act as hosts. Social
situations were not Swallow's forte. Novelist Mark Harris remembered his almost painful attempts at making conversation: "Among
fellow professors and talkative students, he was slow at repartee
and banter, giving the impression of a man either humorless or a
little deaf."[19] Mae Swallow felt self-conscious too, because book-talk
was not something she kept up with. So she occupied herself with

providing a nice event. Her graciousness put everyone at ease and offset Alan's awkwardness, as he stood in the middle of the living room, a whiskey in one hand and flipping peanuts in his mouth with the other, listening and nodding.[20]

In attendance now and then was J. V. (James Vincent) Cunningham. Raised in Denver in a working-class family, Cunningham was Jesuit educated. Speaking of himself in the third person, he said, "the tradition that surrounded him and formed much of the texture of his early years was the tradition of Irish Catholics along the railroads of the West. . . . He was a Catholic by tradition, training, and deep feeling. . . . Hence, his own identity he fenced off, and though it formed part of the terrain it had its property lines."[21] Cunningham was an intense but detached listener, witty at times, not grave. It was true that some part of him was "fenced off"; there was a hint of the patrician in how he deliberately held himself apart—an unspoken assumption that intellectual integrity and self-reliance called for being reserved. Irving Howe, the literary and social critic, sensed tension beneath his polished surface: "Cunningham lived with, believing in and suffering from, an inordinate pride. Pride was the defense a serious man put up against the world—pride and a fifth of bourbon. Pride was a sin, but an enabling sin: it helped one get through one's time."[22]

Cunningham's father had been a steam-shovel operator. The family had arrived in Denver from Montana when Jim was four. At fifteen, he graduated with top honors in Latin and Greek from Regis Jesuit High School. But then his father was killed in an accident at work, and his plans for college were set aside. To help support his mother and siblings, he worked as a copyboy for the *Denver Post* writing headlines, and then as a runner at the Denver Stock Exchange. The Crash of 1929 upended his hopes a second time. Jobless, in September 1930 he and his brother took to the road in an old car. Small-town newspapers and trade magazines paid him by the article for items of interest to merchants, farmers, and businesspeople.

Cunningham wrote to Yvor Winters at Stanford asking for help, because Winters had befriended him when Jim was still in high school and they had corresponded about poetry. Winters urged his young, penniless friend to come from his freezing cabin in northern Arizona to sunny Palo Alto; he could stay in the garden greenhouse temporarily, rent-free, and Winters would see to it that he was admitted to Stanford. He told him which train to take to San Francisco, and he was there waiting on the platform when Cunningham arrived.[23]

Cunningham was ten years older than Williams, but Williams could imagine becoming like him one day—a professor at the University of Chicago, a teacher, a scholar, and a poet. True to the Winters Circle, Cunningham's verses had a kind of "cold grace" about them.[24] He mistrusted emotion. The emphasis was on meter, rhyme, and precise use of language, giving his stanzas the burnish of seventeenth-century poetry, traits that Winters praised. His verse was classically epigrammatic, and his satire had the sting of Juvenal or Martial. In "For My Contemporaries," he salutes (but smiles behind his hand) the groaning efforts of poets to bare their souls:

How time reverses
The proud in heart!
I now make verses
Who aimed at art.

But I sleep well.
Ambitious boys
Whose big lines swell
With spiritual noise,

Despise me not!
And be not queasy
To praise somewhat:
Verse is not easy.

But rage who will.
Time that procured me
Good sense and skill
Of madness cured me.[25]

The madness he has been cured of, the "spiritual noise," was his Catholicism. Without his faith, he was a "renegade" now, he said, although there is a trace of loss in his poetry, a sense that what had been good and consoling could never be recovered. His first wife, the poet Barbara Gibbs, with whom he had a daughter, bitterly compared him in "Accusatory Poem" to "shifting chips of brilliant colored glass," like a shattered stained-glass window.

———————

Williams submitted his first critical essay, "J. V. Cunningham: The Major and the Minor," to *Poetry* magazine in the fall of 1949. The poet Hayden Carruth, the senior editor, might have returned it automatically because Cunningham was a contributing editor, and it would look like an inside job. "I cannot print any commentary—particularly such an extended one—on members of my staff," he wrote. Instead, he responded with a two-page letter about the career politics of publishing criticism in journals. It included some pointed advice:

> You have a chance to do Jim [Cunningham] some good, but you must do it in the right way. Winters has done Jim much more harm than good—though out of the most honest and generous motives—by pushing him too hard, too belligerently, when others were ignoring him. The result is that Jim has come to be known as Winter's boy, and of course, that is neither true nor just. . . . What I mean to say is that your essay should be published out of the Winters's orbit, yet not in the other camp. It should be published in the East. If I were you, I'd try *Hudson Review* first.

As a sidebar, Carruth added that he couldn't accept Williams' claim that there has been no major poem since Milton: "Even limiting ourselves to English, which I suppose you intend, there have been other major poems." Without a stronger premise to defend, the rest of Williams' argument regarding major and minor poets didn't follow: "You are overstepping your evidence by about ten thousand miles."[26]

Carruth's gentle cuffing of him in the ring of heavyweight criticism did Williams a favor. Six months later, in the spring of 1950, the editors at the *Arizona Quarterly* accepted his new draft of the Cunningham essay, saying they were "unanimous in their praise." They, too, however, admitted to being a little confused about Williams' major/minor dichotomy. What did he mean, "'major' poetry is intrinsically preferable to 'minor' poetry, since there is between them no real difference"? But it didn't bother the editors enough to ask for a revision.[27]

Appearing in the *Arizona Quarterly* seemed a good omen, among others, that he should continue for a doctorate. Swallow recommended the University of Missouri, Columbia, where there was a new program combining creative writing with literary scholarship. On Alan Swallow's advice, he applied to Missouri. Columbia beckoned for another reason, as well: Lonnie could complete an advanced teaching degree there.

Williams was following the path of Winters, Cunningham, and Swallow. He felt a kinship with them—intellectually and personally. In particular, the Winters and Cunningham philosophy that combined life and art—independence of thought as a matter of integrity, the power of reason over emotion, and the plain style as an extension of stoicism expressed in prose and poetry—strongly appealed to him.

And yet, although he wanted to belong to the Winters Circle, he seemed not to have realized how different his goals were from those of most academics in the humanities, who cared nothing about writing novels, and looked skeptically at professors who did. Ironing out problems of character development, pacing, motive, and theme generally didn't interest them. Nor would they, moreover, when they were in their mid-twenties, like Williams, have dreamed of showing fiction to an agent.

Williams had only to look at the three men he admired for glimpses of the scholar's life. J. V. Cunningham would distinguish himself with the monograph *Woe or Wonder: The Emotional Effect of Shakespearean Tragedy*, published by Swallow Press. Winters, the older he got, would crossly fight off all claimants to the throne he thought was rightly his as the preeminent American critic of poetry. And Swallow, the professor/independent publisher, might have served as an example of trying to straddle too much, of having too many masters. There was hardly time enough in Swallow's life to do anything well. Regardless of their different circumstances, none of these academics had a professional inclination to spend years on a novel, which John Williams fully intended to do, and hold down a professorship in the bargain.

As he and Lonnie prepared to leave for Columbia in the fall of 1950, he packed the manuscripts and story ideas he was working on.

CHAPTER EIGHT

"Natural Liars Are the Best Writers"

*I write of human experience so that I may understand it
and thereby force myself into some kind of honesty.*

—JOHN WILLIAMS, 1964 INTERVIEW

Ashland Gravel Road in Columbia, Missouri, where new-
lyweds John and Lonnie Williams found an apartment in
the fall of 1950, was only a few blocks from campus. Years
before, it had been out in the country—explaining why, in Williams'
novel, when young Bill Stoner enrolls at Missouri in a time set decades earlier, he boards at his relatives' farm but can walk to class.
What struck Stoner so powerfully in the middle of the university's
quadrangle is still there:

> Sometimes, in the evenings, he wandered in the long open quad-
> rangle, among couples who strolled together and murmured
> softly; though he did not know any of them, and though he did not
> speak to them, he felt a kinship with them. Sometimes he stood in
> the center of the quad, looking at the five huge columns in front of
> Jesse Hall that thrust upward into the night out of the cool grass;
> he had learned that these columns were the remains of the original
> main building of the University, destroyed many years ago by fire.
> Grayish silver in the moonlight, bare and pure, they seemed to him

to represent the way of life he had embraced, as a temple represents a god.[1]

The implication is that the University of Missouri, the first university west of the Mississippi, is a kind of Athens on the edge of the wilderness. It's fitting that Stoner, the son of a farmer, should come to the brink of his vegetable world and view the columns as a kind of outpost of the ancient tradition of thought and inquiry. Enrolled to study agriculture, Stoner grows lonely in this strange world of metaphysics, discussion, and analysis.

Williams, on the other hand, was accustomed to the sociability offered by college life. His first semester, he joined a club, the Tabard Inn, consisting of about twenty-five students and professors, all men, who met twice a month in a banquet room at the Moon Valley Villa, a dine-and-dance restaurant on the eastern edge of Columbia. A "Chaucerian cell," they called themselves in "spiritual affiliation" with "Chaucer's pilgrims who set out from a grog house yclept 'Ye Tabard Inn.'" The club's purpose was to offer camaraderie among men who liked conversation with a literary bent. Within a year of joining, Williams was part of the inner circle. And it was probably here, while the members lingered past midnight to prolong their revels, that he heard the story of a decades-old feud between two professors of English at Missouri, which became one of the inspirations for *Stoner*.

―――――――

Years earlier, about the time of World War I, Robert L. Ramsay and A. (Arthur) H. R. Fairchild had been colleagues and friends at the University of Missouri. Both were "learned," in the quaint phrase of the day, with doctorates from Johns Hopkins and Yale, respectively. Later, their animosity toward each other became legendary.

Ramsay, a southerner born in Sumter, South Carolina, taught courses in the history of the English language. He corresponded with just about every American and English scholar of language of his day. His hobby was investigating the origin of place names in

Missouri—whether they were Native American, French, Spanish, or English, and so on. His love of etymology carried over into his linguistics classes, which were demanding. He wrote energetically on the board, connecting various forms of words and their origins, with chalk lines of red, yellow, or purple, getting the dust on the sleeves of his jacket and sometimes on his snow-white beard.

In his short-story writing course, students were surprised to hear him say that if they were natural liars, then they might succeed as writers. "Many men start life with a natural gift for exaggeration," he pointed out, "but in a short time develop a morbid and unhealthy faculty of truth-telling. If, when you look over your past life and recall those occasions when you ventured to use a lie, you find that you met humiliating failure, then you will not make a writer."

There were other prerequisites for being a writer, he said, such as a yen for "poking [your] nose into other people's business." A writer should also be "an ardent lover of gossip and a confirmed listener to all sorts of scandal." A penchant for cruelty helped, as well: "A genuine artist will never hesitate to deprive his characters of any happiness, to hurt them, mutilate, torture, or even kill them." If these traits made some students uncomfortable, he reassured them: don't worry, because "you may at least be a good citizen."[2]

His gently ironic sense of humor extended to oral examinations of candidates seeking a master's degree. "Well, do you think you've written a masterpiece?" Professor Ramsay would inquire, looking skeptically at the student's thesis.

"Oh, no, sir," was the usual, humble reply.

"No? Why not? What is a masterpiece?"

The student, trying to recall everything he or she could about guilds and journeymen, would explain that a masterpiece was work done to qualify a craftsman for the rank of master.

"So then," Ramsay would say, smiling, "you have written a *master-piece*, haven't you?"[3]

Ramsay's colleague in the English Department, Fairchild, an Elizabethan specialist, was a Canadian from Toronto who limped from an unsuccessful operation in middle age. His lectures tended to be formal and arid—"austere," as someone called them. His logical mind expressed the link between education and success as a syllogism. "In the last analysis," he concluded, "the success of a man in any line of work must depend upon his knowledge of human nature. A man who limits his capacity for understanding human nature limits his ability to deal with his fellows. A widened point of view, a knowledge of our fellowmen, can only be drawn from good books."[4] In 1915, Fairchild married a Miss Workman from Grand Rapids, Michigan, who became a renowned hostess and chairperson of many activities. Invitations to their home for social occasions were prized.

For a time, Ramsay and Fairchild gave public lectures together about developing taste in books, poetry, and Shakespeare—topics of broad interest to residents of a college town who enjoyed a little cultural spillover from the campus. Seated on the dais, side by side, glancing at their notes, they were the epitome of university men— two scholars, both alike in dignity. But then a split occurred, resulting in an antagonism that became, as one department member said, "intense, protracted, and largely inexplicable."[5]

During Fairchild's chairmanship, he slighted Ramsay. Ramsay usually taught the works of Milton to undergraduates. But Fairchild, who believed he was better qualified to teach Milton because he was the department's Renaissance expert, took the course away. Ramsay's fellow instructors rallied around him and created a course at the graduate level called, "Miltonic Criticism." For three decades, Professor Ramsay happily taught the course under the department chair's nose, but Fairchild never forgot how Ramsay had played mutinous Fletcher Christian to his Captain Bligh.

A second quarrel, over splitting the department, came to a head in 1937. Fairchild agreed with a lengthy report from a senior speech professor pointing out that treating speech and drama as separate from the study of literature was becoming a national trend in higher education. But Ramsay didn't see it that way; he blamed Fairchild's imperiousness for creating a rift, writing to him, "Your overbearing attitude and unwillingness to share supreme control [of departmental matters] was, I believe, the primary cause that drove our fourteen brother teachers of speech, oratory, and dramatics to press for the setting up of a separate department—a step I cannot help thinking disastrous for our students and our common interests."[6]

The fight between Ramsay and Fairchild had become notorious by now, and the bad blood trickled into every corner of the department, impossible to ignore. In fact, it poisoned the oral examination of one of Ramsay's doctoral candidates.

Ramsay's student arrived at the examination prepared to defend his thesis about the importance of local color for creating regional literature, such as the dialect found in William Faulkner, John Steinbeck, or Willa Cather. Ramsay and Fairchild, and the rest of the thesis committee, took their seats. Everything seemed to be going well, until it was Fairchild's turn to begin asking questions. Feigning the bewilderment of Socrates, he pressed the candidate to define his terms: the words "regional" and "local" and even "literature"—what did they mean? For example, *Uncle Tom's Cabin*, would that be considered "great regional literature"?

Nervously, the student tried to reply as best he could; but Fairchild continued to badger him, probing, until at last he was ready to spring his trap. "Since Aristotle has established the principle that great literature must be universal," he said, "local color writing, which is your subject, must by its nature be something less than great—wouldn't you agree?"

Ramsay and other examiners were aghast. They understood what Fairchild was doing—his trick question was intended to demean Ramsay and his hobby of collecting the "local color" of place names, which Fairchild thought was a childish pursuit. The candidate was being sacrificed for malicious reasons in front of his adviser's horrified eyes. But before Fairchild could thrust home, Ramsay interceded, and other instructors came to the rescue as well, until the thesis and the student seemed to be on safe ground again. Fairchild retired not long after that, in 1946, having accused Ramsay of stealing postage stamps from the office.[7]

When Williams arrived at the University of Missouri in 1950, there was still the odor of brimstone hanging about the English Department. With few changes, the feud would become a set piece of *Stoner*, appearing in the novel as the decades-long antagonism between Bill Stoner and his nemesis, Hollis Lomax, a professor of Romantic poetry, who not only limps like Fairchild, but has a humped back, too.

———

Everything was "going great guns!" back in Denver, Swallow reported in May 1951. "The writing program and the progress of the university press are the bright spots. Yet the rest promises to be a shambles if we can't hold it together." A distance of seven hundred miles wasn't enough to keep Swallow's problems from becoming Williams', as well. Would he mind, Swallow queried, taking delivery on a five-hundred-pound shipment of printing paper already on its way to his apartment? "I hope you will find it not too inconvenient." An agreement followed, indicating that the cardboard boxes of paper belonged to him and not to Swallow Press. "I'd appreciate it much if you could sign the enclosed," Swallow wrote to Williams, "—and perhaps your landlord would go along with signing to reinforce the situation."[8]

Swallow's difficulties, usually the result of lurching from one project to another, tried Williams' patience at times, but Swallow was meticulous about returning favors and using his influence whenever he could. To thank Lonnie, who was compiling his *Index to Little Magazines* practically for free, Swallow wrote a letter of recommendation to support her application to graduate school at Missouri. And when Williams completed a novel he'd begun in Denver, called *Splendid in Ashes*, he sent it to Swallow, confident that his friend would reply with a candid and detailed opinion.

The title *Splendid in Ashes* comes from Thomas Browne's 1658 *Hydriotaphia, Urn Burial*: "Man is a noble animal, splendid in ashes, and pompous in the grave." The book "smells on every page of the sepulcher," said American essayist Ralph Waldo Emerson, whose poem "Threnody," about the death of his son, is one of the greatest memorializing poems of the nineteenth century.

Williams was intrigued with the possibilities of starting a novel eulogistically by describing a life that has ended. *Splendid in Ashes* begins that way, with the main character, Douglas Morely, already dead, which will be the identical method used on the first page of *Stoner*.

Morely, in *Splendid in Ashes*, is a solitary person, observing life from the other side of an emotional wall. Standing apart from everyone else, he rebuffs attempts to break through to him. He's a Nietzschean hero, straining against the boundaries of a conventional life. All that defines him is creative freedom.

———

Swallow praised it, and thought it so good that it deserved a larger readership than he could reach with Swallow Press. That's what he told Williams, although he may have been trying to avoid having to turn down a friend's submission because it wouldn't sell. *Splendid in Ashes* was another piece of experimental fiction, similar to *Nothing But the Night*, copies of which were in boxes unsold in Swallow's garage. For a second opinion of Williams' newest novel, Swallow put him in touch with Barthold Fles in New York, a Dutch American literary agent and former book reviewer for *The New Republic*. Fles' clients included Bertolt Brecht, Heinrich Mann, Jessica Mitford, and Bruno Walter.

Fles' response to *Splendid in Ashes* was rapturous. "Both my wife and I, as well as my assistant," he wrote Williams, "have now read your novel. It is a pleasure to be able to tell you that we are unanimous in considering it one of the most distinguished pieces of fiction that we have read for a long time. It was an experience to read it."[9] It brought to mind a few parallels. "We mentioned *Wuthering Heights*, *Under the Volcano* and some French novels, when we discussed the book. We feel confident of finding a first rate publisher for this." In short order, Fles distributed *Splendid in Ashes* to every major publisher in New York and Boston.[10]

It would have been better if he hadn't, and had offered Williams some editorial advice instead. But Fles was taking the approach of throwing spaghetti against a wall, because something had to stick. Within weeks of receiving a copy of the novel, many prestigious American publishing houses—Random House, Knopf, Harpers, Simon and Schuster, and a dozen more—returned it. And generally their criticisms were the same. Remarks by Harry Brague at Charles Scribner's and Sons were typical:

> There is a great deal of superlative writing in it, and the character-
> izations for the most part are skillfully developed. But somehow
> when you have gotten through reading the manuscript you are left
> with a puzzled feeling as to what the author is attempting to say,
> and the reader is puzzled as to just what Douglas Morley's problem
> was and not a little impatient over the fact that so many people
> should spend so much time worrying about a basically uninterest-
> ing and irritating character. . . . The book begins by informing
> the reader that Douglas is dead, and as it progresses the reader is
> given no reason for either sorrow or elation over the fact.
>
> To us it seems a shame that a writer of Mr. William's [*sic*]
> obvious capabilities and potentialities should have spent so much
> time delineating a character who is basically not worth it.[11]

Perhaps Barthold Fles hadn't read this letter when he replied ebulliently to Williams from Beverly Hills:

> Your letter updated caught up with me here, which is most unfor-
> tunate, because I would certainly have come down from Iowa to
> see you had it come in time. As it was, we were both anxious to get
> to the West Coast, because of a pending movie deal about which
> we are in constant telephonic touch with Hollywood. . . . We con-
> sider your novel, *Splendid in Ashes*, one of the best we have seen in
> years and a real discovery.[12]

Splendid in Ashes continued to stagger through Manhattan after that, being turned away from every door. From an editor at E. P. Dutton: "Unfortunately, we think that in the present market this manuscript is just too long and too pretentious. This does not mean that there is not a great deal which is powerful and thought-ful, but the material seems to us somehow too elaborate and some-what too posing."[13]

Finally, Fles threw up his hands. "John, this has had endless submissions—twenty in all—and it's just impossible to do in today's fiction market." Bowing out with a tip of his hat, Fles expressed his regrets. "Sorry, but we tried hard—I tried hard."[14] Williams never heard from him again. As Anaïs Nin said when she quit Fles, dissatisfied, "Bonjour, friend, and good-bye, literary agent."[15]

"Dear Slaves," Butch Marsh began a letter to John and Lonnie in October 1952. He and George Rae had relocated to Mexico and were living the life of literary bums. With "both typewriters clacking, and the jug of tequila diminishing as we go"—they were writing to congratulate Lonnie and John on the birth of their first child, Katherine. (John said, "Except for the mustache, she looks like me, God help her.") The Marshes were living in a rented house in the town of Ajijic, south of Guadalajara, a "quietish, friendly, clean little town on the banks of the country's largest lake." They had two floors and seven rooms to themselves above, at street level, an ice factory. They were on the main floor, and upstairs on the third floor was a glassed-in studio overlooking a roof garden with a view of the town, where Butch worked all day. "We find that we can seem to live quite well, in our cozily disordered way, for about seventy-five bucks a month, including everything."[16]

He was getting a lot of work done, Butch informed John, in the new digs, having an "almost pathological obsession with getting everything I turn out into print, somewhere or other—even to the point of using goofy pen names if I am ashamed of both the story and the magazine."[17] His output since moving to Mexico included a fifty-eight-thousand-word novel written in forty days (rejected); a poem published in the *Arizona Quarterly*, and a short story carried in the *Antioch Review*. Random House returned his second novel "for commercial reasons. [The editor] didn't want I should have a novel that would only get mild praise, when I had such manifest gifts, etc. I tell you, there wasn't a dry eye in the house." An editor at G. P. Putnam suggested he revise and then resubmit the manuscript, but by then Butch had lost interest. Now he was a quarter of the way into his third novel, salvaging some of the material from the first. Added to this, he was generating stories and poems constantly, banking on the odds that he could make a few hundred dollars a month at it.

He confessed, tongue-in-cheek, to feeling contrite about the difference in their situations. "I hope you understand that we are not gloating about living in a country where we, of all people, are considered millionaires."[18]

The rough teasing was accepted. Williams didn't begrudge his brother-in-law the freedom to write all day, because he was after bigger game than selling stories to monthly magazines. Many writers were paying the bills that way (before Upton Sinclair became a novelist, he wrote eight thousand words a day for pulp magazines, seven days a week). But the respect of his peers was important to Williams, and he would never submit to *Colliers* or *Argosy* any more than he would to *Spicy Detective*. Besides, added to the demands on him as a new father as well as a student, novelist, and poet, he had a doctoral thesis to write.

His subject was English literature, and his work at Swallow Press, together with Swallow's influence, had led him to the English Renaissance. The press had published, and Williams had read, a revision of Swallow's master's thesis at Louisiana State, "Principles of Wyatt's Composition," retitled as *Some Poems of Sir Thomas Wyatt*. Williams was so taken with Wyatt's "They Flee from Me" that he memorized it, savoring its cadence by reciting the poem aloud.[19] His introduction to Wyatt had coincided with reading Winters' *In Defense of Reason*, also published by the press, which included the essay "The Anatomy of Nonsense," which criticized Romantic poets for using "words denoting emotions . . . loosely and violently, as if the very carelessness expressed emotion."[20]

In Defense of Reason introduced Williams to Winters' canon of the greatest English-language poems, where he found, among the reexamined Elizabethans, Fulke Greville (1st Baron Brooke), a member of the sixteenth-century Essex-Pembroke circle of playwrights, versifiers, and essayists. Winters claimed Greville was one of the most important lyric poets of the age, because his work resembled Drayton's, "although it is far better." "Furthermore," he wrote, "in [Greville's] later work he became a greater poet in every way than any of the associates of his youth. It is my opinion that he should be ranked with Jonson as one of the two great masters of the short poem in the Renaissance."[21]

Greville is not unknown to Elizabethan scholars. As an aristocrat, courtier, soldier, spymaster, patron, dramatist, historian, and poet, he certainly led a colorful life. Some claim he was one of Shakespeare's collaborators. But after his death in 1628, Greville was deemed a lesser light of Elizabethan England's golden age of poetry. He was "uncertainly admired" by Coleridge, Lamb, and Hazlitt; and C. S. Lewis labeled him "imperfectly golden."[22] More attention has always been paid to Greville's closest friend, Philip Sidney, in whose memory Greville wrote *The Life of the Renowned Philip Sidney*. Because of that book, Greville is better remembered as a biographer than as a poet.

By choosing Greville for his dissertation, Williams would be moving toward acceptance in the Winters Circle. By siding with Winters over Greville's importance, he would be linking arms with the famous critic's assessment of an overlooked poet. If his dissertation was then published as a book, he would have a title on the shelf of scholarship declaring that he was a Winterian.

———

Intense reading of the poetry of that era had a salutary effect on his writing style. The benefit of studying the plain style, practiced by many of the greater English poets of the Golden Age, was seeing its genuineness. Editors had faulted him for being tedious and overwrought. But the more he came to appreciate the merits of using simple sentence structures and concrete words and actions, the better he was able to recognize the problems with *Nothing But the Night* and *Splendid in Ashes*. A sentence like, "I shook the rain from my hat and walked into the room," from Mickey Spillane's *I, the Jury*, is purposeful and vivid. Nothing might seem further removed from the traits of classical prose as it was practiced by some

Elizabethans than pulp fiction—Seneca from Sam Spade—but both styles demonstrate the virtues of thinking clearly and writing honestly. When handled well, the result can be poetical.

Williams' challenge was to say what he meant, and to resist his desire to impress. His inclination toward flair, embellishment, and exaggeration—"lying" a bit while telling a good anecdote or polishing up his experiences—did not belong at his desk while he was writing. (The good-humored Professor Ramsay at Missouri oversimplified when he compared fiction-writing to lying.) Winters' beliefs about restraint and rational stoicism commanded Williams to write honorably. "I have found that the knowledgeable act of writing a poem or a novel or an essay," Williams said, "is a means not of self-expression (which is of little importance in a literary sense) but of contemplation. I write of human experience so that I may understand it and thereby force myself into some kind of honesty."[23] The demands of the craft altered his character during the hours he spent trying to establish a real world for his characters to exist in, because truth is paramount in creating readers' belief.

It was a nice coincidence, and a boost to his career, when the editor of the literary quarterly the *Western Review*, Ray B. West, contacted him in early 1953, requesting a review of Winters' *Collected Poems* from Swallow Press. Williams entitled his piece—fitting for Winters' emphasis on intellect over feeling—"The Goddess of Mind." But West shelved the Winters' review for the time being, pleading a backlog of submissions. "It caught me at the end-of-semester rush," West apologized. "Yes, it did come too late for the summer issue. I will use it in the fall."[24]

Disappointed, Williams asked a fellow student, Alan Stephens, a friend from his Denver days, to give the review to Janet Lewis, Winters' wife, who was coming to campus for the Missouri Writers' Workshop. As the workshop's director, Williams thought it might be inappropriate to ask a favor involving her husband when he had invited her as a guest speaker. But Stephens didn't mind helping his friend.

Winters had a reputation of "provoking out of people their ineptitudes," as Swallow put it. Replying to Stephens, Winters gave Williams' review a high grade.[25] "The review by John Williams I liked a great deal, partly, I suppose, because it praised me, but partly also because it gave a very good account of what I was trying to do." But Stephens' poems annoyed him, because they were too similar to his own. Some poets would be flattered to see that younger ones were emulating them, but Winters considered imitation lazy. It was stealing his work, which made him roar.

"There are certain poems in this lot, which are so obviously plagiarized that they could hardly be published; and I cannot see the virtue of that kind of thing as exercise," Winters wrote to Stephens. "If you wish to write well, you must learn to adjust language to subject; you can do this only if the subject is your own and you have come to understand it." He upbraided Stephens for appropriating from him: "When you swipe a subject and a bundle of imagery from someone else, it is not your own, you have not mastered it, and the original poem, in which the subject is well handled is perpetually in your way, so that you can depart from the original only by moving out into inferior treatment. . . . There is too much miscellaneous diction and imagery mopped up from my own verse, even where the subjects are original."[26] Stephens, for his efforts, felt abashed, but Williams had the pleasure of finding out even before his review was published that Winters appreciated his critique.

And then the unthinkable happened. Whether West, at the *Western Review*, discovered that Williams was an editor for Swallow Press, and was worried about a conflict of interest, or he simply didn't get around to reading Williams' review for months, he returned it abruptly that fall. "We all liked it, but agreed finally, that it took too long to make its point." He was "going to have someone else do the review."[27]

Williams was mortified. He was in Winters' good graces now; the "sage of Palo Alto" would be expecting to see the review in print. Quickly, Williams tried to interest other magazines and journals in accepting it, including *Poetry* and the *Sewanee Review*, explaining plaintively that he had been led to believe he had been "commissioned" to write the review. A note of desperation followed: "I feel very strongly that this review should have a hearing, and I assure you that I am not alone in that feeling. I believe that I have something to say about Winters' poetry that has not been said before, and I believe that what I have to say is of some importance."[28]

But it was no use—it was too late. Reviews of *Collected Poems* had been assigned already. Autumn passed, and Williams never heard whether Winters noticed that the favorable review of *Collected Poems* he had read wasn't published. But one thing was certain: he was aware of a young professor named John Williams who admired his work.

———

Williams' dissertation, "The World and God: The Poems and Dramas of Fulke Greville," was accepted in June 1954, and he passed his oral examinations. Alan Swallow added a further measure of happiness by informing him that there were two positions available in the English Department at the University of Denver, and Alan was recommending him and Alan Stephens.

To celebrate, the Williamses chose a long vacation to Mexico. Butch and George Rae, in Ajijic, had been asking for a visit. "In case you should ever have a sabbatical or a little time off why don't you and Lonnie and Kathy come down here for it?"[29] And so, with another couple from the university, Florence and William Hamlin, the Williamses drove to San Miguel de Allende for a three-month stay, with the Marshes dropping in on weekends for parties.

The days were spent relaxing, reading, driving a dusty seven miles to a private pool for a swim, and drinking. To ensure that everyone had enough tomato juice for their morning Bloody Marys, Butch and John went around to every *mercado* in town and bought up their stock, with the result that hotel owners had to come to them, pleading for a share. Florence Hamlin was delighted by John's sense of humor. "We rode the train to Mexico City to see the bullfights," she later said in an interview. "We laughed the entire way. It was just ridiculous. We laughed all the way going to the bullfights. There were six of them in one afternoon."[30] They all read

Ernest Hemingway's *Death in the Afternoon*, which is both a treatise on bullfighting and a manual for fiction. "Find what gave you emotion," Hemingway exhorts, "what the action was that gave you excitement. Then write it down making it clear so that the reader can see it too. Prose is architecture, not interior decoration, and the Baroque is over."

Florence Hamlin, observing Williams, noticed he was happier outside the university.[31] Without the pressure of coursework for the first time in seven years, living loosely like Butch—up early to write; reading in the shade during the long afternoons—he was a pleasure to be around. Hamlin "liked John so much," but found she couldn't get close to Lonnie. "I didn't dislike her," she said, "but I don't think I was fond of her. She was rather cold. John was the one that everyone liked. He was wonderful, just a delightful man."[32]

CHAPTER NINE

Butcher's Crossing

*The essential American soul is hard, isolate, stoic, and a
killer. It has never melted.*

—D. H. LAWRENCE,
STUDIES IN CLASSIC AMERICAN LITERATURE, 1923

At the University of Denver, Alan Swallow was no longer
teaching or directing the creative writing program when
Williams returned in August 1954 from vacationing in
Mexico. An affair with the wife of a university trustee had cost him
everything, and he had resigned acrimoniously. Behind him, the
administration had closed the University of Denver Press.

But he was content. "As you all know," he wrote to Williams, "one
of the prides I had in my publishing was its independence, the fact
that it was frankly only the taste of myself and some friends to aid
me. But the damned thing has mushroomed."[1]

Once he was released from teaching, his days were devoted entirely to running Swallow Press. Bookstore owners in the Denver
area became accustomed to seeing him deliver books in his MG
roadster with the top down, smoking a cigar. For bigger hauls, he
used his Rambler station wagon, loaded with books. The basement
of his home became his sanctuary. There, he typed long, rambling
letters to friends and clients, or stayed up late drinking whiskey
and reading car magazines. "I'll not apply for a job elsewhere," he

assured Williams, "but try to stick it out here in Denver for a year or two, living from publishing, writing, and probably manuscript criticism and consultation."[2] Before his awkward departure from the university, Swallow had recommended Williams as the new director of the creative writing program. After all, besides being an instructor and published author, Williams also brought experience running a public conference about writing, an innovation in its day.[3]

At the University of Missouri, Williams had run a ten-day conference. All the members of the English Department, and their wives, received personal invitations to evening social events, which added, as one of their colleagues gallantly put it, "dignity and charm to the occasion." Participants received individual critiques from English Department instructors and from guest speakers, many of whom were prominent writers of the day, such as Katherine Anne Porter, Nelson Algren, Walter van Tilburg Clark, and James T. Farrell. The guest lecture was free to the public. By the end of the conference, scholars of literature, teachers, and administrators were "flattered to be included for talk with the celebrated, and came away with only the most positive feelings about the worth of the Writing Program."[4]

It was a success at Missouri, and in Denver, Williams would hold an even grander event. He would expand the conference to four weeks, adding summer writing courses to the offerings. Later, his experience went into serving as president of the Association of Writers & Writing Programs (AWP), the largest professional organization of its kind in the United States. The AWP played a foundational role in establishing creative writing as an academic discipline.[5]

––––––––

Swallow believed in Williams and tended to be more relaxed around him than he was with others. He often confided in him. Swallow could be impatient, sometimes "harsh" and unable to "tolerate 'stupid' people who weren't interested in the literary world."[6] One of his former students, Gerald Chapman, who later joined the Denver English Department and rose to chairman, said the friendship between Swallow and Williams operated on several levels: "Alan was John's mentor, in a way. And they had a very great deal in common, including a drinking problem, but I think Alan probably felt John identified with Alan."[7]

The West was Swallow's passion, and they discussed misperceptions of it: how screenwriters had bowdlerized the region's history so much that it became a Christian parable about retaking Eden from heathens; or a paean to "justice at the end of a gun," as moviemakers would have it—buckaroos and sheriffs in silk shirts, blazing away with pearl-handled revolvers. Pulp western magazines and paperbacks—comic strips, too—perpetuated these fantasies. Williams found himself thinking about a show-biz-produced American history "in which 'The West' does not exist, did not ever, exist. It's a dream of the East—almost as if The East made up The West."[8]

The real Old West had lasted only a few decades. It was already part of legend in 1883 when William Frederick "Buffalo Bill" Cody— a former army scout during the Indian Wars—premiered *Buffalo Bill's Wild West*, a three-hour spectacle that toured the country annually for thirty years. Part circus and part historical romance, "Buffalo Bill's Wild West" was a nationalist extravaganza about taking and securing the West.

As a brass band struck up "The Star-Spangled Banner" and audiences got to their feet, cowboys on horseback, whistling and war whooping, stampeded a procession of elk, cattle, and buffalo past the grandstand. Behind them, former Pony Express riders came riding full-tilt, snatching mailbags from startled rodeo clowns who fell over in amazement. Annie Oakley, skipping into the middle of the arena to thunderous cheers, shooed the clowns away, bowed, and shot fifty glass balls being thrown high in the air by her husband, the handsome Frank Butler. Next, at the far end of the ring, a red, white, and blue curtain rose slowly, revealing a sentimental scene: a settlers' cabin and a little family dancing to fiddle music. But then a band of "wild Indians" attacked. A trumpet blast announced the timely arrival of the US cavalry, but the savage enemy was trying to make off with a white child. So Buffalo Bill himself came barreling into the melee driving a stagecoach, the reins clenched in his teeth as he fired at the retreating Indians with a pistol in either hand. And at last came the ear-splitting climax: a reenactment of Custer's Last Stand at the Little Big Horn River, featuring a troop of die-hard US bluecoats commanded by a blond-wigged Lieutenant Colonel George Armstrong Custer, fighting the Lakota Sioux surrounding them to a dramatic, staged "death." Some of the Native Americans in the arena had been at the actual battle.[9]

To millions of Americans—and Europeans who saw the show in Belgium, Germany, Italy, the Netherlands, Great Britain, and France—*Buffalo Bill's Wild West* was an epic story of heroes and villains contending gloriously in a showdown of good versus evil. The knock-off industry it created of B films, cowboy ballads, and third-rate novels about gunslingers helped to explain why eastern literary critics tended to dismiss western fiction as frivolous stuff.

Swallow was willing to wager that he could give the West its due in American literature. He had seen the rise of the Southern Agrarian movement and its standard-bearers—William Faulkner, Katherine Anne Porter, Tennessee Williams, and Zora Neale Hurston, among others. Now he "hoped that the time in the South was achieved," said Gerald Chapman, "and it was the time for the West." According to Chapman, "[Swallow] was interested in cultivating the Western literature, and John picked up a lot of that."[10]

Williams' interest as a novelist, however, was how to redress in fiction the misperceptions about the West. Cultural critic Lewis Mumford, in his influential book *The Golden Day* (1949) suggested that the "vast gap between the hope of the Romantic Movement and the reality of the pioneer period is one of the most sardonic jests of history." The Westward Movement, he said, was the "epic march of the covered wagon, leaving behind it deserted villages, bleak cities, depleted soils, and the sick and exhausted souls. . . . The truth is that the life of the pioneer was bare and insufficient: he did not really face Nature, he merely evaded society."[11]

What if a young man, Williams wondered, steeped in Romantic notions about nature, expecting to meet the divine and invisible, arrives on the Great Plains during the height of the Westward Movement and heads into the wilderness, like Ishmael going to sea in a whaling ship. On the Great Plains, in a wilderness as large as Mexico, what would a New England intellectual flower do? How would a "Har-*var*-dian," accustomed to holiday caroling in Boston, cope with a Rocky Mountain winter?

Historical details would be essential, and Williams had never extensively researched a novel before. From his Texas boyhood he could recall a rusted gate squeaking in the wind, or the smell of a creek that was flat, warm, and ankle-deep. But to re-create the West in the years immediately after the Civil War, to depict a balanced conflict, a fair fight between poetical abstractions and reality, fidelity to time and the environment would be key.

Williams collected maps of the Pike's Peak region in 1860 showing the locations of wagon trails, cattle drives, and towns. The territories in those days were surprisingly unmarked by human habitation. If a rider left Fort Larned in Kansas, for example, heading north, and stopped for supplies at Fort Kearney in Nebraska before continuing on to Fort Randall in the Dakota Territory, he could go for days without seeing another human being. Williams chose a working title that reflected the vastness: *The Naked World*.

But there were great interior seas of buffalo. "Tremendous numbers," Williams wrote in his notes, "whole landscape sometimes seemed a mass of buffalo." An estimated 20 million buffalo lived on the western plains in 1850, the most numerous single species of large wild mammals on Earth. An adult buffalo weighed about two thousand pounds, stood six feet high at the hump, and measured ten feet in length. By the 1840s, the market for buffalo meat and robes among whites was flourishing, and in the Kansas Territory during the 1850s buffalo were hunted for sport. In the winter of 1872–1873, more than 1.5 million buffalo hides were loaded onto trains bound for St. Louis, Chicago, Cleveland, and New York. The despoiling continued until by 1889 only 541 buffalo could be found alive in the United States, sheltering at the foot of the Rocky Mountains.

A parallel exploitation had taken place in fiction, Williams believed, regarding how the story of the Western Movement had been told. He blamed the despoiling on "literary racketeers" and "hired hacks," writers who were "contemptuous of the stories they have to tell, of the people who animate them and of the settings upon which they are played."[12] There were better westerns—a recognized genre by the 1940s. Walter van Tilburg Clark (*The Ox-Bow Incident*), A. B. Guthrie Jr. (*The Big Sky*), and Jack Shaefer (*Shane*) had developed moral complexity. But Williams was convinced that "each of these novelists is, in his own way, guilty of mistaking the real nature of his subject," which should be the interior lives of those who went west. Many had "no precise ideological motive for [their] exploitation" of the land except to change their lives somehow. That experience, more challenging to show than adventure, could be better presented by a mythic quest, "one that is essentially inner."[13]

In literature, myth dares to enter areas that are ambiguous to the soul. The external world becomes a backdrop, offering no law or guidance to the wanderer. And in the American West, a cowpoke could become Ulysses on the illimitable sea—a character driven by the rage to survive and to conquer the dictates of conscience. The outcome of myth, as the *Odyssey* shows, "is always mixed," Williams said, because "its quest is for an order of the self that is gained at the expense of knowing at last the essential chaos of the universe."[14]

Williams anticipated western revisionist novels such as Oakley Halls' *Warlock*, Thomas Berger's *Little Big Man*, Larry McMurtry's *Horseman, Pass By*, and Cormac McCarthy's Border Trilogy.[15] But after a year of research on his novel-in-progress, he moved with the English Department into a three-story, red-brick building that had been a student dormitory, and he lost most of his notes for *The Naked World*.

"You seem to be nicely settled. I guess we are too, as much as we ever are," the Marshes wrote, congratulating John and Lonnie on the birth of their daughter Pamela during John's first semester teaching. Butch was pleased to report that his luck in Ajijic, Mexico, was holding out. "Blessed be the name of Ellery Queen," he said, praising the mystery magazine that had paid well for one of his stories. He was also selling science fiction, a new avenue for him, and the money was enough to keep the Marshes solvent for a few more weeks and to party with the expat writers and artists in town. George Rae mentioned that a friend of theirs, science-fiction writer Theodore Cogswell, whom John knew from the writer's workshop at the University of Missouri, would be applying to graduate school in English at the University of Denver. "Tracy [his wife] and the kids are going to her family or some damn place," she said, indicating that she knew him well enough to know of his marital problems.[16]

It was hard to forget Ted Cogswell once you met him. Handsome, unserious, and offbeat, except when he was depressed, he had joined the Young Communist League (YCL) when he was seventeen and shipped out on the *Aquitania* for Spain in June 1937, to serve in the Spanish Republican Army. He returned after two years ("Most of the time I was hauling cabbages," he reported), completed college, and enlisted in the Army Air Force during World War II, assigned to airfields in India, Burma, and China.[17] His early science-fiction stories, published during the 1950s, proved to be his most popular, beginning with "The Spectre General" and "The Wall Around the World." When Butch and George Rae met him in Mexico, he was an instructor at the University of Minnesota, preparing to motorcycle to the 1953 World Science Fiction Convention in Philadelphia, which would be attended by "all the Young Turks," including Kurt Vonnegut, Robert Silverberg, Harlan Ellison, Isaac Asimov, and Robert Sheckley.[18]

That the Marshes would know a maverick like Cogswell, or be going to bullfights with Norman Mailer, was part of living in Ajijic and why they loved it. The pretty lakeside town had been popular with writers since the 1920s. D. H. Lawrence had written *The Plumed Serpent* there, and Somerset Maugham, *The Razor's Edge*. In the 1940s, Tennessee Williams played poker many nights at the Old Posada hotel, an experience that became part of *A Streetcar Named Desire*. George Rae hoped their house might hold a bit of literary kismet for them, too. "Another bit of interesting anecdote," George Rae wrote:

It was given out by our landlady a few days ago that [Robert
Penn] "Red" Warren wrote *All the King's Men* in the place where
we are living now. She said he was a "nice person with red hair
who drank a lot—and gave wonderful parties." She had no idea of
what she did to me—I'm still going around sniffing the same air
and touching the same walls as Robert Penn Warren and Butch
is hoping that some of his wonderful writing will carry over to
his novel.[19]

Being in a small community of writers, Butch and George Rae
were just as likely to end up as characters in somebody else's novel,
which they did. Ellen Bassing's 1963 novel set in Ajijic, *Where's
Annie?*, features Butch as "Willie Chester" and George Rae as "Sam."
One afternoon, a passerby in the novel peeps in on them while the
chicharras (locusts) are clicking in the heat:

She paused and looked around. She was almost at Willie Chester's
house. He was enshrined there on his patio only half hidden
among the teléfono vines, typing away. He wrote. Merciful God,
how he wrote. A story every day he said, good, bad, indifferent,
sensational, like a nondiscriminating machine, learning, he said,
with each one he wrote, but writing them so fast, so terribly,
frighteningly fast. And he sold some of them, not many. That he
sold any was alarming. He had no reverence, no respect, no fear
of his own possible or impossible talent. He wrote; it was the
answer to everything for him. And there, in the patio behind him,
was his wife . . . Sam. Of course Sam wasn't really her name—that
is, her parents didn't name her Sam when she was born—but it
was the name she had chosen for herself and which she requested
everyone to use. It wasn't used very often, because nobody ever
had anything to ask of her and if anybody did, he just called her
"you." Sam was behind Willie, circling about in a stained and tattered leotard, steadily but badly practicing her ballet. Did she woo
and win him with her twittering, soiled dancing? Oh, turn my eyes
from the vision of their lives . . .[20]

Butch would retaliate later, in *A Week with No Friday*, by turning Ellen Bassing into Martha Blissing, "a lady novelist with a lousy memory." Her husband, Beau, a "fairly entertaining slob," has poodles he can't afford to feed and is possessed of one gift: he can sing "Blue Skies, Nothing But Blue Skies," backward.

———

Losing his notes for *The Naked World* turned into "a most fortunate accident," Williams realized when he began writing the first chapters. "I might have tried to force what I had learned into the novel; as it was, I simply wrote the novel, and I found that when I needed a fact, it would come to me," he later said. "In other words, the accident forced a method on me, and the information was, I hope, wholly subservient to the more important concerns of the novel."[21]

As a counterpoint to Emerson and the transcendentalists—the inspirations for his young hero going west—he had been reading American authors who treated nature as an indifferent presence— neither opposed to, nor supportive of, human hopes. He admired Stephen Crane, Jack London's *Call of the Wild*, and especially Willa Cather's *O, Pioneers!* and *My Antonia*. Cather's desire to suggest "the inexplicable presence of the thing not named, of the overtone divined by the ear but not heard by it," evoked the ancient Greek stage, where forces play out, but are not seen.[22] Naturalists such as Cather didn't seek cause behind events: they found truth from depicting life faithfully. She said of *My Antonia*—the story of several immigrant families becoming Nebraska settlers, "In it there is no love affair, no courtship, no marriage, no broken heart, no struggle for success. I knew I'd ruin my material if I put it in the usual fictional pattern. I just used it the way I thought absolutely true."[23]

The naturalists' influence on Williams was apparent when he sent a completed first draft of *The Naked World* to Janet Lewis at the end of the summer of 1958. "It struck me that the method you use is that of Crane in the 'Open Boat,'" she replied. "You have characters who exist only in the moments of the story, of the immediate account of events. They have no pasts and no futures. This makes the events very intense, and that is exactly right for both experiences. In fact it would seem to be the main point in both experiences. . . . Congratulations. It is the most extraordinary reversal of procedure from your first novel."[24]

Williams' protagonist, Will Andrews, drops out of Harvard in the 1870s and, armed with a small bequest, travels from Massachusetts to Kansas and the desolate town of Butcher's Crossing, a tiny, hardscrabble hamlet. Will is brimming with Romantic ideas about nature, and he's eager for an adventure that will unlock "the Wildness" in his "unalterable self." He wants to become "a part and parcel of God, free and uncontained." Shortly after his arrival, looking for adventure, he impulsively agrees to bankroll a man named Miller, a seasoned hunter, who promises to lead one of the last great buffalo hunts. With them will go Charley Hoge, a wagoner, to haul supplies, and Fred Schneider, a skilled buffalo skinner. Hoge's right arm ends at the wrist, where he lost a hand to frostbite, an omen of what awaits. They saddle up and Miller leads the expedition over the prairie. Yet the spiritual experience Andrews was expecting is nowhere to be found. He feels numbed by "the routine detail of bedding down at night, arising in the morning, drinking black coffee from hot tin cups, packing bedrolls upon gradually wearying horses," the rituals that mark the passing of one monotonous day, and then another. At last, Miller finds the secret pass he was looking for—a sort of chink in the ordinary world—that leads into a Colorado valley that seems to be known only to God:

> A quietness seemed to rise from the valley; it was the quietness, the stillness, the absolute calm of a land where no human foot had touched. Andrews found that despite his exhaustion he was holding his breath; he expelled the air from his lungs as gently as he could, so as not to disturb the silence.
>
> Miller tensed, and touched Andrews's arm. "Look!" He pointed to the southwest.[25]

The buffalo are innumerable, a dark, undulating shadow as if cast by a passing cloud on the sunlit grassland. Miller becomes obsessed with killing every last one of the animals for their hides, and after weeks of shooting and skinning, the valley becomes an abattoir of carcasses, while "the remaining herd strayed placidly among the ruins of their fellows," until nearly all the creatures are dead and Miller is sated. Then, from the clouds, a single snowflake portentously falls—the only hint of supernatural agency that Williams will allow—heralding an apocalyptic winter that arrives within hours. The men are trapped for months under the snow. Hoge, already prone to religious fever, shows signs of going mad. The men survive, but Schneider, the skinner, is killed crossing a river on the way back; the wagon, piled obscenely high with hides, falls over into the water's torrent and gets washed away. The uselessness and cupidity of the whole venture is underlined when they reach Butcher's Crossing and learn that the buffalo hides are worthless—the bottom has fallen out of the market from oversupply. Miller makes a pyre of hundreds of rotting hides, stored in a corral, and sets them afire, the burning stink and sparks rising into the night like an Old Testament sacrifice to appease the anger of Jehovah. Looking on, an easterner appalled by the irrationality and chaos, cries out at the destruction. "Go back," Miller tells him evenly. "Get out of this country. It doesn't want you."

Will Andrews, purged now of sentimental notions about nature learned from books, doesn't want to accept that he's been lied to:

> "'No,' Andrews said. A vague terror crept from the darkness
> that surrounded them, and tightened his voice. 'That's not the
> way it is.'"[26]

Williams started looking for an agent. *The Naked World* had taken four years to write, his most sustained effort. For some reason, he turned for advice not to his university colleagues, or to Alan Swallow, but to someone whose situation he identified with: Morton M. Hunt, a former Army Air Corps pilot he had been friends with in Burma, who was now freelancing in New York. "About an agent for you," Hunt replied. "There are a number of large agencies with glittering names, to which I might recommend you, but I know about them only their general reputation, and have no personal intimate contacts with most of them. I prefer to suggest to you a smaller agency, where I am personally well acquainted with the principal partner, and know her to be a woman of considerable sensitivity, charm, and creative ability."

Her name was Marie Rodell. "She is utterly ethical, well thought of in the business, and perfectly capable of handling contract details, Hunt told him."[27] Hunt had already spoken to her by phone, in fact, before responding to Williams, and she had said she would be delighted to read the manuscript.

"Wild man, wild," Butch wrote when he heard the news.

CHAPTER TEN

Fiasco

*I'm almost physically sick . . . to be classified as a
"Western" novelist could be damn near ruinous to me as
a teacher and a scholar. And don't think the gleeful word
won't get around.*

—JOHN WILLIAMS, 1960

M arie Rodell had been an agent for ten years when she
received Williams' manuscript for *The Naked World* in
1958. She was "world-wise, well-traveled, a sophisticated
New Yorker fluent in four languages who moved comfortably in
many of New York's most elite literary and publishing circles," said
a biographer of Rachel Carson, author of the ecology classic *Silent
Spring* and one of Rodell's clients. Rodell had been an editor at
several large houses until after the war, when layoffs of women in
publishing, to make room for veterans, forced her to strike out on
her own. Briefly, she'd been married to a playwright. Because the
statuette of Edgar Allan Poe awarded to her by the Mystery Writers
of America reminded her of her ex-husband, she kept it in a closet.[1]
Attractive, of average height, with auburn hair that she wore up-
swept, she was a poker player, chain smoker, and gourmet cook.
She was comfortable around men—who liked the contrast between
her femininity and her bawdy sense of humor—but her views about
men and women were conservative, making her a good match for

the traditionally minded Williams. Rodell had resigned as Betty Friedan's agent after reading *The Feminine Mystique* in manuscript. "I think she was threatened by my book, as many women were," Friedan later wrote. "She was a great devotee of Freud and she wanted me to throw out the whole chapter on Freud."[2]

She was not an aggressive agent. She used a light touch with clients' work—reviewing their manuscripts, and offering her reactions and suggestions here and there for improvement, but leaving the close editing of style and syntax to publishing house editors. Her job was selling the book, and she liked coming up with catchy titles. "She does not fight or argue quite as fiercely as some for the last inch of advantage," Morton Hunt had written to Williams, "but I don't conceive that to be important to you. When you sell 150,000 copies of the new book and are ready to do another, that's when you have to do the hard fighting, not now."[3]

"Dear Mr. Williams," Rodell replied in October after having his manuscript for a month, "Both Miss Daves [her assistant] and I have read *A Naked World* and like it very much. You have made a meaningful as well as a highly readable novel of the story, and we'd be delighted to represent you and it."[4] Williams replied that he was pleased because he was convinced *A Naked World* was "something above the run-of-the-mill novel." She asked what else he might be working on. He was reluctant to say because it was hard to summarize. The next one would be about a college professor:

> To all outward appearances, he is a failure; he is not a popular teacher; he is one of the less distinguished members of his department; his personal life is a shambles; his death by cancer at the end of an undistinguished career is meaningless. But the point of the novel will be that he is a kind of saint; or, stated otherwise, it is a novel about a man who finds no meaning in the world or in himself, but who does find meaning and a kind of victory in the honest and dogged pursuit of his profession.[5]

If she had any reservations about a novel by a college professor whose hero was a failed college professor dying of cancer, she didn't say. Instead, Rodell responded warmly to the news that he was already working on his next book.

———————

Seeing John go from strength to strength in his career, Butch had decided perhaps he should give teaching writing a try, too. Having hit a dry spell at the typewriter in Ajijic, he wrote, "Poverty can be amusing, if you like your humor on the ironic side."[6] Not that his "weirdly precarious existence" as an independent writer for ten years had been fruitless.[7] He had a dependable market selling to pulp and men's magazines such as *Playboy, Nugget, Dude, Swank,* and *Rogue.* His smart-alecky, dame-wise characters—projections of himself, really—were suited to male readers. His better work— mysteries, science fiction, and domestic dramas—had appeared in two best-of-the-year short story anthologies, including Random House's *Saturday Evening Post Stories 1954.*

But for George Rae's sake, he believed it was incumbent on him to finish his bachelor's degree as a precaution. She had been able to "enjoy leisure with poverty" long enough. With the help of an ad- viser at the University of Iowa—Paul Engle, soon to become famous as the director of the Iowa Writers' Workshop—Marsh's three years' worth of college credits put him within a semester of receiving his undergraduate degree. But Engle, seeing an opportunity to add an experienced, published writer to his faculty, also offered him a paid assistantship teaching creative writing, provided he stayed to complete his masters. The only other "real professional" on the faculty, Marsh discovered, was Vance Bourjaily, author of *The End of My Life*—a respected postwar novel.

So September 1958 found Willard Marsh—former jazz musician, bohemian, and expat writer—trudging across the Iowa campus as a college instructor.[8] To students, he appeared to be a slightly pudgy, shorthaired, mid-thirties gentleman with a stern expression, wearing thick glasses and letting a cigarette hang from the corner of his mouth. For his brother-in-law's delectation, he described a normal day:

I rise at a civilized hour, unhungover, don a clean shirt and even tie, walk a few clean streets of East Overshoe (unlittered by burro shit and drunken Mexicans) to a room on the campus where twelve to twenty eager youths want to learn how to sell their first short story to the *Saturday Evening Post* and/or the *Yale Review*, and thereby instantly and perpetually become that dashing figure, The Professional Writer.

I figure I'm just the cat to show them how. I don't know who was teaching those things at East Overshoe before I came along, but compared to me, he doesn't know his ass from a hot rock. Could *he* tell them how to con an editor into thinking he's seeing a rewrite of a story he rejected last year? Could he even know which editor should see that story in the first place? Get in and get that big slick dollar, children, like I used to before I became as dated as a celluloid collar; screw that arty-farty literary twaddle. Get in there where the tall cane grows.[9]

Unlike Williams, Marsh didn't think he could ever become "a very nice, dedicated prodigy-Ph.D. like yourself."[10] His ambition was to teach well, get the master's degree, and then return to Ajijic as soon as possible, where he could sit at his desk every day and listen to how his typewriter blended with the *chicharras* buzzing outside, while in the kitchen George Rae prepared another pitcher of margaritas with lemons and limes, rattling with ice cubes.

Williams' hopes for *A Naked World* received an unexpected boost when he received a call from the senior editor at Macmillan, Cecil Scott, saying he happened to be in Denver—could he have a look at the novel? Morton Hunt, who had recommended Rodell as his agent, must have tipped him off, because Rodell hadn't sent out the manuscript yet. Williams said he could, but he instantly wrote to Rodell as a precaution. "I made it quite clear to him that you were handling the book, and that if he became seriously interested that he would have to work through you."[11]

Scott, an erudite Londoner, read about forty pages and seemed excited, Williams thought. A few days later, a note from him arrived, written on the stationery of the posh Hotel Adolphus in Dallas. He had forgotten to mention that Macmillan was offering a new fiction award worth $7,500. *A Naked World* would make an excellent candidate.[12]

It was a bit overwhelming: unexpected compliments from a major publishing house, plus the chance at a prize worth two years of his salary as a college professor. Rodell assured her anxious client there was nothing to worry about. Scott had phoned her, wanting to know whether any other houses had seen it. She told him cagily that "the manuscript was under consideration elsewhere," but she would note that Macmillan was interested. "They [Macmillan] are very far from my favorite house," she informed Williams. "The president retains the attitude most publishers had fifty years ago (but have since been persuaded out of it) that if his house wants to bestow the grace of its imprint on an author's work, that should satisfy him. . . . Since there are many other good houses who don't share this attitude, I stay away when possible."[13] Williams, never before having reached this level in his writing career, put his faith in his new agent; apparently she was a cool customer when it came to doing business: "I do not wish to urge a judgment of mine in an area where you are more knowledgeable," he told her.[14]

Two months passed, but other publishers didn't share Cecil Scott's enthusiasm. "He may be a writer," replied an editor at W. W. Norton. "The main problem, it seems to me, is that the hero's motivation is not made fully clear. The author simply attributes to him a vague yearning to find the meaning of life, not much better defined than that." *Nothing But the Night* had been criticized for the same kind of shortcomings. In fact, at Scribner's, Harry Brague, who had also disliked *Nothing But the Night*, rejected *The Naked World* because it, too, seemed "watery."[15] A rejection from an editor at Viking took a devastatingly condescending tone, as if he were holding the manuscript away from him with a pair of tongs. "*A Naked World* is not a novel. . . . In fact, the book is almost completely static. The hero, William Andrews, leaves Harvard and comes west, and we don't know why. He goes out buffalo hunting and all he learns is how to skin one, and then he leaves we know not whither. I hope Mr. Williams will one day decide to tell just a story."[16]

Mystified, Williams wondered what he should do. He had spent almost four years on the novel—time that might have been spent submitting to journals and advancing his academic career. Thinking that perhaps he should retreat to firmer ground, he asked Rodell if she'd like to see his doctoral dissertation, "The World and God: The Poems and Dramas of Fulke Greville." Greville, the Elizabethan poet and courtier, hadn't received "a book-length study" since 1903—"and that one was quite inadequate," Williams urged.

Rodell was not enchanted by the idea of trying to sell a book about a minor poet in tights, a doublet, and feathered hat. She asked instead if he had any short stories they could offer to magazines such as *Esquire*. He mailed half a dozen, adding, apologetically, "I don't feel that I write very good short stories. I have never taken the form with the seriousness I'm sure it deserves. I'm afraid I reserve my best energies for my novels."[17] In the meantime, his novel about the college professor had come to a halt, he said, because he was under "academic pressures." Likely, he was getting the jitters and couldn't write without some good news.

Rodell advised giving editors another month to reply. Then they should take advantage of Cecil Scott's interest and enter Macmillan's fiction contest. As a courtesy, they would defer any offers until the winner was announced. It would be a gamble. Macmillan might not offer a contract if they lost, but those were the stakes.

Williams began having doubts about the novel's title. Perhaps *A Naked World* was a bit existential-sounding—too pretentious. Maybe just *Butcher's Crossing*, the name of a town, would be better. He asked Cecil Scott's opinion, who replied, "Frankly, I do not like *Butcher's Crossing* as well as *A Naked World*. It seems to me a good title. Obviously the jacket would give some clue to the subject matter and I would prefer *A Naked World* because it would remove any suspicion in the prospective reader's mind that this was another conventional Western. So for the present at least I would prefer to leave the original title."[18] With the results of the contest only a week away now, Williams decided to leave well enough alone.

————

Out of two thousand manuscripts submitted to the Macmillan contest, *A Naked World* came in second. To Williams, Rodell dashed off, "I'm so sorry!" And during the judging, the publisher Little, Brown and Company had made an offer higher than Macmillan's. Cecil Scott counteroffered with even better terms, because "we have the most substantial faith not only in this book but in the author's future." Rodell urged Williams to accept the Macmillan offer. Or perhaps she didn't—it was hard to tell. She tossed the ball back to Williams. "I do not want my own prejudices against Macmillan to influence you unduly." Comparing the two publishers, she said, "Both are honorable imprints. Enthusiasm at Macmillan seems to be more unanimous than at Little Brown." Williams, a novice, "rather dazedly" agreed, his only concern being that Macmillan make a sincere effort to promote the book, even though it had come in second, "to give it a chance to gain some attention. . . . I presume they will not neglect that."[19]

For a second opinion, he turned to Janet Lewis, who complimented him by pointing out that her advance from Doubleday for *The Ghost of Monsieur Scarron* was much less than what Macmillan was offering him, and her novel just missed becoming a Book-of-the-Month Club selection. In the end, she said, publishing is "something of a gamble always." She wished him well. That settled, he accepted Macmillan's offer, his first time doing business with a major trade publisher.

————

With *A Naked World* slated for publication in the spring of 1960, still eight months off, he returned to his next novel, about a midwestern college professor. The time needed to plan it would be about a year, he estimated, and a prestigious Guggenheim Fellowship, awarded to those "who have demonstrated exceptional capacity for productive scholarship or exceptional creative ability in the arts," would relieve him of teaching.[20] He decided to ask J. V. Cunningham, now at Brandeis University outside of Boston, a previous recipient of a Guggenheim, if he could use his name as a reference on his application.

The deferential tone of the letter is uncharacteristic for Williams, who was thirty-eight at the time and an associate professor after six years at the University of Denver. But having Cunningham's respect was important to him. "I realize that you don't know a great deal about my abilities as a novelist—I assume that you have not read my first novel, published by Alan, and I fervently hope that my assumption is correct; it isn't a very good novel, and it certainly does not adequately represent, or even foreshadow, what I am trying to do now."[21] Not immodestly, he mentioned that Janet Lewis compared him to Stephen Crane. Cunningham assured him of his support.

It was the start of some good luck. The University of New Mexico invited him to apply for a position in the English Department. He supplied a two-page autobiographical sketch listing his work in *The American Scholar*, *Arizona Quarterly*, and *A Journal of Modern Culture*, among others. Having a novel that was scheduled for publication looked impressive, too, by any measure. Then came a letter from a former colleague and friend from the University of Missouri, who said he would be happy to consider Williams' dissertation on Fulke Greville as a scholarly book for the university press.

He seemed to be reaching a milestone, a turning point. To celebrate, he went camping in the Rockies, ten thousand feet up and off a dirt road, about a mile from Clear Lake in the Arapahoe National Forest, near a ghost town. While he was camping, he would "descend briefly a couple of times a week" from the mountains to check on the family, and then he was off again. He didn't clear his plans with Lonnie because seeking permission from his wife was not in his nature: where he went, and how long he would be away, was his prerogative. He stayed the latter half of June and all of July, fishing in the Cherry Creek reservoir and cooking his catches over an open fire.[22]

Come September, he went to New York to meet Marie Rodell in person for the first time, and to have lunch with Cecil Scott. They were still dickering about the best title for the novel. Rodell didn't care for *A Naked World*. "I'm inclined to think the word 'Hunt' should be in it and perhaps 'Valley'? No. 'Lost Valley?' Better. If it sets up in book buyers a subconscious association with *Lost Horizon* it can't hurt sales!" Scott was pulling for *A Naked World*. Williams offered *The Crossing, The Hunt, Hunt in the Valley,* and *The Western Path*. "I don't like *The Western Path*," Rodell cautioned, "because I think we have to be careful never to let careless reviewers or bookstore personnel classify this as a Western." Scott, wanting to bring the discussion to an end so he could begin thinking about marketing, told Williams, "Personally I like the best of any of your suggested titles, and better than any title I have come up with myself, *Butcher's Crossing* . . . *Butcher's Crossing* on the right kind of jacket will give the reader a certain clue to the contents. It is a phrase which is easy to remember and it is also mellifluous."[23] Scott, at last, won the day, and he accompanied Williams over to the Macmillan offices on Fifth Avenue to meet the staffers who were already working to meet the *Butcher's Crossing* publication date set for late March.

A few weeks before its release, Williams took a sentimental trip. He drove 875 miles south from Denver to Clarksville, Texas, intersecting with the fictional paths of his four buffalo hunters in *Butcher's Crossing* across Kansas and into the Colorado mountains. In Clarksville, he located the house where he had been born, and walked the brick streets that his mother and father had known. In Paris, Texas, the first town west of Clarksville, the newspaper editor heard of his return and ran an article about the exciting career of "Dr. Williams." An elderly gentleman in Clarksville, who had known the Williams family well, felt moved to write to him in a crabbed hand, congratulating him on his "wonderful achievements in the educational field," adding, "Your Aunt Emmie [Walker] was a wonderful teacher, also."[24] On the eve of publication, advance orders of *Butcher's Crossing* to bookstores exceeded everyone's expectations.

———

Marie Rodell broke the news. "Brace yourself for a bad shock next Sunday. The *New York Times* has reviewed *Butcher's Crossing* as a western, and the idiot who writes the column has of course no small inkling of what the book is about." She was furious. "It's too, too revolting. I told Cecil that if the reviewers had been informed this was the runner-up in the contest, and if the jacket hadn't looked like a western, this wouldn't have happened."[25] On the cover, a man and woman in Hollywood western dress stand in the foreground; behind them, far below on the plain, a wagon train of pioneers passes by. The cover announced, "Through blinding heat across an unyielding land they trekked. Men in search of a burning vision." There was no trek in the novel; it was a buffalo hunt. There was no vision, just the desire to get rich from buffalo hides. There was no Conestoga wagon train with settlers walking beside it, only four men with a string of packhorses behind them. And the only woman in the story is a prostitute who appears at the beginning and at the end.

The review, by Nelson C. Nye, founder of the Western Writers of America (his pen names were Clem Colt and Drake C. Denver), damned the book. It "is practically plotless, an account of four men who go out to hunt buffalo, find them, slaughter them and are caught by cold weather. The work abounds in graphic descriptions, even to the variegated colors of blades of grass. The story, however, contains little excitement and moves as though hauled by a snail through a pond of molasses. You can leave it anytime, a lot of people will."[26]

Williams was horrified. The damage was irreparable and he knew it. A review carried by one of the most respected newspapers in the United States—a source that booksellers and buyers relied on—had branded *Butcher's Crossing* an unreadable bore. "I'm almost physically sick," he wrote to Rodell. "I have just received your letter, have thought about it for an hour, and I get sicker by the moment. God knows, I might be angry at a bad, imperceptive review—but it would be anger and nothing more. But this is really inexcusable—of the *Times*, of course, but mainly of Macmillan. It would have been much better had the book been entirely ignored— at least it would have been better from my point of view." The situation was a "great deal more serious than it might appear." As the director of Denver's creative writing program, he had ventured into mainstream publishing, confident that it was within his power to compete with the best contemporary novelists. He had intended to revive a genre, to contribute to literature. Instead, "to be classified as a 'Western' novelist could be damn near ruinous to me as a teacher and a scholar. And don't think the gleeful word won't get around after next Sunday. One might say that anyone who read the book would realize the falsity of the classification—but who the hell's going to read it after such a tantalizing invitation not to?" He was heartbroken, and if had the money, he would purchase every copy and destroy them.[27]

At Macmillan, Scott took the unusual step of objecting strongly to the editor of the book section of the *New York Times*, arguing that the novel should not have been reviewed in a column about westerns. "*Butcher's Crossing* is not a 'Western' although its background is the early west, any more than [A. B. Guthrie Jr.'s] *The Big Sky* is a 'Western.'" Paul Engle of the Iowa Writers' Workshop, Scott pointed out, had called it "a superb tale of the Old West" on the front page of the book section of the *Chicago Tribune*, and the *Denver Post* had hailed it as "one of the finest novels of the West ever to come out of the West."[28] Scott commiserated with Williams by inveighing against idiot reviewers, and the tendency of people to suspect anything new and different, and tried to persuade him that no serious readers would really pay attention to Nye's column anyway. "The thing you must simply not allow yourself to be is discouraged."[29]

But the novel's chances were ruined. The summer passed and *Butcher's Crossing* sold only a few thousand copies. Come fall, the Guggenheim Foundation turned down his application for a fellowship, leaving him to wonder whether there was a connection between being scorned in the *New York Times* and not receiving the award.

John Edward Jewell, later to become John Williams, with his mother Amelia, about 1924.

Williams' birthplace, Clarksville, Texas, when he was a child. The statue in the square is of a Confederate soldier facing north in perpetual defense.

"The Corner," in Wichita Falls, Texas, where land speculation and oil deals were made on a handshake. Williams' father, John Jewell, would have known this place well.

Williams at Hardin Junior College in Wichita Falls, wearing a silk scarf out of admiration for Ronald Colman, who played Sydney Carton in the 1935 film version of A Tale of Two Cities.

For a short time, and during his first marriage, Williams pursued a career in radio news broadcasting under the name "Jon Williams" in Denton, Texas.

Williams served as a radio operator aboard US Army Air Corps cargo planes in northwestern India, flying "the Hump" over the Himalayas into China.

Yvonne (Stone) Woolf, shortly after her divorce from Williams in 1949.
She married Beat writer Douglas Woolf that year.

George Rae, Williams' sister, and her husband, Willard "Butch" Marsh, in a photograph taken for identification purposes during one of their frequent trips to Mexico.

Left to right: *Florence Roberts, whose husband was an English professor at the University of Missouri, the setting for* Stoner; *John Williams; and Williams' third wife, Avalon Smith, during a vacation to San Miguel de Allende, Mexico, in 1954.*

Williams, when he was writing Butcher's Crossing, *shortly after joining the faculty at the University of Denver.*

Buffalo hunters in Texas about 1870. Butcher's Crossing, published in 1960, was dismissed as a Western, instead of what Williams intended: a debunking of Emersonian ideas about nature and the frontier.

Poet and classicist J. V. Cunningham, a friend of Williams' and the model for professor Bill Stoner in Stoner.

The 1966 faculty of the Bread Loaf Writers' Conference. Rear, left to right: *William Sloane, John Frederick Nims, William Hazlett Upson, David Wagoner, John Aldridge, X. J. Kennedy.* Center, left to right: *Brock Brower, Dan Wakefield, Eunice Blake, John Ciardi, Seymour Epstein, William Lederer.* Front, left to right: *John Williams, Robert Pack, Edward Alexander Martin. The conference was the first time Williams was in the company of other fiction writers and poets, and it helped assuage his loneliness. Robert Pack led a small countercultural revolution that overthrew most of the old guard, including Williams, by 1972.*

Williams in his office, a converted dormitory room at the University of Denver, in 1967, two years after publishing Stoner.

Williams and his fourth wife, Nancy, in the early 1970s.

Williams near the end of his life. Novelist Joanne Greenberg (I Never Promised You a Rose Garden) said, "He had a face like a five-day rain."

PART III

Stoner

CHAPTER ELEVEN

"It Was That Kind of World"

*They wanted to know who was I, apart from papers and
credentials—"Can you do it? Can you do the work? Could
you teach and inspire students?"*

—ROBERT D. RICHARDSON

John's foray into mainstream publishing, where the landscape
was familiar to Butch Marsh, left him bewildered. Likewise,
Butch was finding that academe was another country. "Being
a faculty wife is a rather strange experience for me," George Rae
confided to John, "and here in the South it is a full time job. This
place is crawling with women's clubs, literary societies (made of il-
literates), and social groups. The sole occupation of the members of
these groups is giving Teas, 'Coffee-drop-ins,' and 'little luncheons.'
However, I'm holding up pretty well, and the people are really extremely nice and kind."[1]

She and Butch had left the University of Iowa after he had
completed the coursework for his masters, a few months before the publication of *Butcher's Crossing*, and relocated to Rock
Hill, South Carolina, where he was now an assistant professor of
creative writing at Winthrop College. Their experiment with college
teaching was continuing as they weighed the benefits of security
versus living paycheck-to-paycheck from Butch's fiction. He had
stockpiled about fifty stories, but was too busy teaching to submit

them. He fantasized about a New York editor just dropping by their little apartment at 830 College Avenue and choosing the best for a short story collection. "It isn't as if I'm never going to have a decent novel of my own someday, so I feel I'm worth the visit."[2]

They had purchased a car, their first—a two-door 1952 Nash Rambler, a favorite of suburbanites—sleek, modern, and "frighteningly cute," George Rae said.[3] The wife of the English Department chairman had befriended them and was playing fairy godmother, loaning "Mrs. Willard Marsh," as she was referred to, enough furniture, sofa pillows, and dishware to set up housekeeping. She took George Rae under her wing, "helping me learn the ropes," as George Rae put it. "She also tells me that I may begin to say 'no' to invitations. Thank heavens." On weekends, there was "some very pleasant socializing with the younger, drinking segment of the faculty." The chairman's wife had made it quite clear that the Marshes could stay as long as they liked—indefinitely. Ajijic receded into the distance.

John could have told them that if Winthrop College was cliquish, that was to be expected; it was no different from the English Department at the University of Denver. Everyone belonged to a subset. In the early 1960s, for example, Elizabeth Richardson accompanied her then husband, the biographer Robert D. Richardson, to the University of Denver to begin his instructorship in the English Department. After they arrived, "one or two other women made a real effort to include me," she said. "But I had zero in common with them. We had young kids, so several times we went out to Cherry Creek Reservoir and sat in the sand while the kids played and most of the conversation was complaining about husbands. After a while that got—well, I was a biology major and all those women were English majors, so it seemed I couldn't be part of a conversation that transcended those topics."

Men in the University of Denver English Department—the faculty was male throughout most of the 1960s—had a different experience. Newcomers were invited to join a kind of band of brothers who were outdoorsy, drank hard, and were at the top of their game. Robert Richardson, a New Englander and Harvard-educated, was excited by the West as "open country." For the job interview, he said,

"John did to me what he did to everyone—he took me to a cabin with some faculty members and a few wives and we got drunk. It was a weekend retreat with a cookout, mostly men. They wanted to know who was I, apart from papers and credentials—'Can you do it? Can you do the work? Could you teach and inspire students?'"[4]

It was hard not to warm to John if he liked you. "Always very nattily dressed. Spiffy dresser," said Richardson. "He was low-key, and loved to laugh. 'Hi-*lar*-ious!' he would say, and 'And in this country, it was *bound* to happen.' His small stature didn't matter to him. He felt no need to work against that. He was extremely kind."[5] If John didn't like someone, he tended to be prickly, according to Fred Inglis, a cultural historian; more often he just ignored them. But when he felt sympathy for a person, he tended to extend his help and friendship as a kind of respect. A deciding factor was whether the person seemed genuine. Inglis came to Denver on a fellowship from Oxford University because John had worked out the details with his tutor, a mutual friend. As a Briton arriving at the foot of the Rockies, Inglis felt a little disoriented at first, but "John and I got on instantly," he later recalled. "He was good at that. The friendship was plainly stated, and you knew it was there—you could just reach out a hand and touch it for reassurance without ever making a great to-do about it. He was somebody who lived at the front of a friendship."[6]

It was not only the bonhomie of the department that induced English instructors to come to Denver, either. Williams offered them an opportunity to help build the "Harvard of the West." He was developing a PhD program in creative writing that had the potential to become one of the best in the nation, requiring proficiency in two languages, passing an oral examination, and submitting a thesis—in this case, a novel or a short story or poetry collection. As a result, said Richardson, there were "bright, hard-working students" in the program who earned the respect of instructors who taught English literature and literary criticism. "The department ran with a kind of smooth unity."[7]

"It was that kind of world," said Gerald Chapman, "and John helped us keep it alive. He didn't care for the ponderousness at all, or any pretension would really turn him off quickly. But he loved people who were willing to pitch in and be there."[8]

The ethos of the English Department, being all male, was in agreement about something else, too—sex. Male chauvinism was taken for granted, and affairs, which included sleeping with students, weren't worth mentioning except as gossip. "This was the decade when the east-to-west academic exodus was in full flood," wrote Harvard professor Daniel Aaron in his memoir, *The Americanist*:

> Palo Alto and Berkeley had become gilded Botany Bays for middle-aged East Coast professors in flight from sagging marriages undermined by their irregular romances with students: The West Coast represented a paradigm shift, new love in a new clime. Here was the stuff for a spate of tragic-comic college novels with an archetypal plot: a professor falls in love with a young woman prettier, smarter, and more exciting than his shopworn wife, who has drudged for him, raised their brood in mean surroundings, and grown obsolescent in the process; the professor feels he has earned his eminence and can no longer deny himself what Providence has decreed, so he dumps the wife with varying degrees of anguish and remorse.[9]

During the summers, Williams left for weeks at a time to stay in the mountains where he wrote and fished, accompanied now and then by his third child, Jonathan, who was thrilled to wake up one morning, during hunting season, "with about three inches of snow on us—that was pretty much of an adventure!" Williams purchased a cabin near the town of Pine, Colorado, in remote territory favored by hunters. By going up to the cabin on Thursday, he could get three days of writing done on the screened-in porch.

Lonnie was not in the picture for much of John's life outside of home. To the wife of a department member, the third Mrs. Williams came across as "a Colorado girl, kind of small-town, bright, but not a very forward personality." Gerald Chapman "didn't know Lonnie well. I had dinner at their home and I saw her on various occasions. She and John had some pretty bad quarrels." More than once, Lonnie had wanted to leave a faculty party, but John, drunk and annoyed with her, had wanted to stay.[10] It was known that John was having an affair with Shirley White, the English Department secretary. The romance had been going on for about a year when one day, in the spring of 1960, one of Williams' students—a tall, rosy-cheeked young woman in her mid-twenties—asked him to sign her copy of *Butcher's Crossing*.

———

Her name was Nancy Ann (Gardner) Leavenworth. She was living in Denver with her parents and her four children, having left her husband, James Leavenworth, who had suffered a nervous break-down. Her father was a Denver elementary school principal, her mother a housewife, and Nancy and her sister had been raised in a conservative home and educated at local Catholic schools. During junior high, 1946–1947, she had attended extracurricular classes for young ladies that taught domestic arts, including how to speak politely and practice social graces that would suit her as a wife and mother. In 1950, she had enrolled as an English major at Grinnell College—a small liberal arts college in Grinnell, Iowa—partly be-cause her parents were pleased that it was only an overnight train ride away. When she met James Leavenworth, he was a junior, not long out of the army, and working toward a degree in comparative literature. At the end of her freshmen year, they married after she became pregnant.

James showed promise as a writer, winning awards at Grinnell for original plays and musicals. He might have pursued a career in college teaching, or gone into the arts, but married with two children when he graduated in 1953, he accepted a job writing for General Electric's trade magazine in Western Springs, Illinois. After that, the Leavenworths relocated to upstate Schenectady, New York, to General Electric's huge, campus-like research facility, and then back to Illinois again—typical of a young corporate couple on their way up after the war.

It was around that time that James' behavior and personality changed. His voice lost its highs and lows and he began speaking in a monotone. He shambled, heavy-footed, despite being tall and long-limbed, as if he were a stranger to his body. After losing his job, he became obsessed with a solution to everything. The Leavenworth family needed to escape to the mountains, where they could start over, he insisted. He would be a "mountain man"—answering to no one, and he would provide by building a house, and they could live off the land, the way nature intended. To get ready for hardship, he began sprinkling dirt on his food, because that was what mountain men ate.

Nancy fled with the children on a train to Denver, having witnessed the "cruelest, saddest thing—he didn't know what was wrong." James followed them, wandering about the city helplessly, protesting, wanting the children back, until Nancy's aunt, a pediatrician, prescribed medication to quiet his mind, enough to allow him to return to his family home in southern Michigan.[11] Their divorce was uncontested.

———

By the time Nancy enrolled in Professor Williams' poetry class in the spring of 1960, thinking she might finish her degree in English, Williams had entered a new, and rather splendid, sartorial phrase, perhaps to counter the damage from—or in defiance of—the review in the *New York Times* that had labeled him the author of a terrible western novel. His new plumage stated unequivocally that he was an artist. He replaced his usual Windsor-knotted tie with a dark blue, polka-dotted cravat. For social occasions, around his small waist he drew a cummerbund, purchased in the men's clothing section at the Denver, the best department store in town, which he wore under a blazer (two-piece suits made him look petite). For the final touch, he added a dab of Brylcreem to his hair and combed it before the mirror up and away from his forehead into a pompadour.[12] Before going out the door, he inserted a fresh cigarette into a short holder made of pear wood and brass. By fashioning himself as a cultured, sophisticated loner, like the Hollywood leading man of his youth, Ronald Colman, he restored his self-confidence.

He was a presence as he entered the classroom. "John was a

fairly small man," remembered a student, "with dark hair, glasses, a creased face, and a salt-and-pepper goatee. Being a poet, I thought he looked like a bohemian Black Mountain Poet, perhaps Robert Creeley without the eye patch. . . . He had a certain flair, and an elegance of manner, though with a slight rough edge by way of Texas."[13]

Nancy felt her instructor's big, booming voice conveyed important things. He read aloud from *Butcher's Crossing* now and then, to illustrate his points about rhythm and sense. "I loved to hear him talk about it," she said. "I liked his authority in that it was all earned. He knew what he was talking about. And his wit, of course. It was never dull with John, ever."[14]

Nancy signed up for as many classes taught by Professor Williams as the quarter-system schedule would allow, becoming dependable company in his classrooms, as if she were proof of her conviction about him and his talent. Reading Melville's *The Confidence-Man*, she found a quote that fit young Will Andrews' experience in *Butcher's Crossing*. She copied it out: "Aye, and poets send out the sick spirit to green pastures, like lame horses turned out unshod to the turf to renew their hoofs. A sort of yarb-doctors in their way, poets have it that for sore hearts, as for sore lungs, nature is the grand cure. But who froze to death my teamster on the prairie? And who made an idiot of Peter the Will Boy?"[15]

She took it to his office, along with her copy of *Butcher's Crossing* to sign. He read the quote, smiled, and took the book from her hand. On the title page, he wrote, "To Nancy, in memory of that mad, mad night on the Cap D'Antibes, when . . ." and no more. He handed it back to her.

She understood that he was declaring his intentions.[16]

————

He began courting her—asking her out for coffee, coming over to her house to cook his specialty from his India days, chicken curry and rice. Afterward he would serve her tea and they would talk. He didn't mention Lonnie, and she didn't ask about her. Shirley White, the English Department secretary, had left to take a position at the University of New Mexico, but Nancy wanted to make sure that affair was over. He went to Albuquerque to break it off. On dates, John said hello to people occasionally, but he didn't introduce her, wanting to keep their relationship private. As in *Stoner*: "He had no talent for dissimulation, nor did it occur to him to dissemble his affair with Katherine Driscoll; neither did it occur to him to display it for anyone to see. It did not seem possible to him that anyone on the outside might be aware of their affair, or even be interested in it."

One afternoon while they were sitting in her parents' kitchen, Nancy confessed something that she had been trying to keep from him. She wanted to have his baby, but that wasn't possible, not with his three children and her four. "I wasn't depressed, I was sad and passionate," she later said. He propped his elbows on the table and began telling her a story. "It was about a perfect child—ours. It was never born, it just materialized somehow and it was ours." After that, whenever he came over, he continued the story where he had left off. She didn't have to ask him; in the evenings when he came by to ask how her day had been, he talked about the baby. The child had a name and did funny, endearing things. After a while, she began to laugh when she knew exactly what the baby would do and how they would respond. "He courted me for a year before we made love," Nancy recalled. "I wasn't ready. But by the time the year was up, I was just insane about him. I adored the guy."[17]

Progress on the novel about a college professor named William Stoner was going "slowly," Williams wrote to Marie Rodell in September 1960, "but there's nothing to worry about, I think. I hope to have a draft by Spring." Professor Stoner was having a love affair with a graduate student named Katherine, moving him into an emotional sphere he had never before experienced. Williams' working title for the novel was *A Matter of Light*. Meanwhile, he had high hopes of publishing a collection of his poems, titled *The Shape of the Air*. He needed a victory after the debacle of *Butcher's Crossing*; and, as he told Rodell, "I don't want to sound snobbish about this, but I have spent a good twenty years of my life in a fairly concentrated study of the problem of poetry and poetic method, and I know what I am talking about."[18]

Williams refused to accept that the ideas and methods advanced by the up-and-comers such as John Berryman, Elizabeth Bishop, Gwendolyn Brooks, or Theodore Roethke were legitimate. Like other practitioners of the New Criticism, in "poor simple Walt Whitman," as Alfred Kazin said of that school, Williams could find "no Donne-like tension, paradox, or ambiguity."[19] He greatly admired the 1930s modernist American poet William Carlos Williams, and endorsed his doctrine about the importance of concrete objects—"no ideas but in things"—because it dovetailed with Winters' emphasis on rationality. But further on the timeline of poetry he would not go. Consequently, as the 1960s bloomed, Williams' conservatism as a poet made him difficult to publish. Moreover, his convictions prevented him from becoming a better poet. To write verse well—the kind that is sublime and flashes an image of a thing or experience on the reader's inner eye—he would have needed to be more in touch with those Wordsworthian impulses that he resisted. If he felt them, he forced them and racked them into a frame with so many beats per line. Mastery of technique is not art, or there would be statues of forgers, counterfeiters, rock 'n' roll tribute bands, and plagiarists. Williams' insights about life and human nature, the empathy—the *interiority* of experience—that made him a superior novelist, aren't evident in his verse. He maintained a distance from the material. He kept his greatest strengths out of his poetry.[20]

It showed. "I am very much afraid that our final verdict has been the same as with the earlier manuscript of poetry which you sent us," wrote Cecil Scott from Macmillan. "There simply has not been the sort of enthusiasm on the part of our readers that would warrant our embarking on publication."[21] The rejection annoyed Williams, who was still smarting about the fate of *Butcher's Crossing*. He wondered whether Macmillan's continued negativity about his poetry meant they should offer the new novel, *A Matter of Light*, to another publisher. He expressed these thoughts to Marie Rodell, writing, "I think they did rather a bad job in packaging [*Butcher's Crossing*], that is to say, in a sense they misrepresented it, by the jacket, the jacket copy, and the advertising." But she demurred, saying it wasn't worth breaking with Macmillan "just in order to get the poems published."[22] Eventually, after rejections of his poetry collection had arrived from Harcourt Brace, Scribner's, Viking Press, and New Directions, Williams conceded that perhaps, as a last resort, they might try a small press.

Scott, realizing he was in a position to do a favor for an author who must be unhappy with him, assisted with a related project instead. Williams hadn't given up trying to publish his dissertation about Fulke Greville. But editors hadn't shared his conviction that a book focusing on a lesser-known Elizabethan poet, even edited for the trade market, was needed. Not even his friend and former colleague at the University of Missouri William Peden, editor of the university press, expressed much enthusiasm after he read the manuscript. "Nothing but bad news," Peden wrote to him. "Very regretfully, I have been unable to include your study of Greville in our publications schedule for the next couple of years."[23]

But then Williams saw a practical way of folding Greville into a larger concept—one that would both serve his career as a scholar and honor, at the same time, the portion of the Winters canon that dealt with the 1500s—an anthology, *English Renaissance Poetry: A Collection of Shorter Poems from Skelton to Jonson*. He explained to Scott how, by being specific, it would fill a niche: "The anthologies [currently] available are either critical collections based on what is essentially 19th century taste; or 'representative' collections which include snippets of virtually everything, important or unimportant; or 'period' anthologies designed primarily for lower division survey courses, and inadequate for anything beyond that."[24] Professors who taught the Elizabethans would welcome it in their classrooms, he knew from experience. The era was a staple of upper-level and graduate courses—and anthologies that became the cornerstones of instructors' syllabi could become classics in their own right, enjoying long and profitable lives in college bookstores.

Scott proposed the idea to Macmillan's college textbook department, but the editors, thinking that the collection would be just another paperback of best-loved poems, or something like it, decided the cost couldn't be justified. So Scott, unwilling to give up, went out of his way for Williams. "Would you like me to drop a line to Pyke Johnson at Anchor Books?" he asked. Anchor was an imprint of one of Macmillan's competitors, Doubleday.

No sooner had Williams given his permission—literally within a few days of Scott contacting his fellow editor—than an offer arrived. "Your idea for an anthology of Renaissance poetry strikes us as a very interesting one," Pyke Johnson wrote, "and one that we would be interested in publishing as an Anchor Book." He offered a generous advance—better than many midlist novelists were receiving—along with a first printing of ten thousand books, with an expectation of reaching thirty thousand. He only needed to know when the manuscript would be delivered to finalize a contract.[25] Williams replied that he could finish it in a year—midsummer of 1963, because he already had all the material. He was steeped in Winters, and relied, for classroom instruction, on his three important essays about sixteenth-century lyric poets, which had appeared in issues of *Poetry* magazine in 1939.

It's easy to imagine him rubbing his hands with satisfaction. His admiration for Winters was constant, and his friendship with Winters' wife, Janet Lewis, indicated that Williams might reasonably count himself as part of the Winters Circle. If he published an anthology essentially canonizing the Elizabethan portion of the canon, then he would have done yeomen's work in the service of the "sage of Palo Alto."

Williams exceeded his self-imposed deadline by six months, and the ease with which the anthology came together was the beginning of a tide of small but good things rising around him. To Marie Rodell he reported, in February 1963, that "the novel is coming along so well that I hesitate even to speak of it. When I spoke to you in New York, I predicted optimistically a June 1 completion date for the first draft. Well, that is no longer optimistic; I will almost certainly have it done by then, maybe sooner."[26] He walked in on his typist, a junior in history, while she was finishing "typing chapter 15, and discovered great huge tears coursing down her cheeks. I shall love her forever."[27]

In the English Department, the feeling of fellowship was running high. Gerald Chapman, in his new capacity as department chairman, wrote a letter of praise in support of Williams' application to attend a summer session on Elizabethan poetry at Oxford:

> Professor Williams is, without question, one of the more brilliant artist-scholars in the Rocky Mountain region, and, some may think, in the United States. Only a very few in university circles can be a novelist, a poet, a research scholar, an editor, and a teacher, all with high excellence. Professor Williams is responsible for our having one of the two organized doctoral programs in Creative Writing throughout the United States. . . . He is currently finishing a third novel and planning a fourth. He has published poems, essays and reviews in almost every important journal in the country; his anthology *English Renaissance Poetry* is being published by Anchor Books this spring.

His choice of words is telling. He characterizes Williams as an "artist-scholar" and lists his achievements beginning with his literary ones. Privately, Chapman didn't regard his friend as "that much of a scholar." Later, he said, "His anthology on poetry is an excellent one. But when we talked, he thought he knew more about the Renaissance than he really did. John didn't have a scholarly mind."[28] In any case, Williams was accepted into the six-week summer program at Oxford. Chapman had sweetened the whole experience by giving Williams the fall quarter off to pursue his writing. After Oxford, Williams planned go to Rome for several weeks to think about another novel he was considering.

The trip was important for another reason, too. Lonnie would be accompanying him. Although the marriage was damaged, he felt obligated to share this reward with the person who had supported his career, regardless of the state of their relationship now. He booked passage from New York for the two of them, because the "prospect of a few days on board ship, with nothing to do, is damned attractive right now," he wrote to Rodell. Besides, he said, he had developed a dread of flying.[29]

English Renaissance Poetry was slated for publication in May 1963, a month before their departure for England. Williams' introduction to the anthology, written with students in mind, is an approachable, easygoing discussion, as if he were a professor giving an overview of what the class will cover. He explains that in Renaissance poetry "there was a fairly conscious progression from one set of principles to another, from one method to another, throughout the century," and then sets out to examine those principles and methods. The introduction itself exemplifies the plain, or Native, style that Williams favors, because, in Thomas Wyatt's phrase, it's "graven with diamonds, in letters plain."[30] Williams dismisses the Petrarchan style because "the rhetoric is very nearly the whole poem." Each of the twenty-three poets represented in the anthology receives a brief biography that is very interesting and colorful, preparing the ground for the verse to follow, and there are madrigals, too. It isn't just an anthology of verse: it's about writing poetry and the joy of reading it.

From Anchor Books, Pyke Johnson flew out to Denver to meet Williams for the first time and convey his congratulations on the upcoming publication of the anthology. The two walked around campus, and Williams told Johnson the story of how his interest in Renaissance poetry had begun, principally due to his friendship with Alan Swallow and his reading of Yvor Winters' *In Defense of Reason*.[31]

In mid-June, Williams took the train two thousand miles to New York and met Lonnie, who preferred to fly, at Idlewild Airport (now John F. Kennedy International). Ahead of him, he had mailed a completed draft of *A Matter of Light* to Rodell at her office in Manhattan on East Forty-Eighth Street, just off Fifth Avenue. She was not at all sanguine about the appeal of *A Matter of Light*, a college novel whose protagonist, the narrator admits on the first page, was eminently forgettable:

Stoner's colleagues, who held him in no particular esteem when he was alive, speak of him rarely now; to the older ones, his name is a reminder of the end that awaits them all, and to the younger ones it is merely a sound which evokes no sense of the past and no identity with which they can associate themselves or their careers.

Rodell's pessimism was not unjustified—it was based on what people were reading. Novels at the top of the best-seller lists were richly adorned with description and dialogue—lively stories that favored European settings: Daphne du Maurier's *The Glass Blowers*; Morris L. West's *The Shoes of the Fisherman*; and *The Moon-Spinners* by Mary Stewart. Barring exceptions that year, such as J. D. Salinger's *Raise High the Roof Beam, Carpenters, and Seymour: An Introduction*, and Günter Grass's *The Tin Drum*, Americans generally preferred fiction that prized plot over character, and trusted genres they recognized at a glance: romance, historical fiction, biography, history, and so on.

"I may be totally wrong," Rodell said, speaking as someone who had agented one of the most talked-about books of the previous year, Rachel Carson's *Silent Spring*, "but I don't see this as a novel with high potential sale. Its technique of almost unrelieved narrative is out of fashion, and its theme to the average reader could well be depressing."[32] She knew the market and readers' tastes. *A Matter of Light* was going against the grain of contemporary literature.

Williams, however, seemed not to be listening, replying:

Oh, I have no illusions that it will be a "best seller" or anything like that; but if it is handled right (there's always that [excuse])—that is, if it is not treated as just another "academic novel" by the publisher as *Butcher's Crossing* was treated as "western," it might have a respectable sale. The only thing I'm sure of is that it's a good novel; in time it may even be thought of as a substantially good one. A great deal more is going on in the novel than appears on the surface, and its technique is a great deal more "revolutionary" than it appears to be.[33]

And so, with that, he prepared to sail.

———

The MS *Berlin* had weighed anchor shortly before noon in New York Harbor on a clear, hot day in late June to begin its weeklong journey across the Atlantic to Southampton. As a diversion, Williams kept a journal during the crossing. He intended to relax by jotting down his impressions of what he saw and heard—good practice for a writer. But strangely, strains of unpleasant feelings related to the World War II seem to have intruded on his thoughts.

He may have accidentally invoked them by choosing for the voyage exactly the same kind of composition booklets he'd used in Burma, and this was his first oceanic trip since shipping out for India in 1943. Warming up his pen by journaling, he noticed that shadows of the war seemed everywhere. "I had known it was a German ship, but I had not really anticipated that most of the passengers would be German. But—my God!—they are," he wrote. A sense of history, and the rise and fall of power, had stolen aboard somehow. He caught a little boy goose-stepping up and down the corridor outside his stateroom door. The resentful expressions he saw on the faces of the ships' German laborers, "the deck hands, lowest of the crew members," who picked up the cigarette butts and trash, made him think of the concentration camps: "These are the men—the sergeants, the corporals—who did the physical shoving of the victims into the ovens—laughing perhaps, making jokes—while our ship's officers stood by and shook their heads regretfully, after they had signed the orders."[34]

A topic of conversation in the ship's baronial and high-ceilinged passenger lounge—"English style in oiled walnut and green leather, a peculiar kind of wilderness"—was John F. Kennedy's arrival in West Berlin that week. His refrain of "Ich bin ein Berliner!" within sight of the Berlin Wall, on the knife-edge of the Soviet hegemony, would be met with roars of acclamation from tens of thousands of West Berliners, some of whom, just twenty years earlier, had shouted themselves hoarse swearing their allegiance to the Thousand-Year Reich.

It made Williams think about the mystery of identity. He had heard a story, shortly after the publication of *Butcher's Crossing*, about a scandal during the reign of Caesar Augustus. Despite being emperor of the Western world, he couldn't force his daughter Julia to obey him. Though he trusted her with private secrets, she would not be reined in. Her behavior gave his enemies reason to hope that he was vulnerable. In 2 BC, Augustus exiled his only child to a tiny island called Pandateria, removing her from society. Here in mid-ocean, Williams thought about the human dimension of the conflict: on the throne Augustus was emperor; in his own home, he was a father with a difficult daughter, and the ramifications shook the known world. In Augustus' story, in postwar Germany, and in the novel he was working on, *Stoner*, the question of identity, and which one was truest, intrigued him. It spoke to the person who had been John Jewell, then "Jon" Williams, and the effort to become what he wanted to be.

CHAPTER TWELVE

"The Williams Affair"

I don't wish any communication with Williams unless it is to plead for mercy. . . . I will wreck this book unless you provide proper acknowledgment.

—YVOR WINTERS, 1963

The Williamses unpacked their travel belongings in their rooms at 26 St. Michael's Street in Oxford, a rather dingy three-story rooming house run by a Mrs. McArdle in a neighborhood that wore, as someone said about the face of postwar England, "an insulted look." Their disappointment with the living arrangements contributed to strains between them, until, after just three weeks, Lonnie announced that she was going home early. "I believe she misses the kids," Williams explained to Marie Rodell, minimizing what her sudden departure suggested about the state of their marriage. Williams stayed on, enjoying the tourist-crowded streets of Oxford and discovering, to his surprise, that "the teachers here in the University are no better than you will find in a decent graduate department in the States—perhaps not quite so good, really, though they do speak better and are a great deal wittier and handsomer."[1]

In the meantime, Rodell had given *A Matter of Light* to Cecil Scott at Macmillan. As she predicted, the response was a flat-out no. In fact, Scott and his associate editor, Al Hart, were willing to let

Williams go. "While both of us agree that the writing is excellent, we simply cannot foresee a satisfactory sale, the sort of sale that John would expect and feel entitled to. We understand, too, that this will mean our losing John as an author, which disturbs us because quite obviously he has a bright future in front of him."[2]

Williams was unfazed, and, as Rodell prepared to send the manuscript to other publishers, he expressed relief they were finally free of Macmillan, writing, "I can't really believe that it's going to be impossible for us to find a publisher for the novel, and I suspect that almost anyone we get will be an improvement."[3] He asked her to wait until he could tighten the manuscript a bit more, but she had already sent it on to Little, Brown and Company, along with a letter that sounded like regret: "Here is John Williams' new novel, *A Matter of Light*. This is not the final draft; John wants to do more with the wife's motivations, for one thing."[4]

While he was away in Oxford, Williams' editor at Doubleday Anchor, Pyke Johnson, also took a vacation for most of July. *English Renaissance Poetry* had been in college bookstores since May, ready for the fall semester, and sales of the first printing of ten thousand had been brisk. When Johnson returned to the office, on his desk was an airmail letter from Williams—a nice coincidence for bringing him up to date about the anthology's success. But there was also a small sheaf of correspondence in chronological order, on top of which was a three-page letter from Yvor Winters.

"Dear Sirs," Winters began frostily, "There has recently come to my attention an anthology published by yourselves entitled *English Renaissance Poetry*, edited by John Williams. I regret to inform you that you have been taken. The book is in a large and serious measure pirated from my own publications." To substantiate his claims, Winters had asked a colleague to compare the titles of poems from the Winters Canon against *English Renaissance Poetry*'s table of contents. The overlap was about 80 percent. "You will find not only a surprising number of the titles in Williams' anthology," Winters continued, "but a theory of the history of the sixteenth century lyric which Williams takes over bodily and which no one except myself (or so far as I know has ever) propounded. . . . Williams discusses many of the poets exactly in my terms. This outline of 16th century poetry is original and it is correct, but it is mine, not Williams'. In so far as he departs from it, he departs into fog." Winters said he would have protested to the English Department chairman at the University of Denver, too, if it weren't for the fact that "the poor bastard has a wife and two or three kids, and they need the job."[5]

Underneath this opening salvo was a reply to Winters from Johnson's assistant. "John Williams is presently abroad, so I am afraid we will not be able to contact him about this matter until the fall. Mr. Johnson, the editor of the volume is also on vacation for a few weeks, but I am sure he will give your letter his prompt attention when he returns."[6] Winters, beside himself with anger, replied accordingly. Into a file he labeled "The Williams Affair," he placed a carbon of his response, which carried a threat of retaliation:

> I have your courteous brush-off letter of yesterday. There is not the slightest reason why this matter should wait until Mr. Williams gets back from his tour of Europe or Mr. Johnson from his vacation. In a matter as scandalous as this Doubleday should act at once. If Doubleday does not act, there are more ways I can act than by suing. You are someone's secretary, and doubtless have little understanding of my access to the literary press. I have easy access, however; and I am familiar with the laws of libel. If you people insist on slow action, I will make a quick scandal out of it. I am one of the best-known poets, critics, and scholars now living.[7]

Johnson's assistant, rattled by talk of libel, asked another editor to intercede, who assured Winters that the matter was being taken very seriously; but he refused to be mollified. "I will not wait for Williams to return from his junket in Europe. . . . Besides, there is nothing he can say, and he knows it." He demanded that Anchor Books redress his grievance, and if they didn't, he would "activate the grapevine" against Williams and drag his name through the mud.[8]

Pyke Johnson, looking over this furious exchange that had taken place during his absence, considered what to do. He returned Winters' original three-page letter to his assistant and asked her to retype it, minus the personal attacks on Williams. Then, to accompany the redacted copy, he included a business-like memo to Williams, reducing Winters' fury to a problem that needed looking into. "I arrived back from vacation this morning and found your nice note of July 22nd," he wrote Williams. "Unfortunately, there was also on my desk some material that I bring to your attention most reluctantly, but also most urgently. You will find it enclosed in the form of excerpts from a long letter from Yvor Winters. . . . I am now writing him to say we cannot consider any action until we hear from you."[9]

Winters could accept that someone would plagiarize intellectual content from him—his ego prepared him for that. But what galled him was the lack of attribution, which he believed was deliberate and typical of Williams. "There is no question about Williams knowing my work," he wrote Johnson. "Some years ago, my publisher taught at the University of Denver, and Williams was one of his students. Swallow introduced Williams to my work, and Williams has followed it closely ever since. I understand he has been teaching from it."[10] Johnson chose not to share that allegation with Williams.

Indeed, however, Williams' students did know of their professor's proclivity for borrowing. One of them, the poet Heather McHugh, who later became a MacArthur Fellow, wondered "why a working novelist might occasionally lecture from verbatim hand-transcripts out of a standard text he never acknowledges." She recognized substantial quotations, complete with turns of phrase and rhetoric, from *Literary Criticism: A Short History* by William Kurtz Wimsatt and Cleanth Brooks. "At the time I felt a holy righteousness. . . . [I]f that's teaching, I thought indignantly, why even I could do it!"[11] But to Williams, it was a matter of priorities: he was a writer first and college instructor second. He had taken shortcuts since the beginning of his teaching career: from uncritically embracing Winters' theories about poetry, to piggybacking on Alan Swallow's Wyatt dissertation for his own on Fulke Greville, to compiling a poetry anthology incorporating Winters' scholarship.

Nor was it a matter of being forced to serve one master or the other. It was taken for granted that he would publish fiction—he was the director of the creative writing program at Denver, after all—and it would redound to the university's credit if he became well known. But the reality was that finishing a novel took him four or five years, and he would not take any more time away from his writing than necessary to teach. Unlike Professor St. Peter in one of his favorite Willa Cather novels, *The Professor's House*, he would not say that he had "done full justice to his university lectures, and at the same time carried on an engrossing piece of creative work." Still, his conscience was clear. Choosing between "conflicting integrities," Williams said, "that is, I think, essential drama; it is also essential life—at least, essential civilized life. . . . Life forces us into compromise, and that has nothing to do with integrity. . . . Integrity is a private affair, essentially selfish."[12]

His reply to Winters was of a gentleman caught in an error. "I cannot tell you how miserable I am about this whole unhappy affair," he wrote, but he could not "accept the implications of piracy and dishonesty." There was no way to avoid duplication among the greats of a particular era, although "a large number of my selections do not correspond to your choices." And then, in a particularly telling passage of the long letter, he flew his true banner: he is a writer, first and foremost, making a living as a teacher:

> My only motive for putting together this anthology was to make available some of the poems that you and I and others have admired. I do not think of myself as a critic or a scholar in the professional sense of those words, and I have no ambition to be thought of as such. I am primarily a novelist and secondarily a poet, though perhaps not a very good poet; but I am a teacher, and I put together the anthology as a service to my own students and to others who might not otherwise become acquainted with these poems.

Without admitting to guilt, other than to being influenced by Winters' seminal work on the English Renaissance, he offered to include "in subsequent printings of the volume an explicit statement of my indebtedness to you and to others, in which I will also attempt to suggest that you are not to be held responsible for the distortions I may make to your or anyone else's ideas." He completed a draft of an acknowledgment page for the anthology's second printing, slated for September, paying respect to Winters, who had inspired the "marked increase of critical interest" in the period.[13]

Winters ignored the draft Williams sent him, and to Johnson, dismissed the offer of "some kind of dust-throwing acknowledgement."[14] In the meantime, Anchor Books got busy inserting slips into unshipped books explaining that the volume was based largely on Winters' work. As an extra gesture of goodwill, Johnson mailed Winters a gift: a set of recently published selections from Anchor Books' Seventeenth Century Series, plus an edited edition of *The Psalms of Sir Philip Sidney and the Countess of Pembroke*. "I think that the editing of these volumes will come somewhat closer to meeting your standards," Johnson wrote to him.[15] Several weeks passed and Johnson saw no more "vituperative" letters from Winters on his desk, a man with a "monstrous ego," in his opinion, so he trusted that the matter was closed.[16]

To Winters, however, it would never be closed; he wrote to friends that he would "take care" of Williams in due time.[17] In *Forms of Discovery*, published four years after Williams' anthology, Winters recounted the whole tale as a "most interesting case," adding, archly, "I mention Professor Williams, because I do not wish to give the impression that I am borrowing a large part of my book from him." Williams' anthology would be useful in classrooms, he admitted, but "unfortunately, he often uses inferior versions of poems written by Wyatt and Ralegh." Disputation was not so much an art for Winters as it was a brawl with endless rounds until death sounded the final bell.

Nancy was surprised that John took it so hard. "Yvor was a bit nuts, but that situation upset the living hell out of John," she said later.[18] To have the person he most wanted to impress take his efforts as an insult, and worse, accuse him of plagiarism, was terrible—in fact, beyond the exact reverse of his hopes, because his integrity became the issue. If he had written some ham-fisted criticism, or made a poor decision in his life as a teacher or administrator, it could be written off as a mistake. But Winters' attack implied that he had spent a long time in an endeavor that was intellectually dishonest, and that he had intended to get away with it.

Twice now, Williams had been dismissed as an upstart, a pretender in the royal court of literature. His first major novel, *Butcher's Crossing*, had been whipped out of town in the pages of the *New York Times* as a pretentious western; and his *English Renaissance Poetry* had been damned as arrogant by a famous critic. These humiliations could not be taken lightly. They were happening without the consolation that things would turn out in the long run, or that he would one day be vindicated. Readers of histories and biographies have the advantage of knowing the end of the story, but to the person living it, the darkness is all around. As Williams approached middle age, under the excuse that perhaps it was time he owned up to the limit of his abilities, he might have struck his colors and given up, believing that it's nobler to kill your dreams than to let someone else do it.

It's worth asking, then, why he was considering a third novel, this time set in the classical world. Was it because he was still casting around for a genre he could succeed in? Hadn't he found his niche yet, after all that time? When he was asked about this, his answer was simple: he liked the challenge; he enjoyed the adventure of testing himself each time in a new, imaginary world. "I try never to repeat myself. . . . Why do it again, if you've done it once?"[19]

Williams completed his studies at the University of Oxford in mid-August 1963. Taking the train to Dover, he booked an overnight berth for the Channel crossing and continued on to Rome, eager to begin putting ideas on paper for a prospective novel about the emperor Augustus. For six weeks, he worked uninterrupted in a room at the Bellavista Milton on the Via di Porta Pinciana over-looking the Villa Borghese gardens. The decor was a bit garish and the wine overpriced, as if the establishment were trying to be worthy of its location two blocks from the fashionable Via Veneto, but the solitude delighted him.

"It's amazing what you can get done when you're alone," he wrote Rodell, "and when you don't have desperate students breathing down your neck. I'm seeing the things I need to see for this Augustus novel, and I'm ahead of my schedule on the revision of the William Stoner novel." Regarding the latter, he felt certain, more than ever, that it was a solid piece of work, although the "hardest thing I have ever done."[20]

Williams believed in the Stoner book because it expressed his conviction that novels should "imitate in form the natural world"; or, as he put it another way, "This happens, and then this happens, and then this happens." Time, the iron clock of the universe, goes in one direction, and the business of the novelist is to create "the realized and presented history of a person, or persons, moving through sensibly experienced space and time, between the recognized intervals of birth and death." The closer one adhered, when writing a novel, to life as it's experienced by individuals day by day, he believed, the truer it would be.[21] Joyce's *Ulysses* and Woolf's *Mrs. Dalloway* he admired for their technical virtuosity, but the sensibility of those works was intended to be poetic, and poems are about the "chaos of experience," or sudden realized moments or impressions. This was inauthentic, solipsistic—and, stylistically, "a one-note samba," in one of his favorite phrases used in class, meaning that the effort is clever but ultimately uninteresting. Moreover, it expressed the author's personal truth, which may not be everyone's, or even a few persons'. The novel's strength was that it gave the novelist room to explore, to think in large ways about human nature and moral problems. It graced the author with opportunities to pause along the path of telling the story to observe the way people act, the choices they make, and thereby to illuminate—not in a heavy-handed way, but with craft—certain verities about life.[22]

Come the end of September, he boarded the SS *Constitution* at

Southampton for New York to resume his former life in Denver. The last he'd seen of Lonnie, she was on her way out the door in Oxford, after they'd been together for only three weeks. No doubt the tension in his marriage was rising into a wave that would break over him when he arrived home. "I imagine by this time I'm an almost total stranger to the kids," he mused.[23] His daughter Katherine would be starting high school soon; Pamela was in middle school, and Jonathan was still in elementary school.

"He came in late at night," Jonathan remembered, "and we saw him the next morning, and he had been gone for like three months." At the breakfast table, the children asked about what he'd seen and done, but he didn't regale them with stories. Jonathan didn't expect that he would. "You could go to him and tell him things and he'd be respectful and interact. But he would never come up to you and say: What did you do in school today? How was your day? What did you do today? It just never happened." Via the intuition that children develop about their parents, it was understood they were unhappy, which cast a pall over most things. Within days after his return, John and Lonnie began quarreling again. "They always fought," Jonathan said. "There were times when I remember huddling in the basement and hearing them fight—about what, I have no clue what the fights were about."[24]

When at last Williams had had enough, he stormed out of the house, off to campus, or a bar, or in search of Nancy. At least he was in love with Nancy, who adored him. There was that to sustain him as he began the routines of the fall semester again—teaching, attending department meetings, and reviewing applications to the creative writing program—while in the background his third marriage was becoming increasingly hard for him to tolerate.[25]

Also on his arrival back in Denver, there was a letter waiting for him from his brother-in-law, Butch, who was ensconced once again in Ajijic, footloose and writing full time. He had resigned from Winthrop College, and had taught creative writing briefly at the University of Southern California—a "pretty congenial place"—where they tried to get him to stay on. But it had never been his ambition to teach: it was the writing life for him, and so he and George Rae were back to being literary bums. "How was it on the Oxford/Rome axis?" Butch asked. "We had a wildly relaxing, wildly productive summer in Ajijic, during which time I got so much accomplished on the novel that I can have the mother in the mails before the year's end." The novel was *Week with No Friday*, a marijuana- and booze-infused portrait of the expatriate life in Ajijic among writers and artists. "The advance on the novel, if it's publishable, might get us another year. Therefore, "operating under the belief that thinking beyond six or seven years in the thermonuclear age is pointless, we have seized the day.

"Bring us up to date on your own itinerary down life's highway."[26]

CHAPTER THIRTEEN

Stoner

*And though I may seem to take something away from
Stoner in the end at his death, I don't really; I give him
more than he has had before, and more than any of us
ever gain—his own identity.*

—JOHN WILLIAMS, 1966

News from his agent about *A Matter of Light*—renamed now
A Matter of Love in an effort to give it a fresh start—was
not encouraging. After a desultory period at the end of
1963 when a series of editors returned the manuscript to Marie
Rodell, a response from Simon and Schuster in March confirmed
what she had been warning Williams about from the beginning: the
story of Professor Stoner was depressing. "Several others here have
now read the manuscript," she wrote him, "and we're all in agreement that it is a book to be respected highly but that it has such a
pale grey character that it would be most unlikely to earn its keep in
hard covers and almost impossible to sell to a paperback house. . . .
What a simpatico writer—yet what a problem he presents."[1]

Falling down the ladder of large publishers, rung by rung,
A Matter of Love passed through the hands of Pyke Johnson as
well, editor of the contentious poetry anthology, who said, "I found
it a very moving story, one that might have been told of several professors I met along the academic path, as well as people completely
outside the Groves." But ultimately, Johnson concluded, it wasn't
right for him.[2]

Until now, Williams had been campaigning for his work with zeal, trying to put the sunniest light even on rejections. To Rodell, he speculated that perhaps the book was destined for a more "literary house." It might be slow to find a home, but "I still cannot convince myself that we are going to have an impossible time getting it placed. Whatever its 'commercial' possibilities, I believe finally that its quality will, if nothing else, shame someone into wanting to do it. I may be naïve; but I cannot help believing that somewhere, someone will feel compelled to publish a good novel."[3]

He kept up the good front, but within days of *A Matter of Love* being characterized as having "a pale grey character" and being "impossible to sell," he also received a dispiriting letter from the director of the University of Missouri Press, quoting an outside reader's opinion of his poetry collection, *The Shape of the Air*. "The poems reflect his academic experience," the reader had decided. "Most of the poems . . . lack the vitality which distinguishes the exciting poet from the hand of the craftsman, the passion of the poet is missing. . . . The imagery in the epigraphs is banal and the philosophical content, on which their merit might conceivably rest, is scarcely worthy of serious consideration."[4]

Remarks of that sort seemed to be telling him that he was an academic trying to become something he was not. Signs pointed to the advisability of dropping anchor in the harbor of academia and forgetting about the high seas of literature altogether. A memo from the dean, received the same day as the rejection about *The Shape of the Air*, congratulated him on being promoted to full professor for the fall semester. This came on the heels of the university receiving a grant from the Rockefeller Foundation to create a national literary quarterly, and Williams had been offered the position of editor.[5] He would have the freedom to set the direction of the publication, solicit contributions, review submissions, and put the quarterly into the hands of readers around the country—a far more influential role than having his verse published in little magazines.

His academic career, as opposed to his efforts as a novelist, had a wholeness and symmetry that reflected well on him. Here he was, director of the creative writing program, and soon to be editor of a small press quarterly—very similar to Alan Swallow's achievements at that age. It had taken over fifteen years, but he had equaled or exceeded his mentor in most respects. And yet, it was practically guaranteed that very little would change in his professional life during the coming years: there would be classes to prepare for, students to advise, meetings to attend, dissertations to read, and then the lassitude of summers before it started all over again. By the time he was an old man, his adventures in fiction and poetry would seem, in retrospect, like things he had dabbled in, fond ideas and so on.

Perhaps it was time to take stock. He was forty-two: the age at which Professor Stoner, Williams wrote, "could see nothing before him that he wished to enjoy and little behind him that he cared to remember."[6] After twenty years of trying to make a name for himself as a novelist, he was nowhere. "In those days you could put literary Denver in a phone booth," said Joanne Greenberg, whose 1964 novel, *I Never Promised You a Rose Garden*, would become an international best seller. "And I met John at some literary event. I met him because he was this small, well-made, dapper guy—drink in one hand, cigarette in the other—holding forth. He was very theatrical. 'Who is that?' I asked. 'He writes Westerns,' somebody said."[7]

Students who sought him out for advice found him occupying an untidy office down the hall from the English Department, which was still housed in a former dormitory. No framed awards hung from his walls indicating that anyone would be fortunate to have the benefit of his experience as novelist and poet. When he stayed late at night, he drank from a bottle of whiskey he kept in a desk drawer. A note from one of his graduate students expressed thanks for his help, but also sympathy for someone who was clearly discontented: "Your class lectures were consistently and intensely stimulating. Your opinions, presented in your capacity as my adviser, in some cases saved me much time and energy in many extremely profitable pursuits in the academic field and the field of creative writing." The young man was readying a collection of poems for publication, starting out on the path that Williams had begun many years ago. "In closing let me say that I am aware that, for various reasons, we never became friends. I am aware, too, that there is much anger, and bitterness, and even vehement contempt for what you see in the world. Nevertheless, I do hope that you also feel, for me, at least a modicum of the warm regard I feel for you."[8]

One afternoon, Williams sat quietly at Nancy's house, preoccupied about something. He crushed his cigarette in a tray and exhaled a brooding cloud of smoke. "I don't need to write novels," he said.

She was stunned by how dismissive he sounded. "He was tough. If he said he might quit, he might. He was that type, he could just say, 'Okay, that's it,'" she later said. "But I didn't want him to stop—writing meant everything to him and I was worried that if he quit, he would never be happy."[9]

At 625 Madison Avenue, in the manic heart of "Mad Men" advertising agencies, Viking Press occupied a corner of the book world that authors dreamed about joining. On its list were writers who received splashy reviews in magazines that were bellwethers of new and exciting literature—*Harper's*, *The Atlantic*, the *Saturday Review*, or *Time*, for instance—writers who were in the vanguard of a cultural shift in America, such as Saul Bellow, William S. Burroughs, Robert Coover, Ken Kesey, and Thomas Pynchon. The Viking catalog also included respected works of intellectual history and criticism by Hannah Arendt, Barbara Tuchman, and Lionel Trilling, as well as poetry by Phyllis McGinley, Marianne Moore, and Siegfried Sassoon.

If you were asked to meet with a Viking editor, you took the elevator up to the sixteenth floor, where the office doors were to the left, down the hall. As you entered, you had the impression of a private club. Recessed lights in the ceiling illuminated dark walnut bookcases, with book jackets displayed on the shelves like prints in an art gallery. The receptionist was seated behind a desk that resembled a three-sided pulpit made of the same dark wood; above her hung the company's nickel-plated logo: a Viking ship under full sail, designed by illustrator Rockwell Kent and chosen by the company's founder Harold Ginzburg as a symbol of enterprise, adventure, and exploration in publishing.[10]

"Oh, Mr. Williams," the receptionist might say, "you're expected," and you were invited to wait in one of the leather club chairs, opposite which were rows of black-and-white photographs mounted on the wall in silver frames: James Joyce, Graham Greene, John Steinbeck, Stefan Zweig, Sherwood Anderson—authors from the early days. When you were told you could go in now, you followed a paneled corridor past the office of the founder's son, Thomas Ginzburg, a trim man with Mediterranean features whose suits and shirts were hand-tailored. The chairs in his office were covered in chintz; and, just for whimsy, he had a model train that ran. Although he had the final say on any manuscript an editor wanted to purchase, he relied on one of his best editors—considered brilliant in fiction publishing: Corlies M. Smith.[11]

"Cork," as his friends called him, was another patrician of the book world. He had attended the Episcopal Academy outside Philadelphia, a boys' school that was nearly as old as the United States itself. Tall and good-looking, he'd worked at Lippincott in Philadelphia after graduating from Yale in 1951. The editorial side of publishing at that time was the preserve of Ivy League graduates in tweed suits and button-down shirts—a style Smith personally preferred because, as he said to a colleague, "this is not about fashion."[12] When he left Lippincott in 1963—at one point he had threatened to resign if any of fourteen uses of "screw" and "fuck" were removed from Barbara Probst Solomon's *The Beat of Life*—he brought Thomas Pynchon with him to Viking.

In meetings, he expressed his opinions about authors and submissions in a collegial way to avoid giving the impression that he believed he had unerring instinct. But he was extraordinarily perceptive—a good judge of what mattered, whether the title in question was destined to be hardback literary fiction or a trade paperback for the mass market. Once he got down to working with an author, his method was hands-on, or getting "close-in." His edits were returned with reports referring to specific pages; and, if necessary, he would recommend getting together to discuss changes.

In June 1964, Smith received a manuscript from Marie Rodell, whom he had known since Lippincott days. It was *A Matter of Love* by John Williams. The title was bland, he thought, but he settled in to give it a read.

———

From the first pages, it was clear that Williams had written a novel that was, as he had intended, "somewhat against the 'fashionable' novel." American fiction in the 1960s tended to declare heatedly, as Irving Howe complained, that "something about the experience of our age is unique, a catastrophe without precedent."[13] The story of Professor Stoner ran against that grain. It was strangely profound, despite its subject—the life of an unremarkable man. It proceeded with a deliberate, unhurried step, almost at the stately pace of Greek drama, because, as Williams himself said, he wanted to "hold the attention of the reader without resort to gimmicks and inventions," with a narrative "moving primarily upon that level on which we are moved in life."[14]

For his main character, William Stoner, Williams had looked to his colleague J. V. Cunningham. Cunningham was from a working-class background and had entered university life because an older man, Yvor Winters, had pointed out the way to him. Cunningham's first marriage, to the poet Barbara Gibbs—called "disastrous" by one who knew him well—had produced a daughter, Margie, and he had assumed custody of her.[15]

On the first page of the novel, Williams begins at a point not often dared by writers: the story is already over, and the narrator is merely reporting the events that happened. He had tried it once before in *Splendid in Ashes*. But now, the unemotional tone, the understatement, dispenses with all attempts at literariness. "William Stoner entered the University of Missouri as a freshman in the year 1910, at the age of nineteen. Eight years later, during the height of World War I, he received his Doctor of Philosophy degree and accepted an instructorship at the same University, where he taught until his death in 1956."[16]

The hero's surname, "Stoner," suggests the obdurate life he had led growing up with his parents as dirt farmers in Missouri, an existence of unbroken labor and silence. The longest speech he ever heard his father make occurs one night at the kitchen table; the subject is college. The older man repeats the county agent's remark that "they got new ideas, ways of doing things they teach you at the University."[17] Perhaps young Stoner should enroll in college and study agriculture. Left unsaid is the expectation that, as the couple's only child, he will return to run the farm.

Once enrolled at the University of Missouri, however, "the required survey of English literature troubled and disquieted him in a way nothing had ever done before." He's startled awake by poetic language. A sonnet by Shakespeare, read aloud by his instructor, Professor Sloane, speaks to him across the span of three hundred years, and Stoner experiences a sense of existing, of being aware of himself:

> He looked away from Sloane about the room. Light slanted from the windows and settled upon the faces of his fellow students, so that the illumination seemed to come from within them and go out against a dimness; a student blinked, and a thin shadow fell upon a cheek whose down had caught the sunlight. Stoner became aware that his fingers were unclenching their hard grip on his desk-top. He turned his hands about under his gaze, marveling at their brownness, at the intricate way the nails fit into his blunt finger-ends; he thought he could feel the blood flowing invisibly through the tiny veins and arteries, throbbing delicately and precariously from his fingertips through his body.[18]

Until that moment, Stoner has lived enveloped by the insensate world of nature. But language makes it possible for him to reach new consciousness. Words permit reasoning, which can be used to concretize elusive qualities of life. To make real *futility*, Williams describes the home where Stoner grew up: "The floors [of the house] were of unpainted plank, unevenly spaced and cracking with age, up through which dust steadily seeped and was swept back each day by Stoner's mother."[19] The image is mythic in its power to express, like the task of Sisyphus, the terror of endlessness. The psychological depth Williams had tried to achieve in *Nothing But the Night*, and the forcefulness that eludes him in writing verse, he invokes to tremendous, moving effect in *Stoner*. It's as if he has taken a carpenter's plane to the solipsistic, useless overwriting of *Nothing But the Night*. He "strips the narrative of its rhetoric," in Hilton Als' phrase, and shaves down each sentence to Flaubertian exactness.[20]

Stoner switches his major to English literature without telling his parents, and informs them when they arrive on campus to see him graduate that he will not be returning with them to the farm. They receive his news with the same stoical acceptance as they would the fact that inadequate rainfall that season has killed the fields. They are not people of words. He "watched his father's face, which received those words as a stone receives the repeated blows of a fist. . . . [His mother] was breathing heavily, her face twisted as if in pain, and her closed fists were pressed against her cheeks." His decision not to return has put them under a sentence condemning them to work without the benefit of his help and his "new ideas," contrary to what the county agent promised, for the rest of their lives.[21]

Stoner receives his PhD in English literature in 1918, the year he meets Edith Bostwick, the daughter of a local banker. From the outset, it's clear that their romance is flawed. Stoner's idealized expectations about love are taken from books.[22] In his courses, "Tristan, Iseult the fair, walked before him; Paolo and Francesca whirled in the glowing dark; Helen and bright Paris, their faces bitter with consequence, rose from the gloom."[23] These are only counterfeits of love that a mature couple might discard in time. But what's fatal to Bill Stoner and Edith Bostwick's relationship is that they lack a shared, personal language, the intimate "little language" of lovers, as Jonathan Swift called it. Their inarticulateness is painful:

> "It was a very nice reception," Edith said faintly. "I thought everyone was very nice."
>
> "Oh, yes, of course," Stoner said. "I meant . . ." He did not go on. Edith was silent.

He said, "I understand you and your aunt will be going to
Europe in a little while."

"Yes," she said.

"Europe . . ." He shook his head. "You must be very excited."

She nodded reluctantly.

"Where will you go? I mean—what places?" . . .

Stoner was silent for a moment.[24]

He attempts to corner her into talking; and then suddenly, all in
a rush, she begins "to tell him about herself, as he had asked her to
do. He wanted to tell her to stop, to comfort her, to touch her. He
did not move or speak."[25] She continues on and on, mechanically
relating a litany of facts about herself, deposing everything about
her life because, as we will come to understand, she feels contempt
for sincerity, for love, for everything that's weak or vulnerable. Her
talk is obliging noise. She's a disappointed romantic, and carries on
the courtship with an imperceptible sneer.

Williams' portrait of Edith has been criticized as misogynistic.
But he implies that she has been a victim, and the blame belongs to
an abusive man, her father. "'They were very close,' Edith's mother
said mysteriously. 'Much closer than they seemed.'" On his wedding
night, Stoner "put his hand upon [Edith] and felt beneath the thin
cloth of her nightgown the flesh he had longed for. He moved his
hand upon her; she did not stir; her frown deepened." After inter-
course, she hurries into the bathroom and vomits. Much later, on
the day of her father's funeral, Edith returns to her parents' home
after the service, to the bedroom she had as a girl, and divides her
personal items into two piles: one is for gifts and notes from school
friends and relatives, and the other is for what "her father had given
her and of things with which he had been directly or indirectly
connected." Everything from him—dolls, clothing, pictures—she
smashes, pounds, or burns in the fireplace, "methodically, expres-
sionlessly." This exorcism only partly succeeds. After the ritual, she
goes to the opposite pole, beginning her life again, this time as an
artsy, free-spirited, unconventional woman. The effect is pathetic:
"she seemed happy, though perhaps a bit desperately so."[26]

The marriage will be unhappy, Stoner realizes, because they are fundamentally antagonistic. Edith Bostwick is winter; he, a former farmer, is summer. Their union is impossible, unnatural even. "In her white dress she was like a cold light coming into the room." Her face "was like a mask, expressionless and white." When the couple moves to a house near campus because Edith demands it, she "wanted it white, and he had to put three coats on so that the dark green would not show through," as though burying their relationship under snow. For two months, she is wildly sexual, waiting "crouched in the semidarkness," like a predator. But there is no tenderness; and her "eyes were wide and staring," as if sex were an assault. Her strange behavior stops immediately when she becomes pregnant. After months of sickness, she delivers a baby girl, Grace, with whom Stoner "falls instantly in love"; but for a year, Edith acts troubled and upset when she tries to hold her infant daughter in her arms.[27]

About that time, a new instructor joins the English Department named Hollis N. Lomax, a specialist in nineteenth-century literature. Holding a PhD from Harvard, he delays his appearance until the first department meeting. Then he enters, a figure from Gothic Romance:

> Someone whispered, "It's Lomax," and the sound was sharp and audible through the room.
>
> He had come through the door, closed it, and had advanced a few steps beyond the threshold, where he now stood. He was a man barely over five feet in height, and his body was grotesquely misshapen. A small hump raised his left shoulder to his neck, and his left arm hung laxly at his side. His upper body was heavy and curved, so that he appeared to be always struggling for balance; his legs were thin, and he walked with a hitch in his stiff right leg. For several moments he stood with his blond head bent downward, as if he were inspecting his highly polished black shoes and the sharp crease of his black trousers. Then he lifted his head and shot his right arm out, exposing a stiff white length of cuff with gold links; there was a cigarette in his long pale fingers. He took

a deep drag, inhaled, and expelled the smoke in a thin stream.
And then they could see his face.

It was the face of a matinee idol.[28]

Long ago, John Ed Williams, the teenaged poet of Wichita Falls,
had been dazzled by matinee idol Ronald Colman, and had taken
him for the epitome of the Romantic hero. But in the character of
Lomax, Williams parodies the sentimentality of Romanticism for
teaching that feelings can be relied on as a guide to truth. "I am
Lomax," the visitor intones, after a theatrical pause, in a "deep and
rich" voice—a customary thing to say, but meant to seem profound
because it was delivered melodramatically.[29] There is an air of
charlatanism about Lomax. For Professor Stoner, whose field is
logical thought and the poetry of the classically influenced English
Renaissance, his antithesis has arrived.

Lomax avoids his colleagues, although he is "ironically pleasant"
to them. His classes are popular because he performs: he trades on
the cult of personality. And then, on an unusually cold night in September—Edith-weather, in other words—Lomax surprises everyone
by attending a house-warming party at the Stoners' home. Getting
quite drunk, he stays till almost dawn, talking about his loneliness,
his inadequacies, and how literature had been a refuge. Before he
leaves, he gives Edith a chaste kiss on the lips, and whispers something to her, as if they understand one another. The next day, Stoner
tries to follow up with overtures of friendship; but Lomax—threatened by how his drunkenness made him drop his Byronic mask of
alienation and self-sufficiency—snubs him "with an irony that was
like cold anger."[30] Lomax's resentment never lessens; he becomes
half of the ancient Fairchild-Ramsay feud at the University of Missouri. Probably because Fairchild limped, Williams unconsciously
wrote "Fairchild" sometimes in his manuscript instead of "Lomax."[31]

Stoner carries on, a conscientious but not inspiring teacher.
Despite his love of language, he pulls back uncertainly from con-
veying his passion for it, as if that would be admitting too much.
He publishes a book in his field, awed by his temerity at daring to
make a bid for immortality. When he holds it in his hands, it seems

"delicate and alive, like a child." His affectionate relationship with his daughter, Grace, six years old now, fulfills him, too. The simplicity of his love for her, his instincts as a father, lead him to believe "that it might be possible for him to become a good teacher."[32]

But Edith cannot live comfortably without conflict. Like her complement, Lomax, she is histrionic, a born thespian, because drama gives her a role. She resents the feeling of calm between Stoner and Grace. After her absence following her father's death, when she returns home, Edith says to her daughter, "'Gracie, honey,' . . . in a voice that seemed to [her husband] to be strained and brittle, 'did you miss your mommy? Did you think she was never coming back?'" Surprised that such a frightening thought had never occurred to Grace, Edith determines to give her the education about family relationships that Stoner is failing to give. One evening, when Grace and her father are in his study, "laughing together, senselessly, as if they both were children," Edith enters and tells Grace not to disturb her father. Confused, Grace leaves the room. The "enormity" of his wife's "surprise attack" suddenly becomes clear to Stoner. From now on, Edith will hold Grace hostage in a never-ending game of making her complicit in hurting her father. Wearily, he surrenders to his wife's stratagems, and concedes his happiness at home. "There are wars and defeats and victories of the human race that are not military and that are not recorded in the annals of history," Williams writes. But in another contest, this one in the English Department, Stoner realizes he cannot stand by.[33]

One of Lomax's doctoral students, Charles Walker, comes to Stoner to ask a favor. His area is Romantic poetry, and he's a younger version of his adviser: his left hand hangs "stiffly at his side, and his left foot dragged as he walked."[34] He wants Stoner's permission to enroll in an overloaded, and challenging, seminar on the influence of the Latin tradition on English literature. Professor Lomax has assured him he can handle the work. Stoner listens and decides to give this impulsive young man what he wants.

On the first day of class, Walker is late. Then he interrupts with questions for the sake of drawing attention to himself. His remarks don't stem from curiosity; he wants to demonstrate that Romantic poetry, "*real* poetry," has no need of a classical perspective. After class, Stoner seeks reassurance from Lomax that Walker can indeed do the work. Lomax extolls his protégé's brilliance, adding, with "cheerful malevolence, 'As you may have noticed, he is a cripple.'"[35] The insinuation is that Walker should be given extra consideration; and if Stoner doesn't agree, Lomax will take it personally. Thus Lomax has brushed aside the question of Walker's intellectual ability and made *feelings* the issue.

Walker's dependably off-the-point remarks continue in class, and when it becomes clear that his classmates regard him as a nuisance, he expresses "outrage and resentment." The last straw, however, is an audacious stunt he tries to pull off that makes a mockery of academic study. He pretends to be reading his final paper aloud to the class, when he's really only extemporizing. In a sad imitation of Lomax's fervent style, he makes a rebuttal to a well-researched and thoughtful paper presented earlier by a student named Katherine Driscoll, whose genuine scholarship has earned Stoner's gratitude and respect. Walker's unserious response shows contempt for both him and Driscoll. Stoner gives him an F, to which Walker warns, "You have not heard the last of this."[36]

The confrontation comes, as it did between professors Fairchild and Ramsay, during Walker's preliminary oral examination—with Stoner, Lomax (now the interim department chair), and two other academics at the table. It's clear that Lomax has coached his candidate, whose ignorance is appalling, but Stoner will not let the travesty get by. As a scholar, it's his responsibility to defend the profession, whose primary aim is to elucidate truth through knowledge and reasoning. Predictably, when Stoner refuses to agree to giving Walker a "pass" on the exam, Lomax accuses him of "holding incipiently prejudiced feelings" against Walker. But Stoner stands his ground—at the cost of his career, as it turns out. A corrupt compromise, handed down from higher in the administration, allows Walker to take his oral preliminaries again, this time with a committee selected by the new English Department chairman, Hollis Lomax. Edith laughs at her husband's principles: "Honestly, things are so important to you. What *difference* could it make?" When

Stoner receives his teaching schedule for the new term, Lomax has assigned him courses appropriate for a beginning instructor.[37]

Following this defeat, Williams releases Stoner into a love affair with graduate student Katherine Driscoll; it's a release in the sense that love frees him to learn about what he is capable of. Williams emphasized the need for characters to have a moral identity that is not fixed, but constantly redefining itself, as a way of illustrating the complexity of people's relationships. This is not an argument that art should be moral: it was a practical consideration Williams had learned as an author for developing the identity of characters striving against an indifferent world.[38]

Some of Williams' favorite examples came from Henry James.[39] (He once surprised one of his graduate students by bringing her a stack of James novels. "Never mind what they tell you in class—just read and study these. You have to learn it on your own."[40]) Williams subscribed to James' moral realism, where the "imagination of loving"—the phrase used in *The Portrait of a Lady*—creates circumstances of passion involving moral choices the character can explore.[41]

Although the affair between Stoner and Katherine Driscoll becomes known, "what surprised them both was that it did not seem to matter. No one refused to speak to them; no one gave them black looks; they were not made to suffer by the world they had feared. They began to believe that they could live in the place they had thought to be inimical to their love, and live there with some dignity and ease."[42] However, running against society's strictures has consequences, or, as Williams liked to say, "You pay your money and you take your choice, and you find at last that you can't have it both ways."[43] Chairman Hollis Lomax is prepared to use the affair as an excuse to ruin their academic careers. Stoner is tenured and middle-aged, but Katherine is twenty years younger. For her sake, Stoner breaks off the relationship, and she quietly leaves town. He adjusts himself to accepting loneliness as a condition of his life.

"Stoner does endure too much, he accepts too much, and he doesn't fight enough," Williams wrote a friend. "But if these are vices, they are vices that are merely the obverse of certain virtues—virtues that allow him to endure in one world [his profession] at the expense of his happiness in another [his marriage]."[44]

The years pass, and after learning he has cancer, Stoner retires from teaching. Edith regards his illness as a tiresome inconvenience. Grace, who comes to say goodbye, has become a passive, colorless person; she drinks because she feels rejected.[45] In the final moments of his life, Stoner gazes out the window of his sickbed on a summer afternoon, and then "a sense of his own identity came upon him with a sudden force, and he felt the power of it. He was himself, and he knew what he had been." Williams, who never knew his father, who exaggerated his adventures and created a rather fey persona of the *artiste* to cover his insecurities, gives Stoner the gift of self-knowledge, without the interfering fog of moral expectations or a Christian redemption. As his hero gently tells Katherine, when their love affair must end, "We have come out of this, at least, with ourselves. We know that we are—what we are."[46]

––––––––

Cork Smith at Viking offered a contract for *A Matter of Love* in mid-July 1964. He wasn't crazy about the title ("Unfortunately, I have no brilliant suggestions"), so in the ensuing months, after a three-way correspondence between Smith, Marie Rodell, and Williams, they settled on *Stoner* instead. "I couldn't be more pleased with [Viking]," Williams wrote to Rodell. "Their first list is excellent and never so large as to be unmanageable. On the basis of all I know about the books they publish and seem to like I probably could not have chosen a house that would have pleased me better."[47]

It was the beginning of a series of good things happening to him. Alan Swallow accepted a collection of his poems and brought them out under the title *The Necessary Lie* as part of the press's Verb Poetry Series; Williams' anthology, *English Renaissance Poetry* (with the acknowledgment to Winters added), was a hit among college instructors, as he had predicted, and went into a second edition.

In April, *Stoner* appeared, lightly reviewed. Williams went to New York for an autographing party hosted by Viking and did a few interviews. Two strange things happened, and had Williams been thin-skinned, or superstitious, he might have taken offense. A limousine picked him up at his hotel for a talk show on radio. As he got in, "Chuckles the Clown" was sitting in the rear seat, on his way to the same radio program. He was in full circus regalia: a small man with a red rubber nose, black fright wig, huge white ruff, big shoes, and a baggy red-and-white polka-dotted suit made of silk. Williams regarded his companion's costume and thought to himself, "But this is radio." He was chauffeured next to a circus-themed television show, hosted by "a fat person named Stubby Kaye," which turned out to be a Saturday kiddie show called *Shenanigans*. "I can't seem to get away from clowns," he mentioned dryly to Smith.[48]

By June, sales of *Stoner* stood at 1,700, less than half of Butch Marsh's *Week with No Friday* about artists living a bacchanalian life in Mexico, which had been published the month before *Stoner*. "The book is moving, but slowly," Cork Smith admitted. "This in no way diminishes our feelings about the novel. You were right and we were right."[49]

Then, nearly a year after *Stoner*'s release, in February 1966, a review by Irving Howe in the *New Republic* hailed it as an overlooked discovery:

> Given the quantity of fiction published in this country each year, it seems unavoidable that most novels should be ignored and that among these a few should nonetheless be works of distinction. *Stoner*, a book that received very little notice upon its appearance several months ago, is, I think, such a work: serious, beautiful and affecting. . . . Mr. Williams writes with discipline and strength: he is devoted to the sentence as a form, and free from the allure of imagery. . . . I think there should be a few thousand people in this country who will find pleasure in the book.[50]

The day after the review appeared, Williams arrived early at the English Department office dressed in his best. Howe's praise had come late, but it was reason to celebrate. He knew that a few of his colleagues subscribed to the *New Republic*, so he made himself available in the outer office beside the faculty mailboxes. All day he sat in the reception area opposite the secretary at her desk, drinking coffee and smoking, as his fellow instructors walked past, to and from class. A few congratulated him, but most said nothing. A friend in the department, Robert Pawlowski, wasn't surprised. "Most knew that great jealousy lived in a number of his colleagues and he stoically suffered them," Pawlowski later said. At five o'clock, when the halls had emptied out, Williams went into his office and closed the door behind him.[51]

The review in the *New Republic* didn't make much of a difference in sales. Cork Smith mailed out thirty thousand flyers to high school English teachers, hoping they would make *Stoner* assigned reading. But that didn't improve the numbers, either.

PART IV

Augustus

CHAPTER FOURTEEN

Bread Loaf and "Up on the Hill"

> *I would dearly love to find a kind of colleague with less than the rather staggering total of twenty-five years of service to the Bread Loaf Writers Conference. . . . There are things in* Stoner *that make me think you might be such a person.*
>
> —WILLIAM M. SLOANE TO JOHN WILLIAMS, 1965

N ancy didn't know many "Lonnie people," nor did she want to know them. That part of John's life was his business and she trusted him to take care of it. She had acquiesced to his desire not to flaunt their relationship out of respect for Lonnie and the children. Among his friends, Williams was straightforward about having two households—to Nancy's youngest child, he was her mother's friend, "John Worms," but other than that, the professor and his mistress shared an unspoken bargain about the outside world and keeping it out.[1] That included Alan and Mae Swallow.

From what Nancy gathered, Alan had been largely responsible for John's career. John and Lonnie had met while working for Swallow Press. And after they married, the Swallows visited them a few times in Columbia, Missouri. Since then, for going on fifteen years, the two couples had been regulars out for dinner in Denver.

Alan had slipped from the Denver scene somewhat, because of a traffic accident. Cruising noisily down the streets of Denver on his Indian motorcycle, he'd swerved to miss a turning car and caught his right leg on the handle of the passenger door. There had been a chance he would lose it up to the knee; instead, the surgeon reconnected the shinbone with a steel pin. Still, his foot flailed as he walked. To cope with the pain, he drank and "worked like two men," as a friend said, to continue mailing out an average of fifty thousand books a year, in addition to publishing seventy-five new titles.[2] Six months after the motorcycle crash, he collapsed in the living room on Christmas morning from a heart attack. From his bed he wrote letters to author friends, apologizing for having a body that couldn't keep up with him.

Added to the physical strain, though, was Swallow's spiritual isolation. The academic community in Denver had gradually forgotten him after he resigned in 1954 over the affair with a trustee's wife. At first, he had enjoyed the days spent humming along to the radio in the garage, chewing on a cigar, and corresponding with authors and booksellers, regaling them in multiple-page letters about his prospects. And it was good to see the boxes of finished books, smelling of fresh ink, delivered by a truck backing into his driveway. A delivery meant at least a week of late nights spent wrapping orders, individually or in parcels, and making sure to slip a handwritten invoice inside each one. Stacks of paperwork to be sorted sat on top of the file cabinets.

Swallow Press truly absorbed him, but he missed the old days of noisy autographing parties at his home—he didn't know whom to invite any longer, apart from old friends. Being stricken from the faculty mailing list meant he was out of the loop when it came to special lectures, social events, and English Department matters. He was just a "townie" now. While he'd been director of the creative writing program, publisher of the University of Denver Press, and owner-publisher of Swallow Press, there had been a wonderful synergy that put him at the center of everything he cared about.

His frustration over his estrangement surfaced in a reply to John Williams in March 1963 about some poetry Williams had submitted. Addressing his erstwhile student in the tone of a teacher, Swallow scolded Williams for being too easily distracted and not following through on his work. "There are some good poems here, nicely done on real subject matter. But on the whole, I was disappointed. Too many poems seem to me to lack enough subject or theme to become interesting and test the accomplishment of versification." He chided him for continuing to devote energy to fiction. "It seems possible that . . . in the last ten years or so, you have so concentrated your thought on fiction that the poetic concern has not blossomed as much as it would have otherwise."[3]

In the meantime, Saturdays were sale days at the garage on York Street. In April 1966, Alan once again wrestled the folding tables into position for displays of discounted books—ones that hadn't sold or were spoiled for some reason, with the prices written in pencil on the title page. The walk-in trade wasn't brisk—mainly graduate students and people who stopped by to browse—but he could do paperwork while the shop was open. He assumed his place at a card table near the front with an adding machine at his elbow for checkout. He saw a woman coming up the drive. It was Nancy.

There was no one else around, only the two of them, and after saying hello, Nancy walked slowly around the tables, her fingertips finding covers of books lying on their backs. She chose a few, holding them in the crook of her arm and pressing them against her sweater, until she was carrying five or six poetry and essay books. Alan rose and came to where she was at the far end of the garage. He stood by expectantly. She glanced up at him and offered the books for checkout. Instead, he tossed them on the table and grabbed her by the shoulders.

"Suddenly he slammed me against the wall and pressed himself against me," Nancy later said in an interview years later. "I've never been so scared. He was a barrel-chested guy—not tall, but solid. And there was nothing I could do. I kept saying, 'No, Alan, don't!' and he was groping. I'd not been flirting. I'm not a flirt. I said, 'No, Alan,' enough times that he just as suddenly backed off."

She hurried back to her car, her hands shaking as she tried to unlock the door. In the interview, she said, "Alan was probably thinking, 'This is John's whore,' because he was a friend of Lonnie's. I don't know. He could have killed me."

She drove away wondering whether she should tell John about

what had happened. At first she thought she wouldn't, but she was too upset. She went to the apartment he kept near campus and told him everything. He left her there to wait and was gone an hour.

"And that was the end. He never spoke to Alan again," she said. "After all that nurturing, and everything that Alan meant to John. I kept asking myself, 'Did I do anything? No, I just wanted to look at books.'"[4]

———————

Come June, John looked forward to being on his own for a few weeks once Lonnie and the children departed for Mexico to visit Uncle Butch and Aunt George Rae. He hadn't seen his sister and brother-in-law for twelve years, and he'd wrangled an invitation as part of a summer itinerary that would give him maximum time to do what he wanted. First, he needed to put the third issue of the *Denver Quarterly* to bed; then, at the end of July, he would fly down to Mexico for a couple of weeks with his family in Ajijic. Finally, he'd be off to the Bread Loaf Writers' Conference in Vermont for most of August.

Butch was in fine fettle when John arrived. *Week with No Fridays* was selling well—unlike *Stoner*, which had fallen off the edge of the earth after the first few weeks. In fact, Butch's publisher had taken out a big advertisement in the *New York Times*. Butch had half a dozen photographs taken for publicity—an expat American writer living the sweet life—his sports coat thrown nonchalantly over one shoulder as he strolled around Ajijic. While John was visiting, they talked about Butch's next novel, which would be set in San Francisco, and the published short stories from little magazines he was going to pitch as a collection.[5] John was all for it, and he reciprocated by talking about his next project: a novel about power, consisting of correspondence, he was thinking, between Roman senators, generals, and certain family members who benefited or suffered from the rise of Augustus.

It was to his credit that he never begrudged his brother-in-law's incremental successes—partly out of loyalty to George Rae, who adored Butch—but also because John was wholly focused on his own work. There were too many authors, living and dead, to envy. He was striving for respect as a novelist, and it didn't take anything from him to wish his brother-in-law well. Then, after a couple of weeks spent being dad and husband in Ajijic—the kids' complaints about being bored got on his nerves—Williams flew back to Denver and into Nancy's arms before continuing on to the Bread Loaf Conference in Vermont.

———

He'd been invited to Bread Loaf the year before, unfortunately too late for an instructorship for that session. But William M. Sloane, an editor and fantasy writer who helped run the event, made it clear that Williams was on the "must invite" list. "I would dearly love to find a kind of colleague with less than the rather staggering total of twenty-five years of service to the Bread Loaf Writers Conference," he joked, referring to his own tenure there since World War II, "so that some of what I believe in about this conference can be handed along to someone else who might possibly care very much about it after a year or two of experience. There are things in *Stoner* that make me think you might be such a person."[6] Williams accepted a position teaching poetry and fiction; the fee was an honorarium—a few hundred dollars—but the prestige of teaching at a conference reckoned to be the best in the country meant a lot to a writer in mid-career.

He wished Nancy could accompany him, but she had children and a large vegetable garden that was just coming into season. The strain of trying to have everything he wanted, to meet all of his commitments, personal and professional, was getting to him. "I don't know whether or not I told you about my summer; it's a bitch," he wrote to an acquaintance. "I had hoped to get some work done on my new novel, but the prospects look highly unlikely. . . . We don't need money—we need time."[7] In August 1966, he flew to New York and hitched a ride with the wife of a Bread Loafer instructor and her friend. Together they drove up through Concord, New Hampshire, and then northwest into central Vermont, to an upland valley shaped like a diamond in the Green Mountains.

It was midafternoon when they arrived, the day before the start of the conference, and the grounds were nearly deserted. A few attendees were registering at the rambling, turn-of-the-century Bread Loaf Inn, a gift from a local philanthropist to Middlebury College along with thirty thousand acres of timber forest. Smaller buildings—cottages, a barn, a library—were within walking distance, giving the place the appearance of a streetless village seated on an expanse of grass, dappled with old spreading trees. He was surprised to find the setting so bucolic. It was located "some ten or fifteen miles from Middlebury, the nearest town of any consequence," he later wrote. "It is a land-locked island of a wilderness so soft that it seems almost contrived. A dozen or so buildings— from tiny cottages to spacious three-story houses—are scattered randomly upon many acres of gently rolling fields, and in the near distance Bread Loaf Mountain lies squat upon the horizon."[8]

Middlebury College had convened the first summer school session here in 1920. It was then called the Bread Loaf School of English and offered graduate-level study in English and American literature. Many of the attendees were teachers. Robert Frost, who lived in nearby South Shaftesbury, took an interest because he dreamed of owning a farm that would attract writers annually to a literary summer camp. He joined the first faculty of invited guests during the summer in 1922. Eventually, the two weeks remaining after the official end of summer school became the Bread Loaf Writers' Conference, devoted exclusively to creative writing. And for almost thirty years since then, Frost had been its guiding spirit: Frost, the poet of the life and landscape of New England whose flinty personality made younger writers nervous. Then, in 1963, the first "Frostless summer" after a brief period of interim directors, he passed the baton to his heir apparent, the poet John Ciardi.

Ciardi had attended Bread Loaf before World War II and almost every year thereafter beginning in 1947, making him "the conference's anchor in teaching poetry as surely as his deep baritone found a place in the evening sing-alongs," wrote David Haward Bain in his history of Bread Loaf, *Whose Woods These Are*. Ciardi did have one weakness, however—his "utter (sometimes dismaying) lack of modesty" about his financial success, despite coming from a poor Italian neighborhood in Boston's North End neighborhood.[9] Now the poetry editor of the *Saturday Review* and host of *Accent*, a weekly television magazine program, said he was the first poet in America to own a pink Cadillac DeVille. The car, his proudest possession, was parked outside the fine old Bread Loaf Inn the afternoon Williams checked in.

Ciardi handpicked his faculty. As an editor of the *Saturday Review*, he had definite ideas about who belonged at Bread Loaf: primarily middle-aged white males who were part of the literary establishment and given to looking like Oxford dons, with sports jackets and briar pipes. Seymour Epstein, who didn't have a college degree, thought he had misheard when Ciardi said, cheerily, "We'll have to have you up on the hill next summer." Epstein smiled and nodded, thinking he meant, "We'll have you up to dinner sometime."[10] But Epstein was typical of the kind of Bread Loaf instructor Ciardi was looking for: bright and broadly accepted. Epstein had just published *Leah*, a vivid description of midcentury Manhattan through the eyes of a woman searching for love. Having been tapped by Ciardi himself, he accepted the invitation to come up to "the hill" as a new instructor that summer of 1966, the same as Williams. There was only one woman on staff that year: a children's book editor.

John unpacked his suitcase, hung up his clothes in a closet that was "as big as many a bedroom," and then went downstairs for a walk "into the amber softness of the late Vermont afternoon."[11] Drinks were available at Treman cottage, reserved for faculty, and he headed in that direction.

Dan Wakefield, a freelance journalist and author of *Revolt in the South*, a 1961 collection of reports on the civil rights movement, had never heard of John Williams as he came through the door of the cottage. He later described him as a "short, wiry, intense man with black hair, a sharp beard, and glasses," recalling that "a fellow staff member identified him as the author of *Stoner*, 'a novel that was supposed to be terrific.'"[12] Williams opened a beer and went over to a group making small talk to join the conversation. Within minutes, he and Wakefield got into a nasty argument over the merits of a minor political figure. The atmosphere in the room spoiled, Williams returned to his room and went to bed early, wondering "not for the first time nor the last time in my life why I was where I was."[13]

At breakfast the next morning, Ciardi, wearing a tweed jacket that seemed to billow on his huge, pear-shaped frame, welcomed the staff and students. His mission, he said, was to abide by Frost's "first principle," as he called it, "the center of the Bread Loaf idea: let them come together; let the writers, and the teachers, and the would-be writers, the hopeful and the hopeless come together; let good writers lead their discussion and set the terms of it; and let the talk be of writing from inside the writing process." Wakefield, glancing at *The Crumb*, the daily conference newsletter placed each morning beside everyone's plate, saw that Williams was giving a reading later, and he decided to attend—"only from a sense of noblesse oblige, tinged with curiosity."

He took a seat at the appointed time, waiting for the presenter to begin. A few more Bread Loafers ambled in. Then, for twenty minutes, Williams read from *Stoner* in his deep, rumbling voice, trained for radio broadcasts that went out into the gigantic Texas night, and "the passages read were so eloquent, so moving in their understated passion," Wakefield said, "that I rushed out after the lecture, bought the book, and spent the rest of the day reading it." That evening, seeing his adversary, the "short, wiry, intense man," nursing a drink alone at Treman cottage, Wakefield went over and extended his hand. "Look," he said, "I don't give a *shit* about politics."[14] The two men remained friends for the rest of Williams' life.

The Bread Loaf Conference was a respite and a kind of safe harbor for Williams. In the English Department at Denver, he was a bit of an oddball, a raconteur at parties, an academic who wrote novels. But transported to the foot of Bread Loaf Mountain, he was admired. "I was in awe of John," said one of the students years later. "Deep voice, chain smoker, very intense. He would give a thoughtful answer about the weather. Rock-like, stone-like face, and then suddenly he would break into a big smile. He was gracious, but he said what he thought. He was surprised that people treated him as a true novelist and not an academic."[15]

That fall, too, Alan Swallow attended a symposium on historical fiction in Pullman, Washington. Anyone encountering him there wouldn't have guessed that he was anything other than in good health. Novelist Frederick Manfred shook hands with him warmly. "His leg had at last healed and he was walking around again like a young man. His face had once more the glow of health. He was lively and happy and full of gentle witticisms," he remembered. "We all had a great time together. We were like a bunch of rancher brothers who, after looking for breaks in the fence all day, meet at dusk and sit around the campfire telling stories."[16]

Returning home, Swallow plunged back into the pile of Swallow Press work that was waiting. On Thanksgiving morning 1966, Mae woke up early to start breakfast. Hearing the motor of the electric typewriter whirring in the basement, she assumed that Alan had stayed up all night, and she took him down a cup of coffee. He was seated at his desk, bent forward with his head resting on the typewriter like it was a steel pillow, dead at fifty-one from a heart attack.

CHAPTER FIFTEEN

The Good Guys

Well, I cleaned out my office, and guess what?
I found a dead student.

—JOHN WILLIAMS

"It never rains but it pours," Williams wrote merrily to his Bread Loaf friend Seymour Epstein in February 1967. "And since you mention it, I *will* tell you about my triumphs, my successes, my hopes, my dreams, my fears."[1] He would be leaving in grand style on an ocean liner in May to research *Augustus*, courtesy of a grant. He would return at summer's end for Bread Loaf, then retreat to his mountain cabin in Pine on sabbatical. Come the first of the year, he would begin as writer-in-residence at Smith College in Northampton, Massachusetts. Hence, he would be gone from the University of Denver for an entire year. Sounding a little bemused by this rush of opportunities, he wrote to Epstein, "It is a strange new world."

It was hard to believe that just two years earlier, *Stoner* had come and gone with only Howe's belated review in the *New Republic* praising it. The following year, 1966, he wrote to another friend, seemed to Williams "the worst year of my life, in some ways, as far as time is concerned," because teaching and editing the *Denver Quarterly* had kept him from working on his new novel about Rome.[2] Now, suddenly, he was feeling a measure of success. Unexpectedly, "for me at least," he wrote Epstein, "*Stoner* has paid off handsomely," meaning that the novel had played a role in getting him the grant. "Now, I should have finished the *Augustus* novel by the summer of 1968."[3] But he was going to need a replacement to take his classes, and asked Epstein, who accepted his offer of a temporary position in Denver's creative writing program.

The Augustus novel, as he imagined it, would depict Rome and the life of the emperor through imagined letters and journal entries. Major figures of the era would be put in conversation and conflict with one another: Julius Caesar, Marcus Agrippa, Maecenas, Cicero, Brutus, Mark Antony, Cleopatra, Strabo, Nicolaus of Damascus, Horace, Ovid, Virgil, and Augustus' daughter Julia. The structure would be "webbed," he said. That is, it would "not be straightforwardly chronological, but will cut back and forth in time, getting at Augustus's character from many different angles and points of view," using the novelist's art to illustrate the evolution of Octavian from a mild-mannered young man to Caesar Augustus, ruler of the Western world. "He will become what he will become," says his tutor, the Greek Stoic Athenodorus, "out of the force of his person and the accident of his fate."[4]

But Williams would not try to describe the pageantry of banner-waving Roman legions or ships burning on the Ionian Sea. Too much of that would be a distraction from his main theme, which is how "force of person" meets the grinding forces of circumstance to forge an identity. His method of showing Augustus' development was his favorite: the *bildungsroman*, where the journey is away from security toward self-formation. In *Butcher's Crossing*, Will Anderson goes West to test his notions of himself against the world; in *Stoner*, the farm boy Bill Stoner has an epiphany over a sonnet that sets the direction of his life. Octavian is still a teenager when the catastrophic news reaches him that his uncle, Julius Caesar, has been murdered. His young friends study him for a sign of what he will do, how he will react. "For a long time we watched him, a slight boyish figure walking on the deserted field, moving slowly, this way and that, as if trying to discover a way to go."[5]

And for the second time, as he had in *Stoner*, Williams would turn to the pain caused by a father-daughter relationship that has failed. He detected in Augustus' behavior toward his only daughter and biological child, Julia, "some mystical identification between [her] and Rome; to the one he gave ethical training, education, and love; to the other he gave laws, a sense of order, and the dedication of his immense talent for ruling." When she is eleven, Augustus takes Julia's education and development into his own hands, and as she grows, he confides matters to her that he would trust to few others.

Despite his carefulness, however, Julia defies him with public licentiousness that is politically dangerous. Macrobius records Augustus' remark: "There are two wayward daughters that I have to put up with, the Roman commonwealth and Julia." For the sake of keeping order, he exiles her and her mother to an island. Five years later, she is allowed to return to the mainland, but her father never forgives her betrayal, or how she had placed pleasure above duty. "As we know now, and as her father sensed then," Williams said, "Rome went the way of Julia, not the way of Augustus."[6]

That Williams would be concerned about the pain of being estranged from a child—deeply enough to make it a theme in two novels—would have surprised most of those who knew him. He preferred not to talk about personal matters. Colleagues and friends didn't know much about his war experiences, for instance, outside of a few anecdotes he repeated until they were threadbare. And although he and his fellow instructor Gerald Chapman were both raised in North Texas during the Depression, the coincidence never inspired Williams to talk about growing up in Wichita Falls. "I think for John, that was the furthest topic of interest," Chapman said.[7]

But about his eldest child, Katherine, he was uncharacteristically forthcoming. He exercised full bragging rights as a father, crowing about her successes at school, what she said about a book she was reading, and so on. How much he loved her was apparent to everyone in his circle.[8] To him, a father's break with his child was one of the most traumatic things he could conceive of—perhaps he drew on feelings about his own disappeared father, John Jewell. Katherine was a projection of him, part of his legacy. As a child, she realized her father's approval was somehow tied to writing. At seven, she begged not to have to write a thank-you note to Marie Rodell for a gift because she was afraid it wouldn't be good enough.[9] By the time she was an adolescent, she regaled him at the dinner table with what was going on in her English class. John and Lonnie's middle child, Pamela, resented how her sister steered conversations to what their father preferred to discuss—books, authors, ideas. "My father was a snob," she said bitterly. The youngest, Jonathan, who was interested in mechanical things, also felt left out. "I remember sitting around the dinner table and Kathy and my father would be talking about academic stuff. I got bored with it. It really never interested me at all. I think he resented that a little, because I wasn't following his path."[10]

In May, Williams prepared to sail from New York on the brand new SS *France*, the biggest ocean liner in the world, for a two-month stay in Europe. On a Saturday evening, friends arrived at his room on the promenade deck to see him off, among them Cork Smith, who related to Marie Rodell that the drinking and merry-making was "notable."[11] A week later, the ship arrived in Le Havre, and Williams caught a train to Stuttgart, where he purchased, factory-fresh, a maroon Mercedes-Benz 230 four-door sedan: front-wheel drive, six cylinders, four-speed manual transmission, radial tires, and a retracting sunroof. Tooling through the Alps on his way to Milan and thence to Rome, he cut the figure of a man in his prime. He registered again at the Bellavista Milton. The location had proved lucky for working on the final draft of *Stoner* four years before; now he could get down to the business of planning *Augustus*.

In the early stages of *Butcher's Crossing* and *Stoner*, it had surprised him how much casting a spell of verisimilitude in fiction depends on fact. A novel about buffalo hunting is historical beyond dispute, and he had deeply researched the western frontier. But he had to do almost as much research about the first half of the twentieth century in Missouri for *Stoner*. What would the salary have been of a professor in the 1920s? Would private cars have been common in a small town? The category "historical novel" was so all-inclusive that he could see "no difference between the novel of history and the novel of the near present."[12] When he lectured about his work, he sometimes emphasized this point by quoting the Belgian novelist Marguerite Yourcenar, the author of a novel about the late Roman Empire, the *Memoirs of Hadrian* (1951): "Those who put the historical novel in a category apart are forgetting that what every novelist does is only to interpret, by means of the techniques which his period affords, a certain number of past events; his memories, whether personal or impersonal, are all woven of the same stuff of history itself. The work of Proust is a reconstruction of a lost past quite as much as is *War and Peace*."[13]

Williams undergirded his new novel, although set two thousand years in the past, with facts. To feed a Roman army of sixty thousand men for three months, he calculated, it would take three hundred barrels of olive oil, three hundred tons of grain, one hundred tons of dried fish, fifty tons of cheese, a thousand casks of wine, and sundry other items. To cover them with warm cloaks in the chilly forests of Gaul would take a quarter of a million yards of heavy wool. But he was careful to avoid "antiquarianism"—clogging the text with picayune details—which carries the risk of lulling the author into thinking "that history has created his characters, and that he need do no more than to accede to history, and to repeat and embellish the record, with whatever accuracy he chooses."[14]

He wanted his characters to push forward, out from the factual background, to have the quality of living in their own present, grappling with conflicts between public and private life, between barbarism and civilization, between duty and love. "The difficulty of writing a historical novel is in the history," he said. "You and your readers know what has happened. So I had a technical challenge in creating a sense of discovery in what happened to the characters."[15] The consequences of decisions characters make, they can only guess at, not knowing the future. Williams has Julius Caesar, only weeks before his assassination, write to his adopted son, Augustus, saying that his mind is troubled about his place in history, despite all that he has achieved. "I have conquered the world, and none of it is secure. I have shown liberty to the people, and they flee it as if it were a disease; I despise those whom I can trust, and love those best who would most quickly betray me. And I do not know where we are going, though I lead a nation to its destiny."[16] This is showing "a way of thinking, the life of the mind," in Yvor Winters' phrase, and Williams learned it from studying the methods of the English Renaissance poets.

Unlike those poets, however, Williams does not give his Romans comfort from religious belief. About the soul, gods, and spirituality in general, he expressed little interest, personally or in fiction, as if the question were settled for him. "I knew he was an atheist and he knew I was a practicing Jew," said Joanne Greenberg. "He once said, 'You're an idiot, but you have good instincts.' John was not a believer in any way, shape or form." One of his graduate students in the early 1970s, who later became a Catholic nun, had "the sense that John thought salvation was not available to him." As she got to know him better as her adviser for her dissertation, she discovered "he knew a lot about religious life. He treated me and talked with me as if he understood. But he couldn't believe. Perhaps his experiences in the war had something to do with that."[17]

Williams wasn't against religion or conflicted about it; for him, the black universe was eyeless, uninhabited. As Augustus says in the final pages of the novel, "I have come to believe that in the life of every man, late or soon, there is a moment when he knows beyond whatever else he might understand, and whether he can articulate the knowledge or not, the terrifying fact that he is alone, and separate, and that he can be no other than the poor thing that is himself."[18]

Holed up at the Bellavista Milton in Rome, Williams alternated working and sightseeing: one day at his desk, fortified with a pot of coffee, and capped by a bottle of wine that evening on the hotel terrace; the next day, driving to nearby locations that would play a part in the new novel. Longer excursions took him around the edges of the Mediterranean. "I wanted to experience the quality of the air," he later said. "I went to a large number of places where the Roman Empire extended. I indulged myself in a leisurely, long, meditative look at the places about which I would be writing—Turkey,

Yugoslavia—which was Macedonia in the Roman Empire—and the Greek Isles."[19]

By the end of July, he had finished outlining most of the novel and written chapter summaries. He made arrangements to ship his car to New York so it would be waiting when he arrived. Once home in Denver, he began the process of looking into a larger house for the family, and then in August he rushed off to Bread Loaf to teach at the 1967 session. Back again in September, he went up into the foothills of the Rockies to his cabin near the town of Pine in a hard-to-find spot named Sphinx Park. As autumn turned to winter, he could imagine from the windows of his study that the deep, snow-covered conifer forests cleaving to the slopes were the Teutoburg Forest, where the Gauls lay in ambush for the unsuspecting commander Publius Quinctilius Varus and his legions.

––––––––––

Butch Marsh tapped out a three-page, stream-of-consciousness letter to John—with a pitcher of daiquiris at his elbow—the gist of which was that he was in mid-career but not where he expected to be at this point. *Week with No Friday* had gone into paperback and was now spinning around on vertical metal book racks in bus stations and drugstores, but his publisher, Harper and Row, had rejected his second novel, the one set in San Francisco, and he was broke again.

For more than twenty years, since getting out of the Army Air Corps in 1945, Butch had been writing at white heat—stories, poems, novels—figuring that making it as a full-time author was like playing horses at the racetrack: you spread your bets. Maybe something that took a long time to write wouldn't sell, but a story dashed out in a day might hit the jackpot. Now he was burning out: he was never more than a few hundred bucks ahead of being broke. Much as he hated to say it, he was considering teaching in the United States again.

Ever since John and Butch had begun corresponding, the brothers-in-law had been arguing a point: not about who was the better writer, but over the issue of teaching and writing. Butch taught as a stopgap, although he was good at it. Everywhere he'd been on a faculty—Winthrop College, the University of Iowa, the University of Southern California—he had received high marks and compliments. But he couldn't get any writing done in the meantime.

John didn't see the two occupations as mutually exclusive. "There's no conflict between the roles," he tried convincing Butch, "really, except the inevitable one of time, time to do your best in both roles, each of which is rather demanding. In many ways, each role supports the other: as a teacher, I am paid to think about and discuss with others those concerns that are most important to me as a novelist; as a novelist, I can bring some authority to bear on what I have to say about literature."

Maybe Butch's dilemma was really just a matter of too few choices, he suggested. "The freedom one thinks one finds in Mexico can be a kind of prison; that is to say, though one is free to make choices there, the number of choices possible is fairly limited." He encouraged Butch to mail his résumé to fifty universities, at least. If he was invited to interview, it was almost certain the job was his, "unless you pee on the floor or wear too much rouge." There was no disgrace in teaching; it "will help you as a writer, and it is a decent life."[20]

Butch replied that he would think about it. He had a title anyway for the story collection he was putting together—*Beachhead in Bohemia*.

———

In January 1968, Williams got ready to depart for Smith College to take up a position as writer-in-residence. The family had just finished moving into a housing development in the Denver suburb of Aurora. He had been a distant father, but even with his marriage to Lonnie uncertain, he did his best to provide for her and the children. He had purchased a lot on a cul-de-sac in Aurora for a split-level, four-bedroom home that would have two fireplaces and three baths. Jonathan, fascinated as he pored over the blueprints showing the house's wiring and ventilation systems, considered the privilege of being involved "a very big deal." As John was packing his belongings in the Mercedes for the two-thousand-mile trip, a letter arrived from John Ciardi inviting him to return to Bread Loaf again for a third summer. Williams dashed off a reply saying he would, of course, adding, "The New Year hasn't been that goddamn happy"—referring indirectly to friction with Lonnie.[21] But August was months away, and in the meantime, Williams was due at Smith.[22]

Williams took a leisurely few days to make the drive. The college had offered him an apartment in Northampton that was on the first floor of a grand, turn-of-the-century home on Bedford Terrace. He could walk through the backyard to reach the campus on the street behind. "I've only been here a few days," he reported to Wakefield, "but it appears that I'm actually going to be able to get some work done. Which will be a novelty, given the last several months." He liked the ambience of Northampton, a small New England town, founded by seventeenth-century English colonists, "but the girls seem to be so goddam *young*; I have been remarkably chaste and aloof all winter, and nary a girl has pressed a grape in my mouth." By the end of February he had completed the first chapter of *Augustus*, and by mid-March, he sensed he had passed "the magic point beyond which it will be all right."[23]

He wrote home fairly regularly, too, but when Jonathan asked his mother what Dad had said, her reply at one point was, "No, you can't read this one." He knew his parents were unhappy, and overhearing a conversation between his mother and a close friend of hers—the wife of an English professor—about divorce worried him. He called his father for an update.

"Hello?" a woman answered. He hung up, thinking he had the wrong number. He dialed again.

"Yes, hello?" It was Nancy, whom he'd never met, but whose voice he recognized later. Until then, he hadn't known there was a woman other than his mother in his father's life.

When John returned in May from Smith College, he moved in with Nancy; several nights a week he spent staying over in Aurora with the children. Lonnie wrote on envelopes addressed to him, "Doesn't live here anymore."

"I don't think we were in that house for more than a year before we moved into a condominium instead and Dad saw us there," Jonathan said. "No, I'm sure we weren't."[24]

––––––––

The August 1968 session of Bread Loaf crackled with dissent. The earlier part of the year had seen the assassinations of Martin Luther King Jr. and Robert Kennedy; civil rights demonstrations over-lapped with anti–Vietnam War protests. The little summer camp for writing was not immune to feelings of restlessness and impatience with authority. Williams was a member of a subset of staffers who called themselves the Good Guys: Dan Wakefield; the poet Maxine Kumin; Miller Williams and Robert Pack, also poets; the magazine journalist Brock Brower, and the novelist Harry Crews. They were a hard-drinking clique, and not everyone looked kindly on their revels, although the Beatnik-bohemian atmosphere at the confer-ence had been growing stronger since the early 1960s.[25] But nothing was going to cramp the Good Guys' style, and as far as their nightly inebriation was concerned, they had the support of Ciardi, who was of the opinion that "it is simply impossible to gather writers, editors, agents, etc. without alcohol."[26] The older heads were not going to accommodate the complaints of counterculture-types attending Frost's "literary summer camp."

Three weeks before the start of the session, Williams had re-ceived a memo addressed to the staff from William Sloane in which he tried to prepare instructors for a change of attitude among their students. Beginning the conference with "the old [Bernard] De Voto approach," of delivering a lecture about theory, "no longer impresses the young who approach writing with the belief that the reader owes them a hearing and that the reader is supposed to absorb the story or the material in such a manner and way as the artistic sensibilities of the writer determine." In other words, the reader should have to work harder to understand the author's meaning, instead of the author trying to court or please the reader. "Fiction is in trouble because everybody thinks it is no longer nec-essary to regard readers as a volunteer audience but a captive one and this is contrary to nature and fact."[27]

Williams believed he knew exactly what the problem was. "Anyone who could afford a ballpoint pen or a typewriter was allowed to think of himself as a poet or a novelist; talent and craft were suspect, more often than not described as 'elitist,' a curseword of the period; and literacy was thought by many to be a species of corruption, a loss of innocence or a kind of damnation."[28] He was schooled in New Criticism, which emphasizes the formal properties of literature, and the idea that self-expression automatically deserved respect, regardless of its merits, was absolutely anathema to him.

However, he was right that the term "elitist" was used to object to many things perceived as undemocratic, including how the staff and attendees were treated as separate but equal. Why was dinner delayed until the instructors had finished their cocktails at Treman cottage? Why were the instructors seated at their own high table in the dining hall?

Ciardi, in his sonorous, baritone voice—like a captain in command speaking to a wayward crew—made it plain that he didn't want to hear any more grumbling about differences in rank. When one of the instructors wanted to know why Ciardi had refused his request to invite a student for a drink at Treman, the director shot him a warning look. "Don't get too near a psychic buzz saw," he said darkly. He was blunt with the administrators of Middlebury College, who had heard rumors of discontent. Ciardi dismissed it as bellyaching. Bread Loaf, he said, was "intense, rapid, informal, and more ego-driven, in most cases, than scholarly. Throw a faculty member to one of the dining room tables with conference members and he would be devoured. Insist on such a policy and half the staff would refuse to come back."[29]

Privately, some wondered if that might not be such a bad thing.

The patriarchy of Bread Loaf was typical of academe, and the arts, for most of the twentieth century. The composition of the faculty at Bread Loaf closely resembled the full-time faculty of the Department of English at the University of Denver: a dozen white, middle-aged men—about a third of them World War II veterans—and one or two women, depending on the year. At Denver in 1968, a female graduate student, pursuing a master's degree in English literature, smiled when her favorite instructor said, "Well, Sally, you're only a girl, but you're the best we've got." Sally Boland, who later cofounded the women's studies program and chaired the English Department at a small private university, later thought about his remark. "The amazing thing, now I look back on it, is not what he said to me, but rather what I said to myself, which was: 'Maybe if I can learn to think more like a man, I'll do better.'"³⁰

Over the years, John Williams had contributed to building Denver's English Department and its creative writing program, both of which were uncontestably male and white. Seymour Epstein, after a year of filling in for him while he was on sabbatical, was welcomed to the club, so to speak, with a permanent position in 1969. For several years after that, they drove out to Bread Loaf together. "Nice not to have the wives along," Williams said to him, sweeping along the interstate in his sports car. "Now we don't have to talk dirty!" Around three or four in the afternoon, it was "as though a light came on," Epstein said, and they pulled over in search of a bar because Williams was in need of a drink.³¹

There was camaraderie, a bond between buddies in the department who, despite some cultural differences, were from the same American phylum. Former faculty members of the Denver English Department in the 1960s recall it as a period of harmony, a decade when a kind of *esprit de corps* guided the direction of things—a "smooth unity," as the instructor and biographer Robert Richardson characterized the times. The connection between men like them—raised during the Depression, tempered by the war years, influenced by mass culture in the 1950s—was very close when it came to interests, ambitions, and what they could expect in life.

Williams felt easiest around men and colleagues who enjoyed a good laugh and bumped along well together. His candid description in a letter accompanying a recommendation for an instructor hints at the kind of person who matched the disposition of the department: "I think I should tell you that he was an exceedingly good undergraduate teacher; how well he might do in graduate courses, I'm just not sure. At least he might do an adequate job, and he might very well do better. . . . He's not a 'swinger' like we were in the old days, but he is in no sense prudish, stuffy, or whatever. He's easy to get along with, does not have the kind of neurotic ego that we often find among our peers."[32]

A newcomer to the department in September 1969, Peggy McIntosh—one of only two women on the English faculty—saw Williams *in situ* in the environment he helped create as he walked the halls between classes, decked out in his ascot and sports jacket, and entering debates about Vietnam by pointing out, "Now your Chinese—as I learned when I was over there in '44 . . ."[33] McIntosh was young, had been raised in New Jersey, and was a graduate of Radcliffe and Harvard. Her days as a leading feminist—and author of a famous essay that introduced the terms "white privilege" and "male privilege" into cultural criticism—were still some years off.[34] She recalled how her arrival in Denver was regarded as an imposition:

> I was this Anglo blonde—short, semi-pretty girl, looking like a girl with my hair in a bun, and I imagined that I just provoked the hell out of John Williams. I imagine he just couldn't stand it that somebody who looked like me and who was interested in Emily Dickinson had come into the department. He never gave me the time of day. He was not interested in conversation with me. Never said anything supportive to me. I was afraid of him. He was so dour, and resentful of women coming into what had been men's territory, that I avoided him. He was one of those who felt, as many men now feel, that the world is closing in on them, with all these "women and minorities"—an illogical phrase—[taking] the place that they were raised to think is rightfully theirs. And I think he felt threatened by the federal government putting pressure on college administrations to hire women.[35]

It was true that the largely male citadel of academe in the 1960s felt blitzed by feminist forces. Robert Richardson's wife at the time remembered her then husband's disgust that a woman had been chosen over him for a position at Harvard. "They *had* to hire a woman, that's all," he had said.[36]

The bombardment from the Left was also aimed at the canon of English and American literature, which Williams was determined to answer with salvos of his own. On that score he wouldn't yield. One of his younger colleagues found his counterattack bracing. "To put it mildly," he later wrote, "Williams had Olympian standards in judging fiction. One could mention virtually any well-known novelist and Williams' reaction would be the same. 'An awfully nice guy,' he'd say, suggesting that he knew everyone worth knowing."[37]

If Williams went out of his way to cold-shoulder McIntosh, it was because he resented federal rules about equality in hiring, which he perceived as wrongheaded and politically motivated—an incursion to be resisted. They were a band of brothers in the department, and of generally one mind about what to teach and how to teach it. For his part, according to McIntosh, he thought she "mothered" her students. McIntosh thought, "He didn't give a damn about his." Perhaps he knew she was listening the day he wandered into the English Department office and announced, "Well, I cleaned out my office, and guess what? I found a dead student."[38]

Williams held the same convictions about the importance of keeping high and low culture separate. From his office window at the University of Denver, he looked out and saw evidence that "the arrows of the barbarians," in his words, were raining down.[39] He was not apolitical; but teach-ins about social justice on the lawn outside struck him as not part of the mission of the university. He worried that English departments were choosing inferior works for their syllabi, too, and teaching too much literary theory, "whereas the whole point of the novel is the experience of reading the novel. Standards have been declared extraliterary."[40]

Everywhere the intellectual life was imperiled, as he saw it. Beyond the University of Denver campus, certain neighborhoods, such as "Desolation Row," consisting of two blocks of head shops and hippie-related stores on East Colfax Avenue, had become hippie enclaves. Williams disliked the counterculture. It placed emotion higher than reason by venerating Thoreau, Whitman, Emerson, transcendentalism, Brook Farm, arts and crafts, and communes. The issues and the times were different, but the slogan among the young, "If it feels good, do it," caught the essential spirit. At Stanford University, Winters was refusing to participate in creative writing courses any longer because he deplored student attitudes. Wallace Stegner had resigned in disgust as director of the Stanford program because Tom Wolfe's book *The Electric Kool-Aid Acid Test* had made Ken Kesey (*One Flew over the Cuckoo's Nest*) and his Merry Pranksters synonymous with the university.

Williams was not against modern literature—the purpose of the *Denver Quarterly*, which he founded and edited, was to explore the idea of the modern in original fiction and verse. But like his intellectual heroes, Winters and J. V. Cunningham, he was alarmed by how quickly new fiction, especially experimental fiction, had been embraced by college English departments. Higher education should be teaching "approved tradition of the elders," as Cunningham put it, for the sake of grounding students in essential texts. Modernism was too heady, too sophisticated, and too likely to be imitated by students. As for everything published after World War II—Susan Sontag, Kurt Vonnegut, Norman Mailer, Günter Grass, Richard Brautigan—that was the kind of new writing one discussed at a party over a beer, or read in *The New Yorker*, in Cunningham's opinion, and Williams echoed it.[41] "The university should be an insulation against the specious kinds of values that are always in the world," Williams maintained. "A kind of protection against them. . . . Once a university becomes what universities often say they are—a reflection of the will of the community, or something like that—well, it's dead. The university more often than not ought to be *opposed* to the aims of the community, the aims of the world around it."[42]

This was not only the principle he stood behind as an academic: it was also his creed as a novelist. At a party in Denver one night, Williams listened to a hippie artisan explain how he ran his jewelry business. The key to success, the young man said, was to "psych out the market"—figure out what kind of jewelry and art people were into—and then make what the public wanted. Williams pointed his finger at the young man and enunciated slowly to make sure he was understood: "No, you are wrong. That is not what you do, as an artist. You figure out what the thing is you most want and need to do, and you do it. You don't try to 'please the public.' You do your best."[43]

At least Williams could turn away from his office window and think about his work on *Augustus*. The ancient voices he was invoking through fiction had endured for two thousand years, which testified to the greatness of what they had to say; by comparison, student takeovers, riots, and peace demonstrations would become a parenthesis in history.[44]

Even so, the golden days of the Good Guys at Bread Loaf were numbered—two more summers at most—and the authority of the "war generation" would come to an end.[45] In a photograph taken during the 1970 session, director Ciardi—large, graying, bespectacled—is seen arguing with a long-haired young man who looks resentful. The issue could have been the war in Vietnam, but actually there was no one on the faculty who was defending it. Instead, the "rabble-rousing," as Ciardi called it, stemmed from differences of opinion about the relationship between politics and art, and the responsibility of an artist.[46]

But Ciardi wanted none of that invading Bread Loaf on his watch. Transient problems of the world must not come to Middlebury. "I feel," he said, "I am trustee for a number of ghosts."[47]

CHAPTER SIXTEEN

"Long Life to the Emperor!"

The world is not a poem.

—JOHN WILLIAMS, *AUGUSTUS*

After twenty years of marriage, John and Lonnie Williams divorced in January 1969. They had shared the new house for less than a year; now John was living permanently at his apartment, and the house was too large for Lonnie and their three children. She found a condominium in Denver six miles north of the University of Denver campus, near the Metropolitan State College, where she had been hired as an instructor. John came over for dinner two nights a week to check on the children. He paid child support. Tight-lipped, as usual, about his personal affairs, however, he didn't tell Nancy how much it was, and she didn't ask. "He had a checking account I never saw," she later said. "I made a point of not knowing."[1]

Nancy had been living in a small house in the Park Hill neighborhood that she had purchased after moving out of her parents' home a few years earlier, near Denver's East High School, where she taught English. She put it up for sale, and she and John started looking for a home of their own. She had toyed on and off with the idea of leaving Denver and starting afresh, but John refused to consider moving away from his children, perhaps thinking of his own childhood. "And I realized," Nancy said, "Would I stay with someone who would do that?"[2]

In March 1970, they chose a home located on a quarter-acre of land at the end of South Madison Street, ten blocks from campus. John liked the "great amount of room in the house itself," and he liked how the property was landscaped—with "fantastic plantings," he told Marie Rodell. He described "a couple of spruces and pines that go up thirty or forty feet," adding, "I'll send you a photo, when I have time to make one."[3] The backyard was big enough for a garden, and he paced off a plot that was twenty by sixty feet. That summer, he planted tomatoes and other vegetables, along with a pumpkin vine for a neighbor child who said he always wanted "the biggest one," but without pesticides, because his grandfather, a farmer, hadn't used them.

In December, after a few months in the house, he and Nancy married, and John's transition from one family to another was complete. He now had a role in the lives of Nancy's three children. For her part, Nancy felt that Pamela and Kathy Williams, his daughters, resented her. "To the girls, I was the wicked stepmother," she said. "I took him away from their mother."[4]

The large garden and house spoke to a part of Williams that liked appearing consequential, someone with roots who knew what he was all about. Parked in the driveway was the imported Mercedes, a similar declaration. He would drive it for the rest of his life, another twenty years, until it became a fixture in Denver, synonymous with John Williams, novelist and professor of literature. And he amended the history of his life to fit the image. When questions of decorum came up, he spoke seriously of an inbred southern code he abided by because he was from Texas—a better biography than growing up poor on a dirt farm in the shadow of oil rigs.[5]

It was a carefully constructed identity, a presentation. Nancy understood its importance when he told her, "In high school, I was Ronald Colman"—not "I *thought* I was." The ascots he tucked under his shirt collars, the fine wool jackets, and the pleated trousers were suitable attire for courting respect. Nancy noticed he was especially careful about his appearance when meeting strangers for the first time, and suspected this "outer John" was a cover-up for shyness. Other women, too, noticed how careful he was about his demeanor. He walked gracefully, reminding one woman who knew him at the time "of the way men from India move: skinny Indian men, loping. It was different from other men. He wasn't jerky." Joanne Greenberg remembered him at a party crossing his legs at the ankles, and lowering himself slowly to a cushion on the floor, "almost like he was making a bow. Almost feminine."[6] Friends said he seemed happiest when he was playing chef in his own kitchen, whipping up his best dishes for dinner guests—soups, stews, chili, biscuits—and beaming at the compliments. Once, when he was seated at someone else's table, at the mention of dessert he announced dramatically, "I make a brilliant mousse!" unaware of the pun and provoking an outburst of laughter.[7]

On campus, his preoccupation with himself could be overbearing at times, but he was proud of belonging to the community of scholars, to the academy, and being a novelist besides. He would never consider throwing it over for the obscure life of the artist in the garret. He must have the certainty of making a living and the automatic status that came with being a tenured professor. "I sometimes hear people, writers, say, 'I will not sell out,' meaning for money," he told an interviewer. "And I always ask them if they've had any offers lately."[8] The fact that he had a beautiful new home and a lovely bride was proof to him that he'd lost nothing by combining the academic life and writing. He felt like he was at the top of his game:

> If I thought that the academic life in itself, was bad for my writing, then I'd quit. . . . [I]t has become one of the many platitudinous ideas that certain kinds of writers throw about nowadays: the academy is the death of creativity, the enemy of poetry, the corrupter of poets, and so forth. . . . And I don't like whiners, either; some of the poets and novelists that keep muttering about the academy remind me of the boy who would run away from home, if only dad would loan him the station wagon.[9]

Meanwhile, work went well on *Augustus*. On days when he didn't have to teach, Williams liked to get up early and be in his study by eight o'clock. He preferred Nancy to be home when he was writing. Occasionally he would get up from his typewriter to see what she was doing, or call out, "Are you there?" She kept disruptions at bay, answering the phone and saying that her husband wasn't available. "I would try to keep his work time inviolate," she said. Sometimes she would see him outside, standing in the garden, not looking at anything in particular, and she would think, "He's stuck on something." He would rather work out a passage silently in his head than make a run at it and have to revise—although he would revise, if necessary, to sharpen the effects. "Since I plan carefully," he wrote, "I am not faced with the problem of major reorganization after a first draft is completed. . . . Though it seems to be so, this is not a mysterious process; it is simply the result of a long period of concentration and work."[10]

He broke for lunch, by which time he usually had finished a page. Two or three pages in a single morning were a triumph. The rest of the afternoon he spent planning for the next day's work. Then, promptly at five, he stopped and went into the kitchen and poured himself a drink and lit a cigarette before ambling over to the sofa with his glass to watch television. He often told Nancy he might just as well have been a carpenter or a plumber. Writing was a job.

———

Things weren't as rosy for Butch. Running out of money, he had reluctantly taken John's advice and gone job-hunting. North Texas State University had invited him for an interview. As a candidate for a position in the English Department, he didn't have a PhD. But with stories in more than seventy periodicals, including *Antioch Review*, *Prairie Schooner*, *Northwest Review*, *Yale Review*, *Esquire*, *Playboy*, and *Saturday Evening Post*, he clearly he was the genuine article, a real writer coming in out of the rain. North Texas State hired him. He and George Rae left Mexico and moved into a prim, whitewashed apartment building called Coral Isles on a side street in Denton. For four semesters and two sessions of summer school in

1968–1970, he met his classes, graded papers, and attended faculty meetings. Since he never did anything by halves, he didn't have time to write anything publishable while he was teaching.

All that looked to change when he and George Rae returned to Mexico, but he was not in the best of shape by then. Butch's heart had been giving him trouble. He was a bit thickset at forty-eight, but not overweight, with large, freckled hands he cupped around a match while lighting a cigarette against the night breezes off Lake Chapalupa. In the collection of stories he was preparing, *Beachhead in Bohemia*, published posthumously, there was one about a man in his forties who feels twinges in his chest: "If pain hit when he was dozing, he would awaken instantly because it was the left side. And even though the pain was in the wrong location, all that his lulled mind could initially report was terror on his left. It was humiliating to be braced in a constant cringe."[11] Butch was glad to be back in the sweet life of writing full-time again, but the pressure was on. He'd gone stale creatively and his inventory of salable stories was low. He was drinking a lot in Ajijic—George was, too—but it seemed to be the only way he could calm down after another day at the typewriter. As he filled his glass, his hand trembled from too much nicotine.

George Rae insisted they make an appointment with a specialist in Guadalajara, the nearest large city. A Dr. Rivera checked him over and admitted him for observation to Hospital Angeles Del Carmen, a brand new and modern facility, just off the office plaza in the center of town. As he was resting in his room for further tests, Butch died from a heart attack on May 27, 1970. The death certificate issued by the American consulate a few days later identified Willard N. Marsh as a vacationing retiree, not as a writer, whose last known address was Denton, Texas.

George couldn't remain in Ajijic without him. "I'm moving back to San Miguel de Allende," she wrote John. "I've gotten a little apartment at the Quinta Loreto where Willard and I lived before in 1967 and '68. Ajijic has just become too dismal for me. It's too full of old retired people who read nothing, see nothing, and do nothing but drink. I didn't mind it when I had Willard, but without him, I just can't take it. If I stay around such people much longer, I'm afraid I'll become just like them—or go mad."[12]

She saw to it that he was interred in the Ajijic municipal cemetery. Then, two years later, a real estate developer cut through the grounds with a street, naming it De Las Flores and desecrating many graves. One of those that disappeared was the last resting place of Willard "Butch" Marsh, novelist, short story writer, and former jazzman.[13]

About the time of his brother-in-law's death, Williams was reminded again of how ephemeral a writer's work can be, when he discovered that *Stoner* had gone out of print after only a year. His publisher hadn't notified him, either—a surprising oversight by his usually careful editor, Cork Smith. The novel's sales had never been robust, but the discourtesy bothered him. It was dismissive, similar to how *Butcher's Crossing* had been lumped in with westerns. He mentioned his frustration to Dan Wakefield, his fellow instructor at Bread Loaf.

As a favor, Wakefield mounted a campaign to get *Stoner* reissued by asking some notable authors and college instructors to write statements endorsing the idea, which he would then forward to Marie Rodell as a friendly petition. Excerpts from their remarks could also serve as blurbs on the cover of a reissue. The one submitted by the poet Miller Williams spoke for many: "*Stoner*? Funny you should ask. Sad that you should have to. . . . I have one copy, which is the only one I've been able to find. It has been read not only by my wife and me, but nine other people whose names I can't recall at the moment. . . . There is no doubt in my mind but that *Stoner* would have the wide reputation it deserves as an American classic if it were possible for readers to buy the book."[14]

Merrily, Wakefield collected the statements of support—"I got a beautiful response," he told John—and added his own cover letter to Rodell, whom he'd never met. It began: "A number of us who are admirers of John Williams' novel *Stoner* have been disturbed to find it out of print." He sent photocopies off to her, and the originals to Williams, feeling the pleasure that comes from doing a good deed.[15]

Rodell was offended at being told her business. "Dear Mr. Wakefield," she replied, "Thank you for your letter of October first and its enclosures." She only wished, she added archly, that the book's advocates had concentrated more on Stoner's literary values, and less on how they couldn't get copies for their college classrooms.[16] Although she didn't say so, she had inferred from receiving a handful of unsolicited requests to reprint *Stoner* from "distinguished writers and teachers" that Williams had been complaining about her. The damage seemed to be spreading when she also received a note from the publishing entrepreneur Seymour Lawrence, who said he'd heard from Wakefield that John Williams' new novel about Augustus Caesar might be available. Could he read the manuscript?[17] It wasn't available, Rodell informed him curtly—it was already under contract to Viking: "I'm sorry you were misinformed."[18]

Williams stepped in and apologized on behalf of his friends. He had been reading aloud from the manuscript of *Augustus* during workshop sessions at Bread Loaf, he explained, and there "are many people who have seemed excited about the novel—staff members, visitors, etc.—and it has occasioned some talk." Thus, he accepted some of the blame; he was just doing his job as a good client.

As it turned out, Wakefield's crusade did help. In January 1971, another publisher, a small paperback house, reissued *Stoner*. Rodell thanked Wakefield for the letters he had so "diligently collected" and assured him that the editor who bought the book "has become as confirmed a 'Stonerite' as you or I."[19]

———

At the end of the term in May 1972, John and Nancy drove to Mexico to check on George Rae. She was living in Ajijic again, part-owner of a discotheque, of all things, and dating Ted Cogswell, the science fiction and fantasy writer who had struck up a friendship with the Marshes years earlier. Nancy knew him not at all, and she was not impressed. In fact, she found him rather frightening. "When George and Ted were together they were drunk a good part of the time," she said. "She'd be completely stone drunk. . . . She stayed at our house. Ted would come over and see her."[20]

Ted liked to ride around Ajijic on his motorcycle wearing a Mickey Mouse costume, complete with the bulbous head, big ears, and imbecilic cartoon expression. Driving around drunk one day, he stopped by the Williams' apartment looking for George Rae. Nancy was alone. For some reason, he had a knife and showed it to her. Then he forgot about it and roared away on the motorcycle, leaving the knife on top of the refrigerator. When John returned, Nancy insisted that Ted not be allowed in the house again.[21]

Apart from George's taste in boyfriends, Nancy was curious about the bond between her and John. Although they were only half-siblings, she noticed they were strikingly alike—they had same petite size and pale coloring, and a similar style of speaking—as alike as "two peas in a pod." And if John seemed—as someone had said about him, "gnomish," with his goatee, deep voice, and penetrating blue eyes—George Rae seemed like a pixie. They had the same theatrical air. In fact, when George Rae talked about how she wanted to get back into theater eventually, John's rough teasing and dismissiveness carried a tone of envy. After all, it had been his ambition before it was hers.

Nancy and John returned to Denver in midsummer, and a few months later, George Rae and Ted married in San Miguel de Allende. The Williamses didn't attend; but a young American writer witnessed the event and the wild send-off that followed:

Like everyone else in the wedding party at the Episcopalian church, including the priest, George Rae was an atheist. The ceremony was followed by the wettest reception I've ever attended, and that was followed by Ted and George getting into her Jeep and heading for their honeymoon suite in Puerto Vallarta. An hour later the reception was winding down when the Jeep came roaring back, stopping between the plaza and the police station for Ted to shove his screaming, cursing bride out on the cobblestones, where bride and groom were immediately arrested for being drunk and very disorderly. Placed in separate cells, Ted made a pillow out of his boots and went to sleep on the thin mattress of the cell's wooden cot. George propped her mattress against her cell's door, set it on fire, and screamed bloody murder until the cops turned them loose at dawn to continue on their honeymoon.[22]

Someone snapped a picture of the pair on their wedding day, standing on a second-floor balcony, wearing matching leather safari jackets like adventurers. Ted is making a face, with one arm around George Rae and flipping the camera the finger with the other.

———

That summer, the axe fell on John Ciardi as director of the Bread Loaf Writers' Conference. Complaints from attendees and a few younger instructors continued to reach the Middlebury College administration. The antagonism was partly generational and ego-driven; Ciardi bristled at talk of deposing the older heads and their lordly "maestro system."[23] Defiantly, he typed a letter of resignation and submitted it, undated, to the president of Middlebury, adding, "When you want it to be time, just fill in the date and I'll be gone." It was time. The president called his bluff and accepted his resignation. Ciardi would be given the 1972 session as his last to run.

The new director would be Robert Pack, also one of the Good Guys, but Pack was determined to recruit fresh blood. The criteria for choosing the staff would not depend on personal friendship or amiability, or how long they had been "up on the hill." They would have to be good teachers and demonstrate respect for beginning writers, both published and unpublished. John Williams had the requisite qualifications. "I was very fond of John," Pack said. "He was a good teacher, a good raconteur, and charming, but he had a drinking problem."[24] And that was the deciding factor—he was not among those invited back after 1972 for what would have been his seventh year.

———

It might appear that too much emphasis is being placed on alcohol abuse, as it affected John Williams and his circle of friends. He himself expressed contempt for "lushes." "John had a sixth sense about who was one," according to Dan Wakefield; as though compared to *that* guy, he didn't have a problem. "He didn't slur his words, or wobble when he walked. He didn't show that he was drunk," said Wakefield.[25]

No one can say when the culture of hard drinking became associated with writing, but liquor and literature seemed to go together: five American authors who won the Nobel Prize during the postwar era were alcoholics—Sinclair Lewis, Eugene O'Neill, William Faulkner, Ernest Hemingway, and John Steinbeck. A character in O'Neill's *Long Day's Journey into Night* rhapsodizes by quoting Baudelaire: "Be always drunken. Nothing else matters: that is the only question. If you would not feel the horrible burden of Time weighing on your shoulders and crushing you to the earth, be drunken continually." A conviction that drinking was somehow tied to the seer's gift—a sign of being in touch with the gods, a spur to prophecy—drew many willing young artists into the stumbling ranks of drunks during those years.[26] Wakefield said it was an expectation: "We were told by other, older writers that if you're going to be a serious writer, you have to be a serious drinker."[27] Williams said as much to a young graduate student, a woman who came to his office to discuss her stories with him. "He opened a desk drawer and poured a shot of Wild Turkey into a glass," she reported. "'If you don't have a drink, you aren't a serious writer.' It seemed like a test and I took it."[28]

People in publishing took it for granted, too, that booze and the making of books went hand in hand, with potentially unfortunate results for Williams when he submitted the finished manuscript of *Augustus* to Cork Smith in the spring of 1972.

Augustus had taken nearly seven years to complete, and he was confident that it was "really a very good novel," predicting to Cork Smith, tongue-in-cheek, "that it might have a good chance to do well on the market, despite that fact."[29] Having read the early sections as they came in, Smith agreed with Marie Rodell that it was "one hell of a book and should be exactly as John Williams wants it."[30] And Smith made a brilliant suggestion about formatting. He recommended omitting numbered chapters—they seemed too modern. Instead, there should be Book 1, Book 2, Book 3, and an Epilogue. Williams concurred immediately, because it also fit with how he had broken the story into three sections, almost like three acts. He was glad the manuscript was in the hands of an editor who understood the spirit of the novel.

And then, suddenly, two months after Williams submitted the final draft, Smith stepped down from Viking. He was being furloughed home from the office indefinitely. His alcoholism was out of control, and the publisher, Thomas Ginzburg, had given him the choice of either drying out or losing his job. It would be up to Ginzburg to decide when, or if, he was ready to return; in the meantime, Smith told Williams, he was going to be "standing back and taking a longish look at myself."[31]

The news upset Williams.[32] Smith had championed *Stoner* from the beginning, and he'd midwifed *Augustus* right up to the point of publication. Now, who would step forward, and who could be trusted to do right by the new book all the way to market? As it turned out, the manuscript went to Alan D. Williams, a skilled and versatile editor whose gifts included the ability to establish a good rapport with authors across various genres. His "open-sensibility," as a fellow editor called it, made him approach a work submitted to him with respect; it was doubly lucky for John that *Augustus* went to him, because he was well versed in classical literature. Under his guidance, Robert Fagles' translations of the *Iliad* and the *Odyssey* later became standards.

While John was waiting for his new editor to read *Augustus* for the first time ("I hope you have read the novel; I hope you liked it," he told Alan Williams), Rodell let him know that Curtis Publishing, owner of a line of inexpensive paperbacks, wanted to reprint *Butcher's Crossing*. The novel had been out of print for ten years; reprinting it would at least guarantee a second chance. Plus, Williams stood to make a little money from the advance. But "the real stumbler," she cautioned, was that the sales staff insisted on marketing it as a western, because "it has to be described as something!" they said.[33]

Williams absolutely refused. He'd rather the book not come out at all. Then Rodell received a similar offer from Popular Books—same advance, same approach: *Butcher's Crossing* would be advertised as a paperback western. And again, he refused, even though his career as a novelist currently was at a standstill. It had been almost twenty-five years since his first novel had appeared, *Nothing But the Night*, which he disavowed as beginner's work. Next, *Stoner* had barely made a ripple when it dropped into the pond of forgotten books. But allowing *Butcher's Crossing* to be reprinted and advertised as a western might permanently label him a second-rate writer. The enjoyment of being able to say he had a novel in print wasn't compensation enough for the blow to his self-respect.[34] He could only hope that *Augustus*, when it was published, would be his vindication.

———

Cork Smith's leave of absence didn't affect the march of *Augustus* toward publication, after all. "LONG LIFE TO THE EMPEROR!" Rodell telegrammed Williams when it appeared in late 1972. The reviews were more widespread, more flattering, and in much greater number than for either of his two previous books. Orville Prescott, the principal reviewer for the *New York Times*, sent a personal note: "I think it ranks with Thornton Wilder's *The Ides of March* as a work of literature and I know it is truer to the facts of Roman history." J. V. Cunningham, ever the classicist, in addition to telling Williams it was an "astonishing book," complimented him on "the observance of decorum in style."[35]

As was John's custom each time he had a new novel out, he took up a prominent spot in the English Department office, where he sat all day smoking and drinking coffee, expecting that some of his colleagues would congratulate him. He waited, making small talk with people coming in to pick up their mail or take a break between classes. The hours passed pleasantly enough, but nothing was said to him about the book. And finally, as the weak December light coming in through the windows began to fade, he went down the nearly empty hallway to his office and closed the door.

PART V

The Sleep of Reason

AN OLD ACTOR TO HIS AUDIENCE

JOHN WILLIAMS

Ford Maddox Ford: 1873–1939

Sirs, I address you out of age, my voice
Gone slack and hoarse, who stood before you once
With some grace and carriage. Ah, time . . .
The face that once was marble now
Is flesh. Motion is impure, and we
Must move, although we break. The voice that was
Your master is your servant now, reminding you
Of its ancient art that once cast up
A substance that could move you out of time,
Our mortal blemish. And you—the wise and foolish
Who listen to an old man's wheezing voice—
Suffered your destruction like a pleasure
Scarcely to be borne, desiring to be deceived
Out of the falsehood of your time and place.

But now I am old, am old, and suppliant
To your most gracious whim. We are the relics
Of our ruined past—although I see you now
As if you were not changed, as if you were
As I created you once long ago
Out of the pride and arrogance
Of my spent youth. To whom do I speak, if not
Myself? If not my own, whose faces stare
At me? Had you given me laurel once,
I would have worn it most carelessly
And spoken my echoing lines in its despite.
But now this pate is bald; bald pates have need
Of bay, for warmth and show. I ask
Your kindness now, and ask forbearance of
These loosening years; they make men foolish,
Who were never wise. I stand before you,
Stripped of years, a beggar.
And yet a supplicant,
I would remind you, who has given service
To you all. Out of these creaking boards
I once created worlds that you could not conceive
And peopled them with what you might have been,
Showing a fairer image of yourself
Than you would dare to dream, and given you
Some instant plucked from time that was your own.
From your deep heart's most lonely need, I have
Dissembled shadows that became your selves
And let them stroll as if they were alive
In the Roman ruins of your northern fields.

CHAPTER SEVENTEEN

"How Can Such a Son of a Bitch Have Such Talent?"

Ah life, that amateur performance.

—JOHN WILLIAMS

On April 11, 1973, the *New York Times* carried a story about controversy in the book world. "In an unprecedented display of public disagreement, the 1973 National Book Award judges announced yesterday that they had split the fiction prize between John Barth's *Chimera* and John Williams' *Augustus*."[1] This had never happened before in the organization's twenty-four-year existence. But lately, nothing seemed immune from dissent. The week before the announcement, the *Saturday Review* had predicted that literary politics would decide the fiction prize because the judges fell into two camps: postmodernists (literary critic and historian Leslie A. Fielder, along with essayist and novelist William Gass), and traditionalists (Evan S. Connell, philosophical novelist Walker Percy, and book critic Jonathan Yardley).[2]

The magazine was right about the likelihood of disagreement: the meeting was "noisy and argumentative," according to the *Times*.[3] The previous year, the historian and journalist Garry Wills had walked out of his committee's meeting when he refused to endorse his fellow judges' choice of the hippie bible, *The Whole Earth*

Catalog, as the contemporary affairs winner. And now, as the judges in different categories adjourned, not only was the award for fiction split, but also the one for the best history. This had never happened before, either.

However, as the book reviewer Jonathan Yardley, a courtly young man from North Carolina, stepped up on the dais in the Biltmore Grand Ballroom in New York to announce the winners, he tried to convey that nothing could have been more natural than a tie. The novels, *Chimera* and *Augustus*, he said, were both books of "uncommon quality . . . similar in subject matter[,] but . . . represent dissimilar approaches to the writing of fiction."[4] *Chimera* was about transforming myth into reality; *Augustus* brought the violent times of imperial Rome to life. Consequently, Barth and Williams would each get half the award money: $500 apiece (which wasn't much more than each of the judges had been paid to read the books). No explanation was given as to why there were two history prizes.

The double deadlock wrecked the organization—not immediately, the big awards ceremony would still go forward—but in the coming weeks. With the publicity value of an author winning cut in half, publishers protested by withdrawing their financial support. No more free books for the judges to read, or luncheons, hotels, transportation, and all the rest. The National Book Committee was forced to disband, and it was not until two years later, when a caretaker administrator for the organization "begged" prospective judges not to split awards, that the contest resumed.[5]

———

In the meantime, news that John Williams had won a major literary award arrived in Denver "on little cat feet," as Joanne Greenberg put it, thinking of Carl Sandburg's poem "Fog."[6] Despite the fact that Williams was the first and only Coloradan ever to receive the National Book Award, the *Denver Post*, the largest newspaper in the state, failed to send a reporter to get his reaction. Likewise, in the English Department, there was no, as one instructor put it, "ecumenical coming together in celebration of John." Instead, there was a lot of headshaking behind closed doors. "Oh my God," one

English professor later said, "if he was difficult to live with before!"[7]
Some of it was envy, but Williams' colleagues knew that receiving
the laurels for fiction would mean that he would now be delivering
his growly pronouncements about literature with even greater authority; the little genie wrapped in cigarette smoke would never go
back into the brass lamp.

The editor of the university alumni magazine wasn't glad to hear
the news, either. Normally, a faculty member receiving a national
honor was tailor-made for encouraging alums to donate more to
the endowment; over the years, however, the editor had tried to
avoid Professor Williams. He was impossible. She disapproved
of his romantic affairs, and of the way he missed class because
he was hung over. She passed the assignment to a newcomer on
the staff, a graduate student in history, Carol DeBoer-Rolloff, who
later became a biographer and a professor at Brown (as Carol
DeBoer-Langworthy).[8]

Carol didn't know Williams, but she had heard of him. "A lot
of people talked about John on campus," she said. "People liked
to gossip about him. He was considered outrageous."[9] When she
knocked on his office door for their appointment, she opened it
gingerly, not sure what kind of person she would find inside. The
room was long and narrow—a rabbit hole that smelled of smoke
and coffee, with sloppily arranged books on shelves and cardboard
boxes on the floor. Seated at a desk was a dark-haired man with a
head that seemed too big for his body. He looked up at her with
enormous blue eyes that swam behind a pair of thick, black-framed
glasses. His face was heavily lined. "This guy is a philanderer?" was
her first thought.[10] He invited her to take the only chair available. In
the middle of his desk, jutting like a rock from a tide pool of papers,
was a large, dark gray typewriter.

The interview went smoothly, though he enjoyed talking about
books more than he did describing his past. In between remarks, he
coughed loudly as he pulled on his cigarette, or had to stop to clear
his throat before continuing. Most experimental novels, he said,
seemed dreadfully stale and forced, and they were always better
the first time around. It was so much easier dealing with theories of

fiction, political issues, and so forth than with relationships—that was the problem with the current state of fiction.

"What do you plan to talk about in your speech at the National Book Awards?" she asked.

His relaxed manner changed suddenly as he leaned forward. "A defense of the goddamn novel," he said.[11]

———

The Williamses' visit to New York City for the ceremony was triumphant. They checked into the forty-seven-story Waldorf Astoria Hotel, known for its striking Art Deco design, lavish dinner parties, galas, and international conferences. The next morning a photojournalist arrived at their suite to take pictures of John for *Time* magazine. Then they went to lunch with Marie Rodell, where John resisted the temptation to start drinking too early. He could wait. Cork Smith, back at Viking part-time, had provided him with an itinerary that included a "Boozerama" at the Tavern on the Green in Central Park after the awards, followed by late-evening drinks and a buffet at publisher Thomas Ginzburg's apartment on Madison Avenue.

At the Lincoln Center for the Performing Arts that evening, hundreds of people from the publishing industry attended a reception, where, among other things, Williams was introduced to his cowinner, John Barth, for the first time. Called "Jack"—a bald, serious-looking man with sideburns down to his jaw—Barth was a professor of English at the State University of New York at Buffalo. Only a few years younger than Williams, he had been nominated twice before for the National Book Award. His newest novel, *Chimera*, was a fabulist, highly theoretical work, not Williams' cup of tea at all. But asked by a reporter about the controversy over splitting the award, they were in the mood to be good sports. If anything, they said, the decision demonstrated that fiction was alive and well, and that literature was roomy enough to accommodate the novel in many forms.[12] Later, on the stage for the program, they sat together. When Williams' turn came to speak, he chose the high road; instead of launching into "a defense of the goddamn novel," he expressed his deep pleasure at being selected and predicted a ringing future for fiction. "My friend Brock Brower, whose novel *The Late Great Creature* was one of the nominees for this award," he remarked, "is said to have said, 'Listen, there's only one stable institution in this country. It's not Princeton . . . it's not marriage, it's the novel.'"

When he arrived home in Denver, there was a warm letter from Barth, who was glad that what might have been a "sticky situation turned out to be really a delightful one."[13]

———

Until now, John Williams had been a kind of extra or chorus member on the literary scene, a spear-carrier in the opera of American fiction, who played his part and then the dusty curtain fell down. So it had been for *Nothing But the Night*, *Butcher's Crossing*, and *Stoner*, all three of which had come and gone with barely a tip of the hat from the public. Also, his success with poetry had been modest. A small magazine would accept a few stanzas occasionally—but even his publisher, Viking, had returned a sheaf of his poems, only a month after the National Book Awards, with an apologetic note saying they preferred younger poets whose work was more experimental.[14]

Nothing, however, could take away the significance of receiving a major literary award for *Augustus*—it proclaimed his rightful place in the annals of contemporary novelists. It was a vindication, and it seemed to him that he was now entitled to extra consideration from the university. After all, over the course of nearly twenty years, he had taught, edited the *Denver Quarterly*, directed the creative writing program, and published literary criticism. These duties weren't out of the ordinary for an academic, of course; but his stature as a novelist added luster to the institution as a whole, and especially the English Department. He deserved a raise, or a bonus—at the very least, more time to write. And, not coincidentally, two weeks after receiving the National Book Award, Brandeis University in Boston had invited him as a visiting professor for two semesters, beginning in September of that year, 1973. He would have the privilege of selecting his students and limiting the enrollment to "numbers agreeable" to him.[15] The time to act on his prerogatives was clearly now—he was in demand—and he went off to see his department chairman, Gerald Chapman, to make his case.

Chapman was not surprised by Williams' visit; he had been expecting it. Williams asked to be relieved of some of his duties; he wanted a lighter schedule, such as having the spring quarter off, so he could begin his summer early. And Chapman appreciated how important it was to John that he be treated with extra consideration.[16]

But as Chapman listened to Williams' requests for privileges that were unusual, he knew he'd have to draw the line. The English Department was small, and special treatment was impossible to give. The opportunity to teach for Brandeis could be arranged; but as for needing time to write and so on, Chapman said, "We all have our problems." Williams left in a rage, complaining bitterly about high-handed "Har-VARD-ians" treating him like a peon.[17] And it wasn't just the English Department. He had also approached the campus library about depositing his papers there, but they weren't interested; Nancy blamed "some prude who didn't approve of John's reputation."[18] His publisher reported "sales resistance" from Denver bookstores about carrying *Augustus*. "What have you been doing and what have you not been doing that you should have been doing?" Rodell asked him.[19]

The offer from Brandeis had come at a good time, and it had the effect of sending John away for a cooling-off period. Arriving in Boston in the late summer of 1973, he and Nancy had the good luck to find an apartment around the corner from Dan Wakefield. Cunningham was still teaching at Brandeis, and that friendship was renewed, too. Nothing would please Williams more than if guest-teaching at Brandeis turned into a permanent position. And to increase the likelihood of that happening, he planned to present himself a little differently.

In the English Department at Denver, he had been adamant that experimental and modernist poets were not yet part of the canon, and had argued against creating new courses that would start with T. S. Eliot—the disease-bringer in the corruption of poetry, in his opinion.[20] By comparison to the older poets, most of the modernists, he insisted, fell short. But at Brandeis, he offered two courses in fiction that were, for him, quite a departure from his traditionalist stance about teaching the greats. During the fall semester, he taught "Modern Fiction: Form and Theory," covering major European and American novelists during the first half of the twentieth century; and then in the spring, he tried out "Contemporary Criticism and the Contemporary Novel," with readings from Lionel Trilling, Leslie Fiedler, Richard Poirier, and the Marxist literary historian György Lukács. The novels assigned were by Thomas Pynchon, Alain Robbe-Grillet, John Barth, Jorge Luis Borges, and several others. He was well thought of there, but his audition as an instructor didn't bring about an offer to join the faculty.

Texas, on the other hand, embraced him as a native son. After winding up his work at Brandeis, he and Nancy went to Houston, where he received the Texas Institute of Letters award for fiction, given to authors who resided in the state or who had spent their formative years in Texas. Following the ceremony, they returned by way of Wichita Falls to see the farm where John had spent his childhood. It was still there, and had hardly changed in forty years. There stood the barn where he had slaughtered his first pig; behind the house were the acres where his grandfather had planted vegetables. Looking around, he talked about spending every moment he could outdoors, just to get away. "I remember feeling sorry for my parents," he said to Nancy, "because they had no privacy" living with his grandparents.[21] From this little farm, he had found his way to becoming a professor and the winner of the National Book Award. But instead of being praised for his literary achievement, he felt resented at Denver.[22] They turned toward home.

———

Williams' students became accustomed to him appearing at the last minute for his nine o'clock class, his hair, combed straight back, still wet from showering to shake off the previous night's drinking.

"That damn metabolism of yours that need forego nothing," Ciardi had once said admiringly. One of Williams' doctoral dissertation students wasn't so sure. "It was a terrible assault on his body," he said years later.[23] And according to one of his seminar students, his health was "very tenuous": "Sometimes in class it would almost bring him to his knees. He was very frail. He smoked heavily and would be coughing."[24] The high altitude, the raw winters in Denver from October to April, and the effort of dealing with deep snows on their property—the last house on a dead-end street—were becoming too much for him.

At parties, Williams became boorish while drunk and could be tiresome. "He wanted to come over and sit next to you and blah, blah, blah, blah, blah at you," said one of the English professors.[25] Another colleague tried to be philosophical. "How can such a son of a bitch be such a great writer? Well, he'll piss on all our graves, that's for sure."[26] At times it seemed inconceivable that John Williams, the man getting insensible with bourbon in the corner, could also be the author of *Stoner* or *Augustus*, novels of almost magisterial restraint and control. Joanne Greenberg attributed his contradictions to a secret that he beat down by drinking—that it was hard for him to act tough, to pretend that he couldn't care less what people thought. "John's admiration of the Romans and Augustus was what he wanted to be. The reticence, the capacity to endure pain, the somewhat cynical approach to life. But he was too sensitive for that."[27]

His students learned to accept that Professor Williams was moody. Normally, he was quiet and straightforward. If a student in his poetry-writing seminar presented a piece that wasn't very good, reading it aloud for criticism, he would listen, "gravely," one former student recalled, "and then, without remotely condemning it, open up the conversation to what the rest of us thought. It was a most civilized occasion." But he could also be testy, uncompromising, and miserly with praise. "Anything other than the obvious to add, Mr. Weaver?" he inquired of another student, who was constantly raising his hand.[28] Sometimes, he could be entertaining, reading verse aloud or reciting it in his deep, sepulchral voice. It was also known that he wouldn't object to a student bringing a jug of wine to pass around at his late-afternoon seminars, and then a Johnsonian atmosphere of rambling conversation replaced the assigned readings. Warmed by the wine, when the breezes of storytelling were running high in him, Williams would invite the class to join him at the tavern down the street. "You repaired to the Stadium Inn and it was wonderful to be with this unassailable figure!," said a former student. Williams liked a good bull session and would retell favorite anecdotes about books and authors until it grew dark and long past dinner.[29] His office desk disappeared under a mound of papers: applications to the graduate program, requests from students asking for updates on their work, and correspondence. His replies often began with the same regret: "I apologize for the delay in responding" (six weeks); "I am sorry to be so long answering your letter" (three months). He delegated the editorial side of the *Denver Quarterly*, but when his overworked assistant demanded to be paid, and the college administration refused his request, Williams' volunteer quit. A student from Stanford University, Baine Kerr, who came to see him about the creative writing program, was taken aback by the appearance of his office. "It was a disaster," he said. "Books piled everywhere. Eight or ten stained coffee cups and papers scattered all around." Kerr was thinking about transferring to Denver, and his initial impression, based on the work environment of the program's director, at least, wasn't favorable. "But when he started talking about writing," Kerr said, "I wanted to be a part of what he was offering."[30]

Williams' dilatoriness about attending to the creative writing program eventually caught up with him. An advisee of his, a candidate for a doctorate who resided in Canada, had been mailing chapters of his novel to him for review. As the weeks passed, the envelopes landed on the white drift of unopened mail atop Williams' desk. Hearing nothing, the student submitted his finished manuscript in fulfillment of part of the requirement for the degree. On his dissertation committee was Seymour Epstein, who realized—after he located the novel in Williams' slush pile and read it—that its inexperienced author hadn't received any guidance, and now his manuscript was completely unacceptable. Furious, Epstein made phone calls up and down the line in the College of Arts and Sciences to figure out what to do. A compromise was reached whereby the candidate would substitute his short stories as a collection, with a preface to fulfill the requirement. In the nick of time, a hastily agreed upon solution saved the day; otherwise, the reputation of the whole creative writing program, and the value of a PhD from it, could have been jeopardized.[31] As of 1975, Williams was no longer director of the program.

That year, too, his agent Marie Rodell died. He had become very close to her over the years, stopping in New York City when he could to take her out to lunch. They signed their letters "Love," to one another, and John, despite the disaster of *Butcher's Crossing*, had trusted her implicitly. For him, she was synonymous with his career as a published author—from his cautious beginnings to winning the National Book Award. Her assistant Frances Collin took over the agency, but it wasn't the same, of course. The two events coming close together—Marie's death and being relieved of the creative writing program—left him feeling disconnected, restless.

One afternoon, while he was serving on an oral examination committee, a small but telling incident occurred. Williams was one of four instructors present to listen to a student in English literature who would be defending a dissertation on fabulism in short stories, using *Don Quixote* as a bridge between fantasy and realism. Eager to impress, the candidate took the full forty-five minutes to make his presentation, answering at length every question he was asked. Slowly, the sky began to darken outside, and it looked as if Colorado was about to have one of its late spring rains mixed with snow. The wind rose and the budding trees swayed. Then the blue-gray clouds thrashed the window with a downpour that made the glass rattle.

Without a word, Williams got up from his chair and went to look at the storm, while the voice of the student droned on behind him. To no one but himself, but overheard by everyone in the room, Williams said quietly, "Oh, my tomatoes . . ."[32]

In Extremis

What I saw was the work—the hours and hours.
So much of his life was dedicated to the work.

— NANCY WILLIAMS

H aving a famous author on the faculty who was unhappy, and vocal about it, presented the University of Denver with a problem, which it solved with a grand gesture. Effective at the beginning of the school year in 1976, Williams occupied an endowed chair. He would only have to teach two quarters each academic year, for three years, and have every third quarter off. John and Nancy began using those ten weeks to visit, first, the Gulf Coast of Texas, then Portugal; several times they circled back to Key West, as if they were experimenting with flyways they would use later as migrating birds to a safe place where John could work on his fourth novel. Of their peregrinations to various locations for the sake of John's health, and his peace of mind, it seemed at last that Key West would suit them the best.

Nevertheless, there was gossip in the English Department office about Professor Williams taking off for Florida whenever he pleased—further evidence, said some knowingly, that the National Book Award had conferred a specialness on him and he was taking advantage of it. His old friend Seymour Epstein said that Williams had become "insufferable," and he was not alone in thinking so. His advisees either had to accept that he would be away for long periods, or, as some did, switch advisers.

Ignoring the complaints, Williams went forward with his plans to relocate. With their children now grown or in college, John and Nancy began moving sideways into semi-retirement. They sold the big house on Madison Street in Denver and moved into a condominium on Pearl Street, where John could stay when he taught during the spring and fall.[1] In Key West, they purchased a small white frame house on the corner of Florida and Duncan Streets, where they "spent about six months remodeling, refurbishing, furnishing, cursing, and so forth," as John put it in a letter to his friend Fred Inglis.[2] He put colored spotlights at the foot of the palm trees shining up into the leaves to catch the Caribbean feel; Nancy noted to a friend, "it is *de rigueur* here to display a number of exotics in tubs arranged cordially on the patio, if you have a patio," which they did, made of mossy brick.[3] When John thought of what it would be like having to return to campus and put up with the pettiness—to say nothing of the effect of pollution and cold on his lungs—he began to dread the idea. "There are no more than two or three other people that I give a damn about seeing back there," he told Inglis.[4]

The verdant little town perched on the flat, fish-shaped island of white sand held strong and agreeable associations for John. It was here that he had arrived shortly after the war, because it was both familiar and exotic. Key West had represented a new beginning in those days as he was finishing his first novel, a time when several roads had been open to him. He might have continued as a news announcer, using his near-perfect voice and delivery to build a career in radio; or he might have taken George Smart's advice and enrolled at the University of Alabama, and then applied for a spot in Hudson Strode's fiction workshop. He also might never have left the island, and become a denizen of the beach-and-town scene, spending his days on a stool at the bar in a local taproom, drinking and telling anyone would who listen how he had an idea for a book.

Key West felt like a homecoming for John for another reason, too; it was a "winter repository of some very good writers, who are also very good friends," he wrote to Inglis.[5] The Williamses stayed for a month at John Ciardi's new three-bedroom bungalow on Windsor Lane, partly because the corpulent poet with the air-conditioned Cadillac was always eager to show off his wealth. "It's you I love," Nancy would say to him, "not your money!" The two men reminisced, ho-ho-hoing about Bread Loaf days, as she languished in the heat, but "John sweats and is happy," she said.[6]

Dan Wakefield came down from Boston hoping to interview John for *Ploughshares*, but Williams wouldn't hear of it until they had drunk deep in the waters of the laid-back life in Key West. Wakefield eventually got his interview, which he published in *Ploughshares*:

> For three days he managed to avoid [the interview] altogether, as he took me around to some of the bars, beaches, and restaurants of the island, dropping in on old friends like the poets Richard Wilbur and John Ciardi, meeting his new friend and Key West neighbor Peter Taylor, the short story writer, going to a party at poet James Merrill's house, drinking wine and talking and eating the Conch Chowder that is the local specialty and John has now added to his culinary repertoire, a favorite right up there with his Texas Jailhouse Chili.[7]

The working title of Williams' new novel was *The Sleep of Reason*, taken from an epigraph by Francisco Goya: "The sleep of reason brings forth monsters." The setting is Washington, DC, during the Nixon years. The central figure is Paul Mathews, in his middle fifties, a senior curator of the paintings in a small but distinguished Washington museum. As a nineteen-year-old corporal during World War II, he had been captured by the Japanese in Burma and held prisoner for several months. It was a period he tries not to think about.

The Sleep of Reason opens on a day when Mathews is trying to establish the authenticity of a painting that has just arrived at the museum, *Peter at the Tomb of the Resurrected Christ* by the great Paduan painter of the Quattrocento, Andrea Mantega. To Mathews, something about it is indefinably wrong, but he can't put his finger on it. His mind is further made uneasy by the unexpected appearance of a man he knew at the time of his capture: former Office of Strategic Services captain Dave Parker, now a rather seedy and defeated-looking operative for the intelligence community. Parker hints that he wants something from his former subordinate. Memory and the long-ago past in art and history have suddenly overlapped, and the question of authenticity—what is true and what isn't—becomes the theme of the novel.

When Baine Kerr, the young man transferring from Stanford who had been enchanted by Williams' passion for writing, went out deep-sea fishing with his instructor one night, Williams talked about the novel—"its aesthetics, and his hope that this would be his masterpiece." Usually, he was reticent about personal things, but on the fishing boat with Kerr, he talked about his childhood years and his parents' poverty, and the hurt he'd felt over the Winters affair, especially because he had tried to promote the work of Winters' wife, Janet Lewis. Back at the house, he read aloud a chapter from his new work, his rhythmic, rumbling voice accentuating the cadence of the sentences. It was memorable, Kerr thought—it was an honor to be treated as an equal. "It was a friendship," said Kerr's wife at the time, Cindy, "with literature at its center."[8]

Disturbing, though, was how Williams' drinking was affecting his behavior. A few years earlier, Kerr had thought nothing of his instructor pouring a glass for himself from the wine jug at seminars, or accompanying his students to the Stadium Inn for a bull session, with pitchers of beer circling the table. But he was not prepared for the "vehemence of his views and his verbal violence" when he was dead drunk. Saddest of all, some of his rage was directed at Nancy. He would become repetitive, and when she tried to correct him on some point, he would lash out, calling her profane names and telling her to shut up. Kerr vacillated between admonishing his old instructor in his own house or holding his tongue. "It was very excruciating at times—to be at the dinner table and hear that," he said. "You wanted to protect and defend Nancy from abuse, but I didn't know how to do that. Why did she take it? Nancy devoutly believed in his genius. She had an understanding of the dark places

where that came from—his war experiences, and his childhood."
Looking on, Cindy concluded that Nancy's devotion to her husband—normally a "sweet man, never given to ridiculing others"—
stemmed from her belief that he would leave a legacy, and it was up
to her to stick by him.[9]

A few weeks after the Kerrs returned to Denver, Williams fired
off a letter to the English Department excoriating them for daring
to amend the curriculum to include form and theory classes with a
modern emphasis while he was out of touch in Florida.[10] But having
thrown his lightning bolt to no effect, he once again withdrew into
silence. He had more important things to think about. The literature
committee at Yaddo, the four-hundred-acre artist colony in upstate
New York, had invited him to stay as their guest from the next May
through September, or for as long as he liked during that time. The
contrast seemed symbolic—the annoyance of academic politics
versus spending months in the company of fellow writers and artists.

But first he would have to attend to a health problem. During
a check-up for his emphysema, an X-ray showed the presence of
a dark spot on his right lung.

———

Given Williams' history of smoking, his physician said the abnor-
mality was almost certainly cancerous. A flexible probe sent pain-
fully into the bottom third of his lung was unable to retrieve tissue
for a biopsy, so he was scheduled for an operation to remove "a
wedge," his doctor called it. Williams preferred to have the procedure done in Denver.[11]

Nancy had been through a similar health issue earlier, and their
support of one another at times like this was unsparing. Following
an operation to remove a melanoma, her incision had become infected and she had experienced toxic shock syndrome. During the
three and a half weeks she remained in the hospital, John canceled
classes and asked friends to help with the children, who were still
at home then. Waking up from time to time in her hospital bed, she
would look over at the chair by the window and he would be there.
"John never left my side," she said.[12]

Admitted to Denver's Presbyterian–St. Luke's Medical Center, Williams sat propped up in bed, wearing a bright blue bathrobe and looking oddly out of uniform without a sports jacket and trousers. His large eyes took in everything from behind his black-framed glasses with an expression of mild boredom and resignation. A few hours later, after the procedure, he was wheeled back into his room. The small nodule in his lung wasn't cancerous, it turned out; but now, he told Fred Inglis, "I have a nice scar like a saber wound that violates my fair white body."[13] He was given the usual advice to stop smoking (which he ignored), and was told to spend as little time in Denver as possible—Key West was a better climate (advice he gladly took). And, the doctor said, it would take a few months to recover his energy (it took a year).

He spent the first half of 1980 resting, on medical leave from the university. During that time, he and Nancy paid a visit to Boston and Dan Wakefield. Wakefield had assumed that after Williams' lung operation, he would have given up chain smoking, but he hadn't. "John would take a puff, then have a paroxysm of coughing, then squirt some medication down his throat, then take another puff, and on and on through the afternoon and night. The next morning the house smelled like gas. I went out to the Public Garden clenching my pipe in my teeth but not smoking and threw away my pipe in a big garbage can and never smoked again. It was like shock treatment."[14]

In July, Williams arrived in upstate New York for a two-month stay at Yaddo to work on *The Sleep of Reason*. "There is no rule against looking for inspiration," said the retreat's welcoming booklet, "but Yaddo cannot guarantee that anyone will find it." The writing went slowly—a handful of sentences before noon. He killed time after lunch by sitting next to the pool in an open shirt and silk scarf, smoking and thinking. A swimmer asked him one afternoon if he was John Williams, who wrote *Stoner*. "So you read it!" he said affably. As 4:00 p.m. approached, he ambled over to the Great Hall, invariably the first to arrive for cocktails before dinner. Above the fireplace where he liked to stand was a glass mosaic depicting a phoenix. He reached for the bottle of Scotch on the hospitality

table and waited for others to arrive. Once, the *New Yorker* artist
Roxie Munro encountered him on his way to cocktail hour and
asked him how his day went. "Great!," he said. "I wrote eight perfect
sentences."[15] Weekends, he went to the famous racetrack nearby to
watch the horses run. He sat on the porch of the clubhouse, where
drinks would stay cool in the shade all day.[16]

—————

The John Williams who entered the classroom in the early 1980s
pulled behind him a small silver oxygen tank on wheels. He used
the clear mask attachment, which he held in one hand, alternating
between inhaling through it and then taking a drag from a burning
cigarette. Like the radio operator he had been during World War II
on supply planes in Burma, he puffed away instinctively. Seated at
his desk in the classroom, he spoke, smoked, and took a breath of
oxygen in a rhythm, the way he had at thirty thousand feet flying
over the Himalayas.

Williams was on the glide path now, finding enjoyment in serving
as an example of a thrice-published novelist in the role of master
to his pupils. "He tended to teach anecdotally; he told wonderful
stories that evoked, vividly, the writers, their craft, and their circle,"
said one former student.[17] With *The Sleep of Reason* stalled at one
hundred pages, nostalgia, for Williams, was overtaking inspiration.
There was no hurry to finish the manuscript, in any case; Corlies
Smith, his longtime editor at Viking, had left to become editorial
director at Ticknor and Fields, and his much younger replacement,
Amanda Vaill, had a cordial relationship with him, but that was all.

Finally, circumstances seemed to indicate that 1985 would be a
good year for him to retire. He was sixty-three; he wasn't the head
or editor of anything any longer, and he didn't want the responsibility.[18] Although he hadn't published a novel for thirteen years, he
was honored by the Academy of Arts and Letters, which inducted
him as a member and awarded him $5,000. (Ciardi hinted to the
secretary of the academy, "He is delighted, of course, and would
like to announce the award in Denver papers as a sort of crown
on his career there.") He also received a prestigious Guggenheim

Fellowship, worth $25,000, to continue writing *The Sleep of Reason*.[19] To help him clear out his office, he hired a local book dealer to take what he wanted from the shelves.

Then, just as he was preparing to return to Key West, he received a phone call from out of the past. His second wife, Yvonne, was in town, and she wanted to see him.

————

Yvonne was now in her late fifties, and looking much younger than the gentleman pulling the oxygen canister behind him who entered the Cruise Room of Denver's Oxford Hotel, casting a fishy eye around the establishment in search of her. The hotel had been a flophouse when John and Yvonne were living together in Denver; now it was the swankiest accommodation of its kind in the city and listed on the National Register of Historic Places. John made his way over to Yvonne's table and eased into the seat opposite her. There was a young woman beside her he didn't recognize. Yvonne introduced her to John as her daughter Gale.

After their divorce in February 1949, Yvonne had married Douglas Woolf, in March. She had now been his wife and untiring supporter for over twenty years. The pattern of their life together had been set the autumn before that, in 1948, when she had fled Denver to meet him in Tucson, Arizona, where, to put food on the table, they had sold plastic housewares door-to-door in the withering heat. Douglas Woolf was an itinerant, and a loner who believed in a semi-mystical way that his surname was part of his character. Yvonne was one of those persons born to be the sidekick, intercessor, friend, and lover of someone who might be a genius. She was tough to an amazing degree.

They had traveled around the West like gypsies. Douglas would take temporary jobs that required no commitment other than to show up: migrant farm worker, ice cream seller, beer and hot dog vendor at baseball games, egg man delivering off a truck; Yvonne worked as a bookkeeper, clerk, or product demonstrator in department stores. When they got enough cash, they would throw it all over and take to the woods or the desert with their two girls and camp out—blankets spread over tree branches for shade, or bedding down in ghost towns.[20] Using the car as his workplace, he wrote and published two novels about escaping the bourgeois life from the perspective of the footloose hero, *Wall to Wall* and *Fade Out*, and a short story collection, *Signs of a Migrant Worrier*.

But Douglas was an alcoholic, and Yvonne had left him in the late 1960s. She was in Denver to attend a conference as part of her job with the federal bankruptcy courts and thought she'd say hello to John.

"I have another daughter besides Gale," she said. "Gale was born in 1949."

John blushed. "What month, 1949?"

This moment was Yvonne's true reason for the reunion. "Let's have a little fun with him," she had said to her daughter, as they watched her former husband make his way to the table.

Before she answered John's question, she paused, as if counting from September 1948 when she'd left him. "Hmm, October."

They could see him doing the arithmetic in his head. And then, "Oh, certainly—I see."[21]

———

With Denver behind him, Williams returned to the island, "out of the snow and smog and into the warmth and air." The university had offered him an honorary degree, but his response had been, "How much?" In other words, could the award translate into money, to help him get on with his writing? In any case, no award of any kind was forthcoming, and Williams interpreted it as another example of being snubbed.[22]

Key West was becoming an even better place for the community of writers now. The annual Key West Literary Seminar—four days of readings, conversations, lectures, panel discussions, and parties—held its first conference in 1983, and Ciardi persuaded Williams to serve on the faculty for the following year. He posed on the beach for a group photo, beaming among the Pulitzer Prize and

National Book Award winners—quite an auspicious start for a new event—and exactly the kind of thing, he joked, that he meant to get away from in retirement.[23]

But he had come to the party too late, in a way. You needed to be young, or at least healthy, to really enjoy the place. And Williams was neither. He needed hospital services periodically because of his bad lungs; moreover, the sea-level mugginess was oppressive, especially when he was hung over. Key West couldn't offer him what he needed professionally, either. There was no large library, no big bookstore.

Nancy began to have similar complaints. In Denver, she had been the director of the Rocky Mountain Women's Institute, and Key West, which was becoming more commercialized and touristy, left her bored. "I was just hanging out for a year," she said. "It was awful. The small island gets smaller."[24] To move again, though, seemed unthinkable after purchasing a home and fixing it up. They had only been settled for less than two winters. Even if they decided to relocate, they couldn't decide where they would be better off.

The monotony was broken by an invitation from the poet Miller Williams, asking John to deliver a series of lectures at the University of Arkansas. There would also be a few old friends from Bread Loaf on the program—a partial convening of the Good Guys. And if that weren't reason enough to visit Fayetteville, Miller wanted to discuss something else. As director of the University of Arkansas Press, he was interested in bringing *Butcher's Crossing* and *Stoner* back into print.

With alacrity, John accepted.

———

Fayetteville is located in the Ozarks in a forested region of highlands, plateaus, rivers, and lakes covering much of the southern half of Missouri and an extensive portion of northwestern and north central Arkansas. The winter weather is mild and generally dry. When the rain stops in midsummer, the high heat begins. Eight hundred miles northwest, within an easy two-day drive, is Denver.

Nancy found the university town of forty thousand "old and

[with] a beauty and character of its own, not grand but rather pretty and nice."[25] As an experiment, she and her husband began looking for a house to rent, and they found one available from John Clellon Holmes, who was on the faculty of the creative writing program there. Holmes' semiautobiographical novel from 1952, *Go*, had been the first to depict the restlessness, disillusionment, and drug-charged lives of the Beats.

Although Holmes had only just turned sixty, he was on his last legs—an alcoholic who was returning to New England where he had been raised to spend what would be the last two years of his life. Allen Ginsburg's long, declamatory poem *Howl*, which alludes to *Go*, begins with the line "I saw the best minds of my generation destroyed by madness," and Holmes' journals, which he intended to publish, were filled with tales of self-destruction.

But now he had become a portly, grandfatherly-looking man with glasses. He and his wife, Shirley, showed their visitors the property. It was near the center of town and the university campus, an older home across from a small park with four bedrooms, two baths, and a fireplace. Holmes took them down into the basement and gave the furnace a derogatory kick, saying it didn't work very well. The house didn't have insulation, and the heating bills during the winter would be higher than the monthly rent. But the Williamses, having spent a good part of their lives in Denver, thought they could use the fireplace to take the chill off.

They signed a lease for their "little gray home in the Ozarks," as Nancy called it, in 1985 and began the arduous business of moving from Key West fifteen hundred miles away. Fayetteville had a "full complement of medical specialists," a research-grade library on campus, and the built-in advantage of a few old friends in town. It seemed perfect. And the University of Arkansas had indeed decided to reprint *Stoner* and *Butcher's Crossing*, long out of print, which would be instrumental, though Williams wouldn't live to see it, in creating renewed interest in his work. "So I seem to be returning to where I began, with a smallish press," John noted with satisfaction. "I'm just as pleased; it has a nice symmetry."[26] By early spring, they were settled in the new house, and spending most mornings having their first cups of coffee in bed, until the ancient furnace bestirred itself to heat the rooms.[27]

Near the end of Williams' finest novel, *Stoner*, the University of Missouri English Department gives a farewell dinner, a grave affair, which tired and ill Professor William Stoner attends. Some of Williams' former colleagues at the University of Denver thought he should have received more recognition at the end of his career. He was, after all, the most famous person in the English Department—the first Colorado author to have won the National Book Award. He had taught for almost thirty years and had been a major figure in adding creative writing to the academy. A junior instructor, remembering how grateful he had been for Williams' encouragement when he had first arrived in Denver, set out to coordinate "A Celebration of John Williams" for a Saturday in March 1986. The event would pay tribute to his body of work with a symposium; Nancy later liked to call it "John Day."[28]

To anchor the event, John Ciardi was invited. He planned to deliver the keynote as part of a six-city speaking tour, beginning with a group of librarians in Topeka, Kansas, who were paying him a large fee. He needed a wheelchair to make his connecting flights at the airport. But it became too much effort, and he couldn't make it back to Denver. "What good is [the money] to a dead man?" he wrote to his biographer, Edward M. Cefelli. "I just don't have Sgt. Ciardi's resilience these days—nor the bastard's legs." He canceled his appearance at "John Day," and three days later he died of a heart attack at home.[29]

Richard Yates, however, did arrive. He would be a panelist for the symposium. Yates, the author of postwar novels such as *Revolutionary Road* and *The Easter Parade*, about the struggles of his generation to adjust to domestic life and peace, was America's "least famous great writer," according to *Esquire*.[30] For ten years he had been living in cockroach-infested apartments, checking himself into the Boston veterans' hospital when he thought he was going mad. Because his reputation preceded him, he was put under the supervision of Williams' former graduate student James Clark, who later said he'd been told "'to keep him company' and 'out of trouble,' which I took to mean 'relatively sober.'"[31]

That evening, Williams arrived at the Denver Public Library to begin a reading of a chapter from his unfinished novel, *The Sleep of Reason*. Before an audience of a hundred or so, he came up to the front of the room, wheeling his oxygen tank behind him although his breathing had been better than usual recently, and took a seat at the high table so he could be seen. Yates, who had gotten drunk at dinner, started to cause a disturbance; Clark had to quiet him before Williams could begin.[32]

"I'm going to read from a novel that's in progress," he said— Chapter 2, because it was "self-contained," he told the audience. He'd been working on the story for ten years, in fact, possibly more. "My energies are not what they once were." It had been difficult for him to make progress. When he went into his study, he might work, or he might try lubricating the muse with a drink.[33] He had completed one hundred pages or so—not much more than what he had in hand when his former student Baine Kerr had listened to him read an excerpt in Key West several years before.

For the next forty minutes, he read his selection slowly, in his warm, dark voice, never varying or stumbling. He'd been over and over it, hundreds of times.[34] But there's something missing in *The Sleep of Reason*, the story of art museum curator Paul Mathews. There's a tone of weariness. Chapter 2, the one Williams read aloud, proceeds at an even pace as Mathews recalls a mysterious mission he participated in as a nineteen-year-old corporal—he was to deliver a briefcase of secret information to a jungle location in Burma. But there is no sense of inevitability, no urgency about events. The details are vivid, drawn as they are from the author's experiences. And, strange as it may sound, perhaps that's the problem. Williams had an aversion to writing about himself. He told Nancy, "Fiction and autobiography don't go together in any sensible way. I bore myself when it's about me."[35] Careful of the persona he maintained as a man of letters, he seems reluctant to drag himself, as the narrator, back into the jungle muck. He'd been alluding to his stretch in the

Army Air Corps at Sookerating for years. He'd talked and talked about it, and embellished his experiences a bit. But, as he said in an interview, "it's difficult to lie when you write a novel."[36] His integrity wouldn't allow it, drinking wouldn't inspire it, and so *The Sleep of Reason* refused to be written.

———

George Rae's second husband, Ted Cogswell, died in 1987. They were living in Pennsylvania when he passed away, and "the idea of another cold, cloudy, snowy winter alone here is more than I can bear," she wrote to the Williamses. "So I'm thinking of heading down toward south Texas when I unload the house."[37] Or maybe Mexico, but she was afraid to be alone there. John said she should come to Fayetteville and be near them. When she arrived, it was clear that heavy drinking had affected her. She told Nancy she could understand what the birds were saying. She wanted to try acting again.

Unfinished business bothered John, too. "I need to ask a favor of you," he wrote to his agent Frances Collin in 1989 when he was sixty-seven, "but the asking needs a little background." His textbook anthology, *English Renaissance Poetry*, published in 1963, had become a classic in classrooms during the ten years it had been in print. He pointed out that "a book can sell only a few hundred copies and still be an 'important' literary text." It had been allowed to go out of print, and he was trying to get an answer from the publisher about how to have the rights revert to him. His letters had gone unanswered. The University of Arkansas Press wanted to reprint it. "There is some urgency involved," he wrote. The problem of rights was taken care of easily; but by involving himself in the matter, he felt he was working, urging on the writing career that, by this time, was over. During a return visit to Key West, he added "OLD?!! Humbug! Nonsense! Young whippersnappers!!" to the bottom of a postcard to his Denver friends. He and Nancy were vacationing with his daughter Kathy, a PhD in literature now and a college professor.

That was the last time John would be there.

———

Medication was giving him strange dreams. He dreamed that he and Nancy were staying in a casino. They needed money. A friend had told him that playing "the one-armed bandit"—the slot machines—would be a good investment. Their investment would pay 10 percent regularly. But he couldn't leave his room to go down to the game room, so he asked Nancy to go instead. She tried, but she lost all the money and came back to him for more. He woke up worried.

He fell in 1992 and required a long hospital stay. To be near the university hospital, John and Nancy moved into the smallest house they'd ever owned. As John had grown weaker and less able to negotiate the features of larger homes—stairs, high cabinets, and so on—they had moved several times within Fayetteville, trying to find a floor plan that would accommodate him. His world had become more and more circumscribed, and they were now in their third house in less than ten years.

In January 1994, George Rae stopped by to check on John and found him lying on the floor like he was asleep. Nancy agreed it was time for him to receive hospice care in his bedroom. A visiting nurse assigned to him insisted that he get all the morphine he wanted. If he was having a good day, Nancy called some of his friends, including Miller Williams from his Bread Loaf days, and told them to bring over beer and sandwiches. They sat by his bed talking about sports.

John said to Nancy, "I never expected to live this long." She sat beside him.

"We said goodbye a hundred times," Nancy said. "He'd be lying there, and it was so hard to breathe. He'd say it was almost not worth it. But I would hear that word 'almost.'"[38]

He died of respiratory failure on March 3, 1994, at the age of seventy-two.

John Williams Redux

O bituaries about John Williams seemed more interested in how the National Book Award was split for the first time in its history in the year he received it for *Augustus*, 1973, and the "unusual display of public disagreement among the judges," than in what his works had contributed to American literature. Perhaps it was because his novels were out of joint with the times and mid-twentieth-century literature in general.

None of his three major works—*Butcher's Crossing, Stoner,* or *Augustus*—held a mirror up to present-day society the way the struggles of Saul Bellow's *Herzog* did, or James Baldwin's short story collection about race, *Going to Meet the Man,* both of which were being talked about in 1965, the year *Stoner* appeared. That year, too, while readers pored over Alex Haley's *The Autobiography of Malcolm X,* Alabama state troopers had clubbed civil rights marchers to their knees in Selma; riots had broken out in the Los Angeles neighborhood of Watts, and the first American combat troops arrived in Vietnam. Williams' stories about a buffalo hunt, an undistinguished professor, and a Roman emperor seemed almost belligerently indifferent to what was going on. Thus his uniqueness, which might have distinguished him in other, less restive times, became the millstone that sank him.

Every decade or so, the name "John Williams" and *Stoner* would reemerge, the way a summer drought sometimes reveals a forgotten edifice standing on the bottom of an ancient lake. People had heard a rumor of it, and there it was again—intriguing, puzzling, a curiosity from the past. In 1973, C. P. Snow had asked about *Stoner* in the *Financial Times*, "Why isn't this book famous?" In 1981, Dan Wakefield had combined an overview of Williams' career as an author with an interview of him in the literary quarterly *Ploughshares*. Morris Dickstein, a literary and cultural historian, devoted a 2007 *New York Times* article, "The Inner Lives of Men," to *Stoner*, acclaiming it as "the perfect novel." Then somehow, by a process that was "mysterious, even alchemical," said a commentator on National Public Radio, *Stoner* rose from the depths to become a best seller in Europe by 2013.

But there was more to it than that. The process of resurrecting *Stoner*, and thereby John Williams, was by no means a matter of magic; it started as a result of conversations between people who love books.

————

Crawford Doyle Booksellers, on a stretch of Madison Avenue on the Upper East Side of New York—a neighborhood near the Metropolitan Museum of Art that used to be replete with independent bookshops—has survived the slow incursion of boutiques, art galleries, and cafés on the block since 1995. The street-level shop has a mix of rare and contemporary books in the window and a bargain bin outside. Past the door, it has the book-walled coziness of a floor-to-ceiling private library with an up and downstairs. The husband and wife owners, Judith Crawford and John Doyle, are handsellers—bibliophiles who act as guides for customers hunting for something. To a woman who inquired about a nonfiction study of the Paris sewer system, Judith replied, "Which one are you looking for? There were two published in English, and I could get you the one by Harvard's Professor Reid within the week."

One day at the shop in the early 2000s, Doyle happened to mention to Edwin Frank, editor of the *New York Review of Books* Classics series, that he couldn't carry enough copies of *Stoner*, a title he liked to recommend. Perhaps the publishing side of the *Review* should consider adding it to their selected series of overlooked titles. Doyle and his wife had done well with the *Review*'s curated collection of titles by Georges Simenon, Jessica Mitford, Nikolai Gogol, Stefan Zweig, and many others.

Frank reached Nancy Williams through one of John's former students. From her, he learned that the University of Arkansas Press had reprinted *Stoner* in 1993. He bought up their surplus stock and reissued *Stoner* in 2006 under the *New York Review of Books* Classics imprint.

A book reissued with a spanking new cover is a little like wearing a new suit to the office: it gets attention. Frank's tight, handsome-looking edition of *Stoner*, graced by American realist painter Thomas Eakins' *The Thinker, Portrait of Louis H. Kenton*, caught the asceticism of the story; Irish novelist John McGahern's introduction redoubled the effect by informing readers that the novel ahead was "about work, the hard unyielding work of the farms; the work of living within a destructive marriage and bringing up a daughter with patient mutability in a poisoned household; the work of teaching literature to mostly unresponsive students. How Williams manages to dramatize this almost impossible material is itself a small miracle."

Frank was a bit disappointed when sales equaled about what they were when Viking published it in 1965—a few thousand copies. Admittedly, he said, "It's not an easy book to pitch—a midcentury, midwestern novel about a man who is a medievalist and whose life is a failure." It was Morris Dickstein's praise in the *New York Times* the following year that gave the *New York Review of Books* edition "a jump and got it going," Frank said.[1]

Meanwhile, French novelist Anna Gavalda had read Colum

McCann's list in the *Guardian* of his favorite top ten novels, with *Stoner* in first place. "I have bought at least fifty copies of it in the past few years, using it as a gift for friends," McCann wrote. "It is universally adored by writers and readers alike."[2]

Gavalda purchased a copy in English, and she wished at the end that she had written it herself. Stoner's "rectitude, his intelligence, his finesse, his tenderness. I didn't warm up to him, I fell in love with him. I like men who don't talk a lot, but who are attentive to the slightest detail." She persuaded her publisher, Le Dilettante, to license the French rights in 2007. But attempts to find a satisfactory translator brought her around to "what I already knew, that William Stoner—it was me, and it was up to me to stick to it." The task of rendering the novel into French—"I took liberties so that it would be as beautiful in my language as it is in his"—would take several years while she continued with her own writing. When it was released in 2011, the French edition of *Stoner* became a best seller.[3]

Even before the French edition, however, Gavalda's attention to the work sparked interest elsewhere in Europe. In Spain, Tito Expósito, at Ediciones Baile del Sol, read an interview with Gavalda and decided, "if she liked this novel, and I liked Gavalda, then surely I would also like *Stoner*." In 2009, the first translation of *Stoner* in Europe appeared in Spanish; and then in February 2012, Elido Fazi of Fazi Editore published the first Italian edition. The Fazi edition drew critical acclaim in the Italian newspaper *Corriere della Sera* by Paolo Giordano, a winner of Italy's most prestigious literary award, the Strega Prize, along with praise by Irene Bignardi in the Italian newspaper *La Repubblica*; Mario Fortunato in a weekly magazine, *L'Espresso*; Roberto Bertinetti in the business newspaper *Il Sole 24 Ore*; and Niccolò Ammaniti, winner of the 2007 Strega Prize. A new word entered the world of books and publishing: "Stonermania." Although the phenomenon began as a word-of-mouth recommendation from readers, it wasn't long before the character of William Stoner also began appearing in articles and discussions not strictly about the novel, but on the theme of the importance in a person's life of rectitude and incorruptibility.[4]

But strangely, readers in the United States still seemed resistant to *Stoner*. During one of his regular visits to New York, Oscar van Gelderen of Lebowski Publishers in Amsterdam heard that some of the younger editors at HarperCollins were reading it for their own pleasure. Van Gelderen purchased a copy at a bookshop, went to his hotel, and read the book in one sitting. Despite the story being "spectacularly unspectacular," he was surprised by how good it was. "Stoner is a teacher. And then he dies. Well, let's hope the author is very good-looking," he thought, "and in his or her mid-thirties to help sell that kind of story," which wasn't the case, of course.[5] There would be no talk shows, no promotional brainstorming with the author because, as Van Gelderen was later informed, John Williams had been dead for twenty years.

But the novel was being read in Europe, and becoming popular in Italy, France, and Israel, even if Williams wasn't being honored in his own land. Consequently, after acquiring the rights, Van Gelderen became, as he put it, a "Jehovah's Witness for *Stoner*." Lebowski Publishers placed it as the lead title in their September 2012 catalog, gave the book a strong, iconic cover, and sent galleys to booksellers that summer accompanied by a printed "love letter" about the novel from the publisher. It was the start of a six-month-long campaign, Van Gelderen said, "from door to door, from one bookseller to the next, from one journalist to the next," to reintroduce a forty-seven-year-old book as though it were a new, contemporary piece of hot fiction. Salespeople were instructed to ask booksellers for blurbs, to get them involved, and to offer customers a money-back guarantee. Customers did come back—not because they were dissatisfied, but to buy another copy. "I wanted booksellers to feel proud that they were up on the latest—give them a reason to say to customers, 'Listen, this is something special.'" Van Gelderen posted the eye-catching cover of a gray-bearded older man against a jet-black background close to four hundred times on Facebook and Twitter.[6]

After six months, by March 2013, *Stoner* was the best-selling book in the Netherlands, and it remained at the top of the list for five weeks in a row—an unprecedented record for a "lost classic."

Van Gelderen continued to promote the book at the April London Book Fair. Sales of the book were so striking that journalists in the United States, at *The Millions*, and *Publishers Weekly*, for example, wrote about the success in Holland, which kick-started more reviews and *Stoner* articles in the United Kingdom and the United States.

Clara Nelson, who was then with Penguin Random House in the United Kingdom, seeing that sales for the Dutch edition were taking off—two hundred thousand copies—decided to adapt Lebowski's approach of intense exposure, but keep the spotlight trained on *Stoner* even longer. "We aimed to do a piece of publicity every week for a year in the United Kingdom national press," part of which included giving Williams "a voice again through champions in the literary community." During the campaign, reviews by Julian Barnes and Bret Easton Ellis, along the lines of "upon first looking into Williams' *Stoner*," had a domino effect of persuading journalists that they ought to find out what all the fuss was about. Bryan Appleyard, a nonfiction author and reviewer, said in the *Sunday Times*, "This is the story of the greatest novel you have never read. I can be confident you have never read it because so few people have. In recent weeks, I have come across academics specializing in American literature who have never even heard of it. Yet it is, without question, one of the great novels in English of the twentieth century. It's certainly the most surprising." Ian McEwan echoed the same opinion on BBC Radio in June, telling his listeners that if they were readers who kept up on the latest books everyone was talking about, here was one that may have gotten past them.

Waterstones named it Book of the Year in 2013, by which time rights had been sold in twenty-one countries—including China—and by riding the best-seller lists in Germany, France, Israel, Holland, and the United Kingdom, *Stoner*'s success encouraged some publishers to bring out *Butcher's Crossing* and *Augustus* as well.

———

Edwin Frank at New York Review Books has a theory about why *Stoner*, in particular, is embraced in Europe, more so than in the

United States. "I think it's of an era that occurred *before* its publication," he said. "There's an existentialist edge to it, and I would point that out to European publishers, because I was confident that *Stoner* would find a European audience for that reason. It's an American book like an Edward Hopper painting. It has that long-shadowed, lonely feeling. Loneliness is a big part of twentieth-century fiction. You might put *Stoner* in the company of *The Plague*, *The Stranger*, and other enduring, existentialist books of that era." Cristina Marino, who obtained the book for Fazi Editore, believes that Italians don't share the optimism of Americans. "We are more accepting of human failings, of people being fragile."[7]

Frank believes that *Stoner's* slow rise in popularity in the United States has been largely a word-of-mouth phenomenon—proof of the fundamental importance of readers recommending and discussing books, especially at a time when social media promotes flash fiction, listicles, videos and pictures, and nonliterary discourse. "It's a book about a person who loves books, and published at a time when people feel passionately that they need to defend the precincts of book culture," he said.[8]

From the last page of the novel, when Professor Stoner is dying:

He opened the book; and as he did so it became not his own.
He let his fingers riffle through the pages and felt a tingling, as if
those pages were alive. The tingling came through his fingers and
coursed through his flesh and bone; he was minutely aware of
it, and he waited until it contained him, until the old excitement
that was like terror fixed him where he lay. The sunlight, passing
his window, shone upon the page, and he could not see what was
written there. The fingers loosened, and the book they had held
moved slowly and then swiftly across the still body and fell into
the silence of the room.[9]

Acknowledgments

Williams' papers at the University of Arkansas, Fayetteville, are deep and detailed. They contain extensive personal and official correspondence, notes and manuscripts of all the novels, official documents, photocopies of newspaper clippings, printed materials, essays on Williams' work, interviews, photographs, and a scrapbook. Papers belonging to some of his literary friends are available elsewhere—including Yvor Winters, Alan Swallow, and J. V. Cunningham, at Stanford University, the University of Syracuse, and the University of Chicago, respectively. Papers belonging to a few of Williams' colleagues can be found at the University of Denver.

Special thanks go to Jim Clark, the Red River Historical Society; Lindsay M. Morecraft, Special Collections, University of Iowa Archives; the University of Arkansas Special Collections Library; Geoffrey Stark, Reading Room supervisor, Special Collections, University of Arkansas; Halley Grogan, Texas State Library and Archives Commission; Katherine Crowe, curator, Special Collections and Archives, University of Denver; Mark A. Greene, director,

American Heritage Center, University of Wyoming; Giana Ricci, Tamiment Library and Robert F. Wagner Labor Archives; Lita Watson, Wichita County Historical Commission; Chloe Morse-Harding, Robert D. Farber University Archives and Special Collections, Brandeis University; David K. Frasier, the Lilly Library, Indiana University; Becky Morrison, Wichita Falls Public Library; and Laura Russo, Howard Gotlieb Archival Research Center, Boston University. Tony Burton, literary historian of American writers in Mexico, was most helpful.

Williams' friends, colleagues, fellow authors, former students, and family members who graciously made themselves available for interviews include Michelle Latiolais, Cindy Carlisle, David Milofsky, Joe Nigg, Robert Richardson, Robert Pack, Dan Wakefield, Sherman Leavenworth, Sandra Cordon, Martin and Joyce Shoemaker, Jim Clark, Angela Ball, Brock Bower, Anne Marie Candido, Victor Castellani, David Haward Bain, Steve Wiegenstein, Doug Devaux, Gerald Chapman, R. H. Epstein, Thomas E. Kennedy, Miriam Epstein, Nancy Esterlin, Gale Woolf, Ben Kilpea, Eric Gould, Joanne Greenberg, Steve Heller, Fred Inglis, Jean James, Baine P. Kerr, Carol DeBoer-Langworthy, Nancy L. Easterlin, Heather McHugh, Jonathan Williams, Pamela Williams, Katherine Williams, Peggy McIntosh, David Milofsky, Roxie Munro, Edward M. Cifelli, Sherry Christie, Mike Dabrishus, David Myers, David Nemec, Jay Neugeboren, Joe Nigg, Robert Pawlowski, Alan Prendergast, Burton Raffel, Bin Ramke, Elizabeth Richardson, Florence Roberts, Joan Saalfeld, Amanda Vaill, Gordon Weaver, Michael White, Geary Hobson, Timothy Steele, Marc Yacht, Sandra Braman, William Giraldi, and William Zaranka.

Matthew Carter, William Zaranka, Robert T. Tally, and Gerald Chapman generously made time to read the manuscript or answer questions related to it. Deb Stone uncovered documents and public records that had eluded discovery; Linda Justice transcribed interviews with lightning speed; graduate students Isobel Strobing at Boston University, and J. Edward Shockley at Midwestern State University (formerly Hardin Junior College), assisted in research.

At Folio Literary Management, Molly Jaffa and Jeff Kleinman, my agent, were the keys to connecting with Oscar van Gelderen at Lebowski Publishers and my perceptive, encouraging editor Stijn de Vries.

Frances Collin, friend and partner to John Williams' agent Marie Rodell, and Collin's associate, Sarah Yake, spurred the creation of this book immensely by sharing materials and correspondence from their files. Their belief in this biography never wavered and led directly to its publication. Elido Fazi and Valentina Bortolamedi of Fazi Editore, Cristina Marino of Rizzoli, Edwin Frank of New York Review Books, Patricia Reimann of DTV Literature, Netta Gurevitch of Yedioth Books, Tito Expósito of Ediciones Baile del Sol, Frances MacMillan of Random House UK, Clara Nelson of Michael O'Mara Books, Claude Tarrène of Le Dilettante, novelist and translator Anna Gavalda, and Oscar van Gelderen graciously retraced their steps in explaining how they rediscovered *Stoner*.

Nancy Williams spent several days answering questions about her late husband and sharing her memories. Without her, much of her late husband's past would have been lost forever.

Notes

PART I. *NOTHING BUT THE NIGHT*

Chapter One. He Comes from Texas

1. Nancy Williams, interview, October 10, 2014.

2. Williams' marriage, his second, to Yvonne Elyse Stone, State of California, Certificate of Registry of Marriage, #26401, September 2, 1947.

3. Nancy Williams, interview, October 10, 2014.

4. Ibid.

5. Dedication to George Rae Williams by her husband, Willard Marsh, in *Week with No Friday* (New York: Harper and Row, 1965).

6. Nancy Williams, interview, October 10, 2014.

7. John Williams, *Stoner* (New York: New York Review Books, 2006).

8. Dan Wakefield, "John Williams, Plain Writer," *Ploughshares* 7, nos. 3–4 (Fall/Winter 1981): 15.

9. Ibid.

10. Frank Gruber, *Zane Grey: A Biography* (Mattituck, NY: Amereon, 1969), 213.

11. Nancy Williams, interview, October 10, 2014. Nancy said, "Things began to make sense to John after that about his family."

12. Wakefield, "John Williams, Plain Writer," 15.

13. Nancy Williams, interview, October 10, 2014.

14. Ibid. The description of slaughtering the pig is based on common practice.

15. John Williams, *Butcher's Crossing* (New York: New York Review Books, 2007).

Chapter Two. "Ho, Ho! Wasn't I the Character Then?"

1. Nancy Williams, interview, October 9, 2014.

2. John Williams, "The 'Western': Definition of the Myth," *The Nation* 43, no. 17 (November 18, 1961).

3. Nancy Williams, interview, October 9, 2014.

4. The scene fades to black and the words appear: "I am the resurrection and the life"—an example of Hollywood hitting the audience over the head and pitching the film to churchgoers who might not approve of movies. The novel ends differently.

5. Dan Wakefield, "John Williams, Plain Writer," *Ploughshares* 7, nos. 3–4 (Fall/Winter 1981).

6. Note from an interview conducted by Jody McCall with Williams, apparently for a local newspaper. Williams Papers, University of Arkansas, Fayetteville (Williams Papers hereafter), Series 10 (Interviews), Box 27, Folders 9–10.

7. Brian Wooley, "An Interview with John Williams," *Denver Quarterly* (Winter 1986): 13.

8. Wakefield, "John Williams, Plain Writer," 15.

9. "These Books Not Really Over His Head," *Wichita Daily Times*, March 6, 1938.

10. Bin Ramke, interview, October 7, 2014. Ramke was a colleague of Williams' at the University of Denver.

11. "Young Wichitan Accidentally Shot," *Wichita Daily Times*, June 30, 1940.

12. McCall notes, Williams Papers.

13. Wooley, "Interview with John Williams," 30.

14. Wakefield, "John Williams, Plain Writer," 15.

15. Ibid., 18.

16. Newsom and Coleman had landed parts for the summer at the county playhouse in Suffern, NY. Vesta Kelling, "Actors Take a Busman's Holiday—And Act!," *Evening Independent*, July 12, 1941, 6, 9. Newsom became a Hollywood writer; Coleman's interest in theater trailed off during the war.

17. "Playgoers Await Unique 'Our Town,'" *Wichita Daily Times*, December 8, 1940.

18. Wooley, "Interview with John Williams," 15.

19. Michael Shannon, "The History of KDNT Radio in Denton, Texas, Part I: 1938–46," Dallas–Fort Worth Radio & Television History, n.d., dfwretroplex.com.

20. Martin (Alyeene's nephew) and Joyce Shoemaker, interview, June 4, 2015.

21. "Miss Bryan, Mr. Williams Married Methodist Church," *Hood County Tablet*, April 9, 1942.

22. Ibid.

Chapter Three. Rough Draft

1. "Mechanics Still Are Wanted by Air Corps," *Lubbock Morning Avalanche*, September 26, 1942.

2. Dan Wakefield, "John Williams, Plain Writer," *Ploughshares* 7, nos. 3–4 (Fall/Winter 1981): 21.

3. Conrad Black, *Franklin Delano Roosevelt, Champion of Freedom* (New York: PublicAffairs, 2003), 603–605.

4. *Hood County Tablet*, November 19, 1942, 8.

5. *Hood County Tablet*, December 24, 1942, 1.

6. Donovan Webster, *The Burma Road: The Epic Story of the China-Burma-India Theater in World War II* (New York: Harper Perennial, 2004), 129.

7. Thomas Ray Foltz, "My Life as a GI Joe in World War II," China-Burma-India: Remembering the Forgotten Theater of World War II, 2007, cbi-theater .com/gijoe/gijoe.html.

8. Ibid.

9. Theodore White, "The Hump: The Historic Airway to China Was Created by US Heroes," *Life*, September 11, 1944.

10. Memoirs of World War II radiomen report that this was common practice.

11. Douglas F. Devaux, "China, Burma and India from the Back Seat: Memories from the China-Burma-India Theater," China-Burma-India: Remembering the Forgotten Theater of World War II, 2001 (adapted for internet 2016), cbi-theater. com/backseat/backseat.html.

12. Still, the efforts of the Hump-fliers were weakened by corruption on the other end. The supplies that landed in China didn't always end up in the proper hands—the bane of international charity—and the black market was booming in and around the drop-off point of Kunming. Unscrupulous hoarders built fortunes from selling supplies shipped from Indian bases. As Donovan Webster writes in *The Burma Road: The Epic Story of the China-Burma-India Theater in World War II* (New York: Farrar, Straus and Giroux, 2003), "troops were living on gruel, Spam, and rice, while those close to Hump deliveries in China grew fat on American-bought pork, beef, and chicken" (128).

13. Williams, reading aloud from his manuscript during an honorary symposium about him, March 29, 1984, CD-ROM, included in the Williams Papers collection.

14. Alan Prendergast, "Sixteen Years After His Death, Not-So-Famous Novelist John Williams Is Finding His Audience," *Westword*, November 3, 2010.

15. Nancy Williams, interview, October 10, 2014.

16. USAAF/USAF Aircraft Accidents 1942–1955 for India: Military Aviation Incident Reports, aviationarcheology.com; National Archives, College Park, Maryland, Lists of Allied Air Crashes, compiled 09/1939–03/1945, ARC Identifier 7373711/MLR Number A1 2109-C Series, Record Group 92: Records of the Office of the Quartermaster General, 1774–1985.

17. Wakefield, "John Williams, Plain Writer," 21.

18. Barbara Tuchman, *Stilwell and the American Experience in China* (New York: Grove Press, 1970); Nancy Williams, interview, October 10, 2014. Nancy said, "His nightmares continued for years and gradually lessened—the guilt."

19. James McWilliams, "The Examined Lie: A Meditation on Memory," *American Scholar*, Summer 2015.

20. Katherine Williams, email, May 2, 2015.

21. Dan Wakefield, interview, November 11, 2013.

22. Nancy Williams, interview, October 10, 2014.

23. From a booklet dated March 1944, Williams Papers. That month the 1st and 2nd Troop Carrier Squadrons flew seventeen low-altitude missions, parachuting supplies to Merrill's Marauders, an Allied guerrilla force in the Burmese jungle—more than twenty tons every other day. Instead of keeping a soldier's diary of events, Williams may have preferred writing fiction as a gesture of faith that he would survive to be published one day.

24. Brian Wooley, "An Interview with John Williams," *Denver Quarterly* (Winter 1986): 5.

25. Satyavati C. Jordan to Williams, March 25, 1945, Williams Papers.

26. Satyavati C. Jordan to Williams, March 29, 1945, Williams Papers.

27. Jack Newsom to Williams, October 22, 1944, Williams Papers.

Chapter Four. Key West

1. Nancy Williams, interview, October 9, 2014. When Williams was in India, he and the men drank something the locals brewed—they called it "spot-bottle"— drops of which stained their uniforms white.

2. Nancy Williams, interview, October 9, 2014.

3. Brian Wooley, "Interview with John Williams," *Denver Quarterly* (Winter 1986): 25. If Williams wrote half a dozen sentences he liked in a day's work, he was satisfied.

4. Edward Stone, *A Certain Morbidness: A View of American Literature* (Carbondale: Southern Illinois University Press, 1969), 18.

5. All quotations here and in the passage that follows are from John Williams, *Nothing But the Night* (Fayetteville: University of Arkansas Press, 1990).

6. Before the war, Smart had published a study of private libraries in colonial Virginia that other scholars would still be citing sixty years later. About this role as an adviser to students, later, at the University of Miami, a student named Marc Yacht sought out Smart, his creative writing teacher. Yacht was in pre-med and wanted to be a doctor, but he was rethinking that decision. Smart had been a member of the pre-med club at the University of Alabama, so he understood. Yacht decided to drop out for a while, but later he enrolled in medical school and enjoyed a long career as a physician. Marc Yacht, MD, interview, June 13, 2015.

7. Smart was a heavy drinker and intimated that it was a problem in his later correspondence.

8. George K. Smart to Williams, July 7, 1946, Williams Papers.

9. Aswell succeeded Maxwell Perkins as administrator of the Thomas Wolfe estate in 1947.

10. *Paris News*, September 10, 1937, 9.

11. John M. Spottswood to Williams, December 6, 1945, Williams Papers.

12. Dan Wakefield, "John Williams, Plain Writer," *Ploughshares* 7, nos. 3–4 (Fall/Winter 1981): 16.

Chapter Five. Alan Swallow

1. Ten years later, the house fell beneath the bulldozers digging for the Ventura Freeway.

2. "Texas Memories: 1932," *Denver Quarterly* (Winter 1986): 129. Nancy Williams said, "John loved his mother too much to talk about her." Nancy Williams, interview, October 9, 2014.

3. Edward Aswell to Williams, June 19, 1946, and George K. Smart to Williams, July 7, 1946, Williams Papers.

4. Alan Swallow to Williams, November 2, 1946, Williams Papers.

5. Gale Woolf (Yvonne's daughter), interview, June 8, 2015.

6. Yvonne (Stone) Woolf to Williams, May 21 and 22, 1947, Williams Papers.

7. Alan Swallow to Williams, December 14, 1946, Williams Papers.

8. Dale W. Nelson, *The Imprint of Alan Swallow: Quality Publishing in the West* (Syracuse, NY: Syracuse University Press, 2010), 159.

9. Ibid., 11.

10. The Blue Books were favorites of William S. Burroughs, Jack Kerouac, Richard Byrd (the polar explorer), Louis L'Amour (who said, "The Little Blue Books were a godsend to wandering men and no doubt to many others"), Harlan Ellison (who called them "moveable schoolrooms at ten cents a shot"), Saul Bellow, Gore Vidal, and Margaret Mead (who took a suitcase full of them to the Samoan Islands). Studs Terkel, who was raised in a Chicago boardinghouse, loved overhearing discussions between boarders about titles in the series. FBI director J. Edgar Hoover regarded the political, religious, and economic tracts as threats to the nation and arranged to have Haldeman-Julius arrested for tax evasion. The popularity of the Little Blue Books declined, however, during the Red Scare of the 1950s.

11. In 1938, Warren Brooks published a textbook, *Understanding Poetry*, that codified many of the New Critical ideas into a coherent approach to literary study. The book, and its companion volume, *Understanding Fiction* (1943), revolutionized the teaching of literature in universities well into the 1960s.

12. Quoted in Richard Ellman, "Publisher for Poets," *Saturday Review*, July 22, 1961, 33–34; Nelson, *Imprint of Alan Swallow*, 57, 78.

13. Nelson, *Imprint of Alan Swallow*, 75.

14. Donna Ippolito and Shirley Kopatz, "Alan Swallow: Platten Press Publisher," *Journal of the West* 8 (1969): 476.

15. Ibid., 476.

16. Robert Giroux to Williams, January 13, 1947, Williams Papers.

17. George K. Smart to Williams, May 5, 1947, Williams Papers.

18. Alan Swallow to Williams, April 29, 1947, Williams Papers.

19. Ibid.

20. Alan Swallow to Williams, August 5, 1947, Williams Papers.

21. George K. Smart to Williams, September 9, 1947, Williams Papers.

22. Historians Charles Graham and Robert Perkin, as well as Mayor Stapleton, are quoted in R. Laurie Simmons and Thomas H. Simmons, "Historic Resources of Downtown Denver," National Register of Historic Places, Multiple Property Documentation Form, US Department of the Interior, National Park Service, http://legacy.historycolorado.org/sites/default/files/files/OAHP/crforms_edumat/pdfs/646.pdf.

23. "Our Literary Alumni," *University of Denver Magazine*, September 1964.

24. John Williams, *Stoner* (New York: New York Review Books, 2006), 7.

25. Michelle Latiolais, interview, December 14, 2013. Latiolais was one of Williams' graduate students at the University of Denver.

Chapter Six. Love

1. Yvonne Williams to Elbert and Adair (?), April 25, 1948, Williams Papers. Elbert and Adair had a little boy, Harry, according to Yvonne's letter, so this is not John's grandfather Elbert Walker, who was in his nineties.

2. She edited Swallow's annual *Index to Little Magazines* from 1948 to 1951.

3. George K. Smart to Williams, September 7, 1948, Williams Papers.

4. Yvonne Williams, April 25, 1948, Williams Papers.

5. Yvonne Woolf, "DW [Douglas Woolf]: A Memoir" (unpublished, undated), provided by Gale Woolf, her daughter.

6. Willard Marsh to Williams, May 4, circa 1958, Williams Papers.

7. George Rae Williams to Williams, March 16, 1948, Williams Papers.

8. Willard Marsh to Williams, March 23, 1948, Williams Papers.

9. Woolf, "DW"; Yvonne Williams, April 25, 1948, Williams Papers.

10. In *Wall to Wall*, Woolf wrote:

There was nothing unusual about the truck parked by itself a little beyond the camp, it was an ordinary open-bed truck, Dodge, similar to the old-fashioned garbage truck. . . . No garbage truck I'd ever seen had smelled like that. I knew at once what was causing it, but I walked over for a look anyway, or perhaps because. The driver must have been waiting in the chowline with everyone else . . . so I was all alone. . . . He had a full load of soldiers in his truck, thrown in, their arms and legs and heads in various positions and attitudes that I'd never seen before. They were mostly French, a few Arabs, and despite their uniforms they didn't look very important any more. Later I learned that if you watched men die, especially if you've known them at all, they still look important afterward no matter what you have to do with them, but I was inexperienced then." (Douglas Woolf, *Wall to Wall* [New York: Grove Press, 1962], 80–81)

11. Douglas Woolf, *Hypocritic Days and Other Tales*, edited by Sandra Braman (Santa Barbara, CA: Black Sparrow Press, 1993), 396.

12. Robert Creeley, "Reading Douglas Woolf's Ya! & John-Juan," Dalkey Archive Press website, www.dalkeyarchive.com/reading-douglas-woolfs-ya -john-juan.

13. Gale Woolf, interview, June 8, 2015.

14. Woolf, "DW"; Gale Woolf, interview, June 8, 2015.

15. Woolf, *Wall to Wall*; Gale Woolf, interview, June 8, 2015.

16. Alan Swallow to John Pauker, August 17, 1948, Williams Papers. Pauker, a commentator for the Voice of America during World War II, later became a poet, playwright, editor, and translator.

17. Yvor Winters, *Primitivism and Decadence: A Study of American Experimental Poetry* (New York: Arrow Editions, 1937).

18. Billie Watson to Williams, July 9, 1948, Williams Papers.

19. John Williams, *Butcher's Crossing* (New York: New York Review Books, 2007), 63.

20. John Williams, *Stoner* (New York: New York Review Books, 2006), 193.

21. Undated draft of "The Summer," Williams Papers.

22. George Rae Williams to Williams, July 11, 1948, Williams Papers; Woolf, "DW."

23. Woolf, "DW."

24. Gale Woolf, interview, June 8, 2015.

25. Woolf, "DW."

26. Willard Marsh to Williams, October 14, 1948, Williams Papers.

27. Letters from George Rae and Willard Marsh to Williams, October 11 and 14, 1948, Williams Papers.

28. George Rae Marsh to Williams, December 4, 1948, Williams Papers.

29. Willard Marsh to Williams, December 4, 1948, Williams Papers.

30. George Rae Marsh to Williams, December 10, 1948, Williams Papers.

31. John Williams, *The Broken Landscape* (Denver: Swallow Press, 1949), 23.

32. Willard Marsh to Williams, January 1, 1949, Williams Papers.

PART II. *BUTCHER'S CROSSING*
Chapter Seven. The Winters Circle

1. Dale W. Nelson, *The Imprint of Alan Swallow: Quality Publishing in the West* (Syracuse, NY: Syracuse University Press, 2010), 86. Not all of Swallow's books were for intellectuals. Virgil Scott's *The Hickory Stick* (1947) was crime fiction. On August 20, 1947, *Kirkus Reviews* said, "Self-portrait of a heel, this, in its cold criminal conduct, its lust without love, its tough, tense narrative stands up well against (but does not necessarily derivate from) James Cain."

2. Quoted in Nelson, *Imprint of Alan Swallow*, 98.

3. Alan Swallow to Williams, August 26, 1948, Williams Papers.

4. Kenneth Fields, "True to His Word," *Stanford Alumni Magazine*, November-December 2000, https://alumni.stanford.edu/get/page/magazine/article/?article _id=39395. The memory of hearing Winters reading verses moved Robert Lowell

to say, "His voice and measures still ring in my ears. They pass [poet A. E.] Housman's test for true poetry: if I remembered them while shaving, I would cut myself." Kenneth Fields, "Winters's Wild West," *Los Angeles Review of Books*, September 10, 2013, https://lareviewofbooks.org/article/winterss-wild-west/#!.

5. Fields, "Winters's Wild West." See also Stanley Edgar Hyman, "Yvor Winters and Evaluation in Criticism," in *The Armed Vision: A Study in the Methods of Modern Literary Criticism* (New York: Alfred A. Knopf, 1955), 23–53. It was true: Winters was born three centuries too late, and he was a thoroughly Johnsonian character. His marriage to Janet Lewis, however, was tender and they were devoted to each other.

6. David Yezzi, "The Seriousness of Yvor Winters," *New Criterion*, June 1997, 26.

7. R. L. Barth, ed., *The Selected Letters of Yvor Winters* (Athens: Swallow Press / Ohio University Press, 2000).

8. A. Alvarez, "Yvor Winters," in *Beyond All This Fiddle: Essays, 1955–1967* (New York: Random House, 1968), 255–259 (originally published in *The New Statesman*, 1960).

9. Hugh Lloyd-Jones, Regius Professor of Greek at Oxford, quoted in Joseph Epstein, "Father of History: Herodotus and the Human Dimension in the Past," *Weekly Standard*, October 20, 2014.

10. Yvor Winters, "Individual Poets and Modes of Poetry: The 16th Century Lyric in England. A Critical and Historical Reinterpretation," in Paul J. Alpers, ed., *Elizabethan Poetry: Modern Essays in Criticism* (New York: Oxford University Press, 1967), 98; originally published in *Poetry Magazine* 53 (1939).

11. Quoted in Yezzi, "Seriousness of Yvor Winters"; Kenneth Rexroth, *American Poetry in the Twentieth Century* (New York: Seabury Press, 1971), 92–93.

12. Yvor Winters, *In Defense of Reason* (Denver: Swallow Press, 1947).

13. Frederick Seidel, "Robert Lowell, The Art of Poetry No. 3," *Paris Review* (Winter-Spring 1961).

14. Winters was also a moral figure to his students, which meant he had as profound an influence on them as any academic knowledge they picked up in his classes. He and Janet Lewis vigorously protested the internment of Japanese Americans during World War II. They were founding members of the California branch of the NAACP (National Association for the Advancement of Colored People); they organized the retrial of a man unjustly convicted of murder; and they were both concerned with the plight and history of Native Americans.

15. George K. Smart to Williams, circa early 1949, Williams Papers.

16. Martha Hume, "Artist of Diversity: John Williams," *Dust* (Winter 1966): 18.

17. Willard Marsh to Williams, January 20, 1949, Williams Papers. Marsh sometimes poured himself a drink, or several, when he wrote letters, so his tone has to be taken with a grain of salt.

18. Nelson, *Imprint of Alan Swallow*, 85.

19. Ibid., 98.

20. Jean James, interview, June 20, 2015. Her husband, Stuart James, was later chair of the English Department at the University of Denver. She said,

Alan, he was impatient, with people who weren't interested in ideas, who weren't interested in the literary world. I don't think he tolerated stupid people very well. He was just kind of harsh in many ways. He never was to Stewart or to me, but I think he was to others. I saw that at many gatherings. He liked working. And many writers, or people of that ilk, that's the way they are, they are always thinking about writing. They are always thinking about ideas. And so to be in a world where they would consider it frivolous, they just don't want to bother.

21. J. V. Cunningham, *The Collected Essays of J. V. Cunningham* (Chicago: Swallow Press, 1976), 421.

22. Irving Howe, *A Margin of Hope* (New York: Harcourt Brace Jovanovich, 1982), 190.

23. Timothy Steele, "An Interview with J. V. Cunningham," *Iowa Review* (Fall 1985).

24. Francis Fike, "Cold Grace: Christian Faith and Stoicism in the Poetry of J. V. Cunningham," *Renascence: Essays on Values in Literature* (Milwaukee, WI: Marquette University Press, 2007), 141–158.

25. J. V. Cunningham, "For My Contemporaries," from *The Exclusions of a Rhyme: Poems and Epigrams* (Athens: Ohio University Press/Swallow Press, 1960).

26. Hayden Carruth to Williams, October 31, 1949, Williams Papers.

27. Desmond Powell to Williams, April 6, 1950, Williams Papers.

Chapter Eight. "Natural Liars Are the Best Writers"

1. John Williams, *Stoner* (New York: New York Review Books, 2006), 15.

2. Quoted in "Natural Liars Are the Best Writers," *Moberly (MO) Monitor-Index,* October 8, 1936.

3. Leon T. Dickinson, *An Historical Sketch of the Department of English, University of Missouri–Columbia* (Columbia: Department of English, University of Missouri, 1986).

4. "A.H.R. Fairchild Talks on Value of Knowledge of Human Nature as Learned from Books," *Columbia (MO) Evening Missourian,* October 30, 1922.

5. Dickinson, *Sketch.*

6. Ibid.

7. Ibid.

8. Alan Swallow to Williams, February 9, 1951, Williams Papers.

9. Barthold Fles to Williams, September 10, 1951, Williams Papers.

10. Alan Swallow to Williams, September 19, 1951, Williams Papers.

11. Harry Brague to Williams, November 11, 1951, Williams Papers. The legendary Maxwell Perkins hired Brague in 1946. He was Kurt Vonnegut's editor for *Player Piano* and became Hemingway's editor in the late 1950s. A colorful description of New York publishing as a decrepit old boys' club after the war appears in an essay by Charles Scribner Jr., "I, Who Knew Nothing, Was in Charge," *New York Times,* December 9, 1990.

12. Barthold Fles to Williams, July 19, 1952, Williams Papers.

13. Harry Shaw to Barthold Fles, June 21, 1954, Williams Papers.

14. Barthold Fles to Williams, June 21, 1954, Williams Papers.

15. Anaïs Nin, *Fire: From "A Journal of Love, 1934–1937* (Reprint, New York: Houghton Mifflin Harcourt, 1995), 280.

16. Willard Marsh to Williams, October 22, 1952, Williams Papers.

17. Willard Marsh to Williams, undated, Williams Papers.

18. Willard Marsh to Williams, October 22, 1952, Williams Papers.

19. A number of Williams' students over the years remembered his delight in reciting Wyatt during class.

20. Yvor Winters, *In Defense of Reason* (Denver: Swallow Press, 1947). One of the editions is available online at archive.org.

21. Yvor Winters, *Forms of Discovery* (Denver: Swallow Press, 1967), 44. Twenty years after publishing *In Defense of Reason*, Winters still thought so much of Greville that he devoted ten pages to him in *Forms of Discovery*.

22. Williams, "Fulke Greville: The World and God," *Denver Quarterly* (Summer 1975). "Imperfectly golden" seems like a generous assessment of a poet who addressed his mistress as "Faire dog" in "Sonnet II."

23. "Our Literary Alumni," *University of Denver Magazine*, September 1964.

24. Ray B. West to Williams, June 8, 1953, Williams Papers.

25. Alan Swallow to Williams, February 22, 1953, Williams Papers.

26. Yvor Winters to Alan Stephens, August 21, 1953, Williams Papers.

27. Ray B. West to Williams, circa late 1953, Williams Papers.

28. Williams to The Editors, *Poetry*, January 20, 1954.

29. Willard Marsh to Williams, March 18, 1953, Williams Papers.

30. Florence Roberts, interview, June 6, 2015.

31. Ibid.

32. Ibid.

Chapter Nine. *Butcher's Crossing*

1. Alan Swallow to Williams, February 8, 1953, Williams Papers.

2. Martha H. Hume, "Alan Swallow: In Memoriam," *Small Press Review* (Spring 1967); Alan Swallow to Williams, January 1, 1954, Williams Papers.

3. Though commonplace today, in the 1950s there were no professional associations of writers in the United States, and only a handful of master of fine arts (MFA) programs. Some faculty resisted convening panels and workshops about writing for market, maintaining it was outside the mission of academe. Others looked askance at writing courses whose purpose was to produce writers; it sounded ironic—maybe even a little Kafkaesque. Allen Tate, a leader of the New Criticism who later taught creative writing at Princeton, voiced a complaint in 1964 that has become perennial: "The academically certified Creative Writer goes out to teach Creative Writing, and produces other Creative Writers who are not writers, but who produce still other Creative Writers who are not writers."

4. Leon T. Dickinson, *An Historical Sketch of the Department of English, University of Missouri-Columbia* (Columbia: Department of English, University of Missouri–Columbia, 1986).

5. Associated Writing Programs Newsletter, "John Williams to Head AWP," 1974. The association supports writing programs in over 500 colleges and universities as well as 130 writers' conferences and centers.

6. Jean James, interview, June 20, 2015. Ms. James came to Denver as a student in 1959 and married Stuart James, an English instructor who became department chairman.

7. Gerald Chapman, interview, May 10, 2015.

8. Dan Wakefield, "John Williams, Plain Writer," *Ploughshares* 7, nos. 3–4 (Fall/Winter 1981): 19.

9. Program for "Buffalo Bill's Wild West and Congress of Rough Riders of the World," 1893, https://archive.org/details/buffalobillswild00buff. For several seasons of the show, Sitting Bull, the Lakota holy man who had a vision predicting victory over the soldiers, walked somberly into the middle of the ring as the finale to the mock battle. Unexpectedly, he became a figure of respect among whites. Indian agency police killed him in 1890, fearing that he would use his influence to further inspire the mystical Ghost Dance movement.

10. Gerald Chapman, interview, May 10, 2015.

11. Lewis Mumford, *The Golden Day: A Study in American Experience and Culture* (New York: Liveright, 1926), 79.

12. Williams, "The 'Western': Definition of the Myth," *The Nation*, November 18, 1961.

13. Ibid.

14. Ibid.

15. Revisionist western films include *3:10 to Yuma* (1957, 2007); *Jeremiah Johnson* (1972); *Dances with Wolves* (1990); and *Unforgiven* (1992).

16. Willard and George Rae Marsh to Williams, November 11, 1954, Williams Papers.

17. Theodore R. Cogswell to Art Landis, March 14, 1978, Arthur Landis Papers, Tamiment Library and Robert F. Wagner Labor Archives, New York.

18. This is the convention, renamed the Milford Science Fiction Convention in Kurt Vonnegut's *God Bless You, Mr. Rosewater*, at which Rosewater blurts out drunkenly to the assemblage, "I love you sons of bitches. You're all I read anymore."

19. George Rae Marsh to Williams, January 25, 1955, Williams Papers.

20. Eileen Bassing, *Where's Annie?* (New York: Random House, 1956), 54. This sketch of George Rae as a ditzy muse does injustice to her career as a writer and playwright. As George Rae Williams, she wrote five published plays: *Mind over Mumps: A One-Act Farce* (Franklin, OH: Eldridge Publishing Company, 1951); *Augie Evans: Private Eye: A One-Act Farce* (Franklin, OH: Eldridge Publishing Company, 1951); *Leave It to Laurie: A Comedy in One Act* (Minneapolis: Northwestern Press, 1952); *Keeping It in the Family: A Comedy in One Act* (Minneapolis: Northwestern Press, 1953); and *A Will and a Way: A Three Act Comedy*

(Franklin, OH: Eldridge Publishing Company, 1962). As George Rae Cogswell, she wrote (with her second husband, Ted) the short story "Contact Point" (1975), and they contributed a coauthored story to *Six Science Fiction Plays* (New York: Pocket Books, 1975). In 1979, as Georgia Cogswell, she published *Golden Obsession* (New York: Kensington, 1979). Tony Burton, "George Rae Marsh (Williams), aka Georgia Cogswell (1925–1997)," Sombrero Books, September 14, 2015, sombrerobooks.com/?p=2689.

21. Martha Hume, "John Williams: Artist of Diversity," *Dust* (Winter 1966): 24.

22. Willa Cather, *Not Under Forty* (New York: Alfred A. Knopf, 1936), 50.

23. Flora Merrill, "A Short Story Course Can Only Delay, It Cannot Kill an Artist, Says Willa Cather," reprinted in *Nebraska State Journal* (April 25 1925): 11.

24. Janet Lewis to Williams, September 3, 1958, Williams Papers.

25. John Williams, *Butcher's Crossing* (New York: New York Review Books, 2007), 117.

26. Ibid., 250.

27. Morton M. Hunt to Williams, August 28, 1958. Hunt authored popular nonfiction books about healthy approaches to relationships and living.

Chapter Ten. Fiasco

1. Linda Lear, *Rachel Carson: Witness for Nature* (New York: Houghton-Mifflin, 1997).

2. Betty Friedan, *Life So Far* (New York: Simon and Schuster, 2006), 138. Rodell was also Martin Luther King Jr.'s literary agent during the publication of his first book, *Stride Toward Freedom*.

3. Morton M. Hunt to Williams, August 28, 1958, Williams Papers.

4. Marie Rodell to Williams, October 20, 1958, Frances Collin Papers, private collection (Collin Papers hereafter). Collin became a partner in the agency after Rodell retired.

5. Williams to Rodell, September 1958, Williams Papers.

6. Willard Marsh to Williams, undated, circa 1958, Williams Papers.

7. Ibid.

8. Ibid.

9. Ibid.

10. Willard Marsh to Williams, August 8 1958, Williams Papers.

11. Williams to Rodell, October 31, 1958, Collin Papers.

12. During his career, until his retirement in 1965, Scott edited James Michener's *Tales of the South Pacific*; Elizabeth Stevenson's *The Crooked Corridor*; and Barbara Tuchman's *The Guns of August*, all winners of the Pulitzer Prize.

13. Rodell to Williams, November 31, 1958, Collin Papers.

14. Williams to Rodell, November 7, 1958, Williams Papers.

15. Editor at W. W. Norton to Joan Daves, December 9, 1958, Collin Papers; Harry Brague to Rodell, January 30, 1959, Collin Papers.

16. Pascal Covici to Rodell, March 2, 1959, Collin Papers.

17. Williams to Rodell, February 18, 1959, Collin Papers. Williams was a good judge of his own ability. The short story form wasn't his forté. His novel-length voice sounded unhurried, removed even, and a sense of immediacy is critical in short stories.

18. Cecil Scott to Williams, May 7, 1959, Williams Papers.

19. Cecil Scott to Rodell, May 12, 1959, Collin Papers; Rodell to Williams, May 13, 1959, Collin Papers; Rodell to Williams, May 13, 1959, Williams Papers. By reversing herself about Macmillan, she confused Williams. He would have been content with Little, Brown. She wrote, "It's a very good house, I think; at least, I have no serious quarrel with the quality of their list."

20. Williams to J. V. Cunningham, June 11, 1959, Williams Papers.

21. Ibid.

22. Williams to Rodell, June 18, 1959, Collin Papers. Nancy Williams said there was no point in asking John where he was going. "Out," he responded.

23. Rodell to Williams, July 20 and 22, 1959, Williams Papers; Williams to Rodell, August 2, 1959, Williams Papers; Rodell to Williams, August 6, 1959, Williams Papers; Williams to Rodell, August 11, 1959, Williams Papers. All of this correspondence was about choosing a title.

24. W. L. Rice to Williams, April 19, 1960, Williams Papers. Rice waited a few weeks after the article appeared to write to Williams.

25. Rodell to Williams, March 29, 1960, Williams Papers.

26. Nelson Nye, "Roundup," *New York Times*, April 4, 1960.

27. Williams to Rodell, March 31, 1960, Collin Papers.

28. Cecil Scott to Francis Bacon, *New York Times*, March 31, 1960, Collin Papers.

29. Cecil Scott to Williams, April 12, 1960, Williams Papers.

PART III. *STONER*

Chapter Eleven. "It Was That Kind of World"

1. George Rae Marsh to Williams, January 18, 1960, Williams Papers.

2. Willard Marsh to Williams, circa early 1960, Williams Papers.

3. Nash Ramblers resemble cars drawn by Robert Crumb in his 1960s underground comics. The model Butch and George Rae owned was the same as the one driven by Lois Lane in the *Superman* television series.

4. Robert B. Richardson, interview, December 12, 2013.

5. Ibid.

6. Fred Inglis, interview, September 5, 2014.

7. Robert B. Richardson, interview, December 12, 2013.

8. Gerald Chapman, interview, May 10, 2015.

9. Daniel Aaron, *The Americanist* (Ann Arbor: University of Michigan Press, 2007), 144–145. Aaron was the author of *Writers on the Left* (New York: Columbia University Press, 1992), his classic study of the radical American activists and novelists of the 1920s and '30s.

10. Jean James, interview, June 20, 2015; Gerald Chapman, interview, May 10, 2015.

11. Nancy Williams, interview, October 9, 2014.

12. Jonathan Williams, interview, October 9, 2014.

13. Jim Clark, letter, February 27, 2015.

14. Nancy Williams, interview, October 9, 2014.

15. "Yarb" is a vernacular mispronunciation of "herb"; "yarb-doctors" were folk medicine healers.

16. Nancy Williams, interview, October 9, 2014.

17. Nancy Williams, interview, October 10, 2014.

18. Williams to Marie Rodell, December 14, 1960, Collin Papers.

19. Alfred Kazin, *Writing Was Everything* (Cambridge, MA: Harvard University Press, 1995), 10.

20. Bin Ramke, interview, October 7, 2014. Ramke was a friend and former colleague of Williams at Denver. His collection of poems, *The Difference Between Night and Day* (1978), won the Yale Younger Poets Prize; *The Massacre of the Innocents* (1994) and *Wake* (1998) were awarded the Iowa Poetry Prize.

21. Cecil Scott to Williams, September 14, 1960, Williams Papers.

22. Williams to Rodell, September 26, 1960, Williams Papers.

23. William Peden to Williams, July 21, 1960, Williams Papers.

24. John Williams, "Prospectus: An Anthology of the Shorter Poems of the English Renaissance," undated, Williams Papers.

25. Pyke Johnson to Williams, May 7, 1962, Williams Papers.

26. Williams to Rodell, February 2, 1963, Collin Papers.

27. Williams to Rodell, June 13, 1963, Williams Papers.

28. Gerald Chapman to R. C. Hadley, March 8, 1963, Williams Papers; Chapman, interview, May 10, 2015.

29. Williams to Rodell, April 2, 1963, Collin Papers.

30. John Edward Williams, *English Renaissance Poetry: A Collection of Shorter Poems from Skelton to Jonson* (New York: New York Review of Books, 2016), xxiv.

31. Pyke Johnson to Williams, July 29, 1963. "I can't help remembering how you and I discussed Mr. Winters during our rambles around the Denver campus."

32. Rodell to Williams, June 11, 1963, Collin Papers.

33. Williams to Rodell, June 13, 1963, Williams Papers.

34. John Williams, "'63 Journal" (in his handwriting), beginning June 21, 1963, Williams Papers.

Chapter Twelve. "The Williams Affair"

1. Williams to Marie Rodell, July 19, 1963, Collin Papers.

2. Cecil Scott to Rodell, July 12, 1963, Collin Papers. Al Hart was later Ian Fleming's editor at Macmillan.

3. Williams to Rodell, July 19, 1963, Collin Papers.

4. Rodell to Alan Williams, July 17, 1963, Collin Papers.

NOTES TO PAGES 155–161 **273**

5. Yvor Winters to Doubleday Anchor Books, July 19, 1963, Yvor Winters and Janet Lewis Papers, Department of Special Collections and University Archives, Stanford University Libraries, Stanford, California (Winters/Lewis Papers hereafter).

6. Johnson's assistant was Helen D'Alessandro, who later became Harlan Ellison's editor.

7. Yvor Winters to Helen D'Alessandro, July 23, 1963, Winters/Lewis Papers.

8. Yvor Winters to Anne Freedgood, July 25, 1963, Winters/Lewis Papers.

9. Winters to "Dear Sirs," July 19, 1963, Winters/Lewis Papers.

10. Recounting the situation two years later to a professor friend, Winters was still angry:

And his students know [he cribs from my lectures]. One of my students brought me a copy of the Williams anthology shortly after it appeared, almost two years ago. . . . I wrote to Anchor and told them they had been taken. They checked. They finally made Williams write a page of acknowledgement, which I accepted, although it was pretty sleazy. . . . Williams teaches at the U. of Denver; Swallow tells me that he has been lecturing verbatim from my essays for a long time, without acknowledgment, and that his students know it. He . . . publish[es] poems here and there which are ghastly imitations and piracies, mostly of me. (Yvor Winters to Gerald Graff, December 21, 1965, email from David Myers, November 15, 2013 [Myers collection hereafter])

11. Heather McHugh, email, May 12, 2015.

12. Martha Hume, "John Williams: Artist of Diversity," *Dust* (Winter 1966): 16.

13. Williams to Yvor Winters, August 8, 1963, Williams Papers. While the draft acknowledgment was making its way to California, Winters told Johnson on the phone, "I don't wish any communication with Williams unless it is to plead for mercy. . . . I will wreck this book unless you provide proper acknowledgment." Pyke Johnson to Williams, August 9, 1963, Williams Papers.

14. Pyke Johnson to Williams, August 14, 1963, Williams Papers. "I don't see what else we can do now," Pyke wrote, "and I am beginning to doubt whether we will ever be able to satisfy him. However, let's try."

15. Pyke Johnson to Yvor Winters, September 25, 1963, Winters/Lewis Papers.

16. Pyke Johnson to Williams, August 26, 1963, Williams Papers.

17. Yvor Winters to Gerald Graff, December 21, 1965, Myers collection.

18. Nancy Williams, interview, October 10, 2014.

19. Hume, "Artist of Diversity: John Williams," 17.

20. Williams to Rodell, November 21, 1963, Collin Papers.

21. John Williams, "The Future of the Novel," in *Contemporary Literary Experience*, David Madden, ed. (Pasadena, CA: Salem Press, 1974).

22. "Our Literary Alumni," *University of Denver Magazine* (September 1964). Williams couldn't abide the solipsism of the Beat writers and poets.

23. Williams to Rodell, September 16, 1963, Williams Papers.

24. Jonathan Williams, interview, October 9, 2014.

25. Several years later, Dan Wakefield recalled visiting Williams at his home. He said, "Lonnie was really icy and you could feel the tension. Very unpleasant. Finally John said, 'Let's get out of here.' We drove over to the home of a woman who was lovely. And I then realized, 'This is his girlfriend!'"

26. Willard Marsh to Williams, October 15, 1963, Williams Papers.

Chapter Thirteen. *Stoner*

1. Marie Rodell to Williams, March 11, 1964, Williams Papers.

2. Pyke Johnson to Williams, March 26, 1964, Williams Papers.

3. Williams to Rodell, November 21, 1963, Collin Papers.

4. Robert L. Morris to Williams, March 16, 1964, Williams Papers.

5. The University of Denver received $50,000 to establish the quarterly, which seemed like an enormous amount at the time—the equivalent of four or five instructors' salaries. *The Denver Quarterly*, of which Williams was the first editor, celebrated its fiftieth year in 2015 and has long been considered a leading literary magazine. Williams discovered he enjoyed creating it from the ground up—contacting writers for submissions, planning the look of the publication, and editing the inaugural issue slated for early 1965. It suited him because he made the quarterly reflect his opinions. Concerned about the "insidious ways that middle class culture" was unduly influencing popular taste, he urged contributors to submit "good essays done on such things as the 'new avant-garde' novel, new-wave cinema, the New York Review of Books, the literary magazines (in general or in particular), modern art, virtually all of the performing arts, and so forth."

6. John Williams, *Stoner* (New York: New York Review Books, 2006), 181.

7. Joanne Greenberg, interview, October 8, 2014.

8. Bob Johnson to Williams, June 5, 1963, Williams Papers.

9. Nancy Williams, interview, October 10, 2014.

10. Amanda Vail, interview, September 9, 2014. Vail, later an acclaimed biographer, was the editor at Viking who later replaced Smith.

11. Gerald Howard, "Jacket Required: Thomas Pynchon's V," Graywolf Press December 12, 2013, https://www.graywolfpress.org/blogs/jacket-required -thomas-pynchons-v. Howard, who worked with Smith, later became an executive editor at Doubleday.

12. Amanda Vail, interview, September 9, 2014.

13. Undated response to questionnaire submitted by a student to Williams, Williams Papers; Williams to Jeremy Larner, April 22, 1966, Williams Papers; Irving Howe, "The Culture of Modernism," *Commentary*, November 1, 1967.

14. Responses to questionnaire, Williams Papers.

15. David Myers, interview, December 16, 2013. Myers, a student of Cunningham's, said, "I know for a fact that Cunningham was the model for Stoner. Stoner's marriage to Edith is Cunningham's wife, Barbara Gibbs" (the poet). Williams spoke often of *My Mortal Enemy* (1926), Willa Cather's portrait of a marriage that

disintegrated over many years. Regarding Cunningham's relationship with his daughter, Timothy Steele said, "He raised her, and, as far as I could judge, they had a good relationship." Email, July 3, 2015. Steele is the editor of *The Poems of J. V. Cunningham* (Athens, OH: Swallow Press, 1997).

16. Williams, *Stoner*, 3.

17. Ibid., 6.

18. Ibid., 13.

19. Ibid., 5.

20. The novelist Baine P. Kerr was a student of Williams': "He would explain brilliantly Flaubert's methods—light glinting off leaves, smells." Kerr, interview, October 8, 2014. Hilton Als, in *Joan Didion: The Center Will Not Hold*, Griffin Dunne, director (2017).

21. Williams, *Stoner*, 23.

22. Responses to questionnaire, Williams Papers.

23. Williams, *Stoner*, 16.

24. Ibid., 51.

25. Ibid., 53.

26. Ibid., 117, 119.

27. Ibid., 65–66, 85–86, 95.

28. Ibid., 91.

29. Ibid., 92.

30. Ibid., 99.

31. Williams Papers, Box 11.

32. Williams, *Stoner*, 111–112.

33. Ibid., 37.

34. Ibid., 131.

35. Ibid., 137.

36. Ibid., 148.

37. Ibid., 174.

38. Moral identity is by no means just a literary construct. How it defines who we are is clear from an incident in medical history. In 1848, an explosion launched a thirteen-pound tamping iron through the skull of a twenty-five-year-old railroad worker named Phineas Gage, taking a chunk of his brain with it. Formerly mild-mannered and responsible, Gage emerged from the accident impulsive and foul-tempered. His character changed so markedly that those who knew him said he was "no longer Gage." Recent experiments conducted in human behavior demonstrate that "moral traits—more than any other mental faculty—are considered the most essential part of identity, the self, and the soul." And so it is with creating strong characters in fiction who operate from a moral identity that is established through choice, behavior, and response to conflict. Nina Strohminger and Shaun Nichols, "The Essential Moral Self," *Cognition* 131 (2014): 159–171.

39. Sr. Joan Saalfeld, email, February 26, 2016.

40. Michelle Latiolais, interview, December 14, 2013.

41. Christof Wegelin, *"The Imagination of Loving: Henry James's Legacy to the*

Novel by Naomi Lebowitz" (review), *Southwest Review* (Spring 1966): 197–199. Winters used a similar method for putting teeth into his poetry. "Every poem of Winters'," wrote the critic Alvin B. Kernan, "is a dramatization of the conflict between the moral perceiver and a spiritually empty world which is nevertheless so solid and real that the confrontation cannot be avoided" (John Fraser, "Leavis, Winters and 'Tradition,'" in *Southern Review*, Vol. 7, No. 4, Autumn 1971, 963–985.

42. Williams, *Stoner*, 203.

43. Williams to Jeremy Larner, April 22, 1966, Williams Papers.

44. Williams to Fred Inglis, January 10, 1966, Williams Papers.

45. Williams wrote, "Grace is one of those mysterious people, as I suggest in the novel, whose moral nature is of such frailty and delicacy that it must be nurtured with infinite care. The fact is, the world does not nurture with such care, and such people are usually destroyed. The question of whether or not this should be so is irrelevant; it simply *is* so [his italics]. If all the world could have loved Grace as Stoner did, she might have been saved; but the world did not." Williams to Fred Inglis, January 10, 1966, Williams Papers.

46. Williams, *Stoner*, 215.

47. Marie Rodell, quoting Williams in a letter to Cork Smith, August 3, 1964, Collin Papers.

48. Dan Wakefield, interview, November 13, 2013. To Cork Smith, Williams wrote, "I can't seem to get away from clowns." Williams to Smith, May 21, 1965, Williams Papers. Stubby Kaye was not as incidental a performer as Williams thought. He was a Broadway musical actor whose role in *Guys and Dolls* was reprised in the 1955 film version with Marlon Brando and Frank Sinatra.

49. Cork Smith to Williams, October 19, 1965, Williams Papers.

50. Irving Howe, "The Virtues of Failure," *The New Republic*, February 22, 1966.

51. Robert Pawlowski, email, April 19, 2015. Jean James about the scene in the English Department—Williams seated alone in a chair all day—from her husband, Stuart, the department head, in interview on June 18, 2016.

PART IV. *AUGUSTUS*

Chapter Fourteen. Bread Loaf and "Up on the Hill"

1. Nancy Williams, interview, October 10, 2014; Robert B. Richardson, interview, December 12, 2013.

2. Dale W. Nelson, *The Imprint of Alan Swallow: Quality Publishing in the West* (Syracuse, NY: Syracuse University Press, 2010), 108; Frederick Manfred, "Alan Swallow, Poet and Publisher," *Chicago Tribune*, December 18, 1966.

3. Alan Swallow to Williams, March 13, 1963, Williams Papers.

4. Nancy Williams, interview, October 10, 2014.

5. Willard Marsh to Williams, June 2, 1965, Williams Papers.

6. William Sloane to Williams, July 25, 1965, Williams Papers.

7. Williams to Wayne Carver, May 13, 1966, Williams Papers. Williams taught

a writing seminar at Carleton College in Northfield, Minnesota, at Carver's invitation.

8. John Williams, "Looking for John Ciardi at Bread Loaf," in Vincente Clemente, ed., *John Ciardi: Measure of the Man* (Fayetteville: University of Arkansas Press, 1987).

9. David Haward Bain and Mary Smyth Duffy, eds., *Whose Woods These Are: A History of the Bread Loaf Writers' Conference, 1926–1992* (Hopewell, NJ: Ecco Press, 1993), 61.

10. Ibid., 95.

11. Williams, "Looking for John Ciardi at Bread Loaf."

12. Dan Wakefield, "John Williams, Plain Writer," *Ploughshares* 7, nos. 3–4 (Fall/Winter 1981): 9.

13. Williams, "Looking for John Ciardi at Bread Loaf."

14. Dan Wakefield, interview, November 13, 2013.

15. Jay Neugeboren, interview, September 3, 2014.

16. Manfred, "Alan Swallow, Poet and Publisher."

Chapter Fifteen. The Good Guys

1. Williams to Seymour Epstein, February 17, 1967, Williams Papers. He also expressed his satisfaction with Marie Rodell in this letter, despite the contretemps he'd suffered in connection with *Butcher's Crossing*, saying she was "the most honest and straightforward agent I have ever known, a real professional, and totally respected among the editors and publishers. . . . *If* she talks to you about your writing, she will talk to you about it as if she were your friend, not your critic, and she will have respect for you, what you do, and your own decisions."

2. Williams to Harry H. Taylor, Ball State University English Department, June 7, 1966, Williams Papers.

3. Williams to Marie Rodell, June 6, 1966, Collin Papers.

4. John Williams, "Statement of Project" to the Rockefeller Foundation, April 12, 1966, Williams Papers.

5. John Williams, *Augustus* (New York: New York Review Books, 2014), 22.

6. John Williams, "Statement of Project" to the Rockefeller Foundation, April 12, 1966, Williams Papers.

7. Gerald Chapman interview, July 12, 2015.

8. Fred Inglis, interview, June 22, 2014. Inglis was a visiting professor from England during the late 1960s and became one of Williams' closest friends.

9. Williams to Rodell, September 14, 1959, Collin Papers.

10. Jonathan Williams, interview, October 9, 2014. Katherine's career is similar to her father's. She received her PhD from the CUNY Graduate School, which specializes in seventeenth-century, romantic, and Victorian British literature. She received a bachelor's degree in French from the University of Denver. As of this writing, she is an associate professor and chair of the English Department at New York Institute of Technology.

11. Rodell to Williams, June 6, 1967, Williams Papers.

12. John Williams, "Fact in Fiction: Problems for the Historical Novelist," *Denver Quarterly* 7, no. 4 (Winter 1973): 1–12. Williams was influenced in his thinking by a paper given by Janet Lewis at the 1966 University of Denver summer writing workshop. It was titled "The Problems of the Historical Novelist." Winters/ Lewis Papers.

13. Williams, "Fact in Fiction," 5.

14. Ibid.

15. Richard Johnson, "Interview: John Williams," *Empire, Denver Post*, June 9, 1985. As Harold Rosenberg wrote, "A generation is fashion: but there is more to history than costume and jargon. The people of an era must either carry the burden of change assigned to their time or die under its weight in the wilderness." "Death in the Wilderness," in *The Tradition of the New* (New York: Da Capo Press, 1994), 255.

16. Williams, *Augustus*, 18–19. Williams' view of life seems almost Russian at times, especially Tolstoyan, as in *The Death of Ivan Ilyich*, where the hero seeks some kind of transcendence that will reveal his purpose before he dies.

17. Joanne Greenberg, interview, October 8, 2014; Sr. Joan Saalfeld, SNJM (Sisters of the Holy Names of Jesus and Mary), interview, October 7, 2014.

18. Williams, *Augustus*, 293.

19. Johnson, "Interview: John Williams."

20. Williams to Willard Marsh, October 11, 1967, Willard Marsh Papers, Special Collections, University of Iowa Libraries, Iowa City, Iowa.

21. Williams to John Ciardi, January 22, 1968, Williams Papers.

22. Ibid.

23. Williams to Dan Wakefield, March 8, 1968, Wakefield Papers, Lilly Library, Indiana University.

24. Jonathan Williams, interview, October 9, 2014.

25. Blake Bailey recounts the legend of Richard Yates, who, in a fit of mania abetted by alcohol, climbed up on the roof of Treman cottage and assumed the spread-arm position of Christ crucified. *A Tragic Honesty: The Life and Work of Richard Yates* (Reprint, New York: Picador, 2004). He had to be talked down.

According to David Haward Bain and Mary Smyth Duffy, eds., *Whose Woods These Are: A History of the Bread Loaf Writers' Conference, 1926–1992* (Hopewell, NJ: Ecco Press, 1993), the "torrid romance of 1963" was between the forty-one-year-old novelist John Hawkes and Joan Didion, who was twenty-eight years old at the time and had come to Bread Loaf on a fellowship. "'They were like tragic teenagers,' snickered one Bread Loafer. *'Two weeks left to live!'*—before they had to go back to their respective lives" (p. 89, italics in original). A staff member suffered a nervous breakdown during Ciardi's tenure as director. "God did not intend for all those writers to gather in one place at one time," he warned from his hospital bed (p. 101).

"We are all madmen, which we already knew," Wakefield wrote to Williams in 1969.

26. Bain and Duffy, eds., *Whose Woods These Are*, 98.

27. William Sloane, July 18, 1968, Williams Papers.

28. Bain and Duffy, eds., *Whose Woods These Are*, 102.

29. Ibid., 98.

30. Sally Boland, "Acceptance Speech for the 1997 Kalikow Award," June 29, 1997, Plymouth State University, Plymouth, New Hampshire.

31. Alan Prendergast, "Sixteen Years After His Death, Not-So-Famous Novelist John Williams Is Finding His Audience," *Westword*, November 3, 2010.

32. Williams to William Hamlin, Chairman, Division of Humanities, University of Missouri at St. Louis, December 7, 1965. Hamlin and his wife, Florence, accompanied John and Lonnie on the vacation to Mexico in 1954, which should be taken into account regarding the breezy tone of Williams' letter.

33. Gerald Chapman, interview, May 20, 2015.

34. Peggy McIntosh, "White Privilege and Male Privilege: A Personal Account of Coming to See Correspondences through Work in Women's Studies," Working Paper (Wellesley College, Center for Research on Women), 1988, no. 189.

35. Peggy McIntosh, interview, March 17, 2015.

36. Elizabeth Richardson, interview, May 18, 2015. The woman chosen over Richardson was American literary critic Helen Vendler.

37. David Milofsky, "John Williams Deserves to Be Read Today," *Denver Post*, July 1, 2007.

38. Peggy McIntosh, interview, March 17, 2015.

39. Brian Wooley, "An Interview with John Williams," *Denver Quarterly* (Winter 1986): 19.

40. Johnson, "Interview: John Williams."

41. Timothy Steele, email, March 1, 2015. Steele is a poet and author. He edited *The Poems of J. V. Cunningham* (Athens, OH: Swallow Press, 1997).

42. Wooley, "Interview with John Williams."

43. Dan Wakefield, "A Matter of Style," *Denver Quarterly* (Winter 1986): 139.

44. *Stoner* fans often wonder whether Bill Stoner and John Williams are similar. In their convictions about the academy, they are. Julian Barnes wrote, discussing Professor Stoner, "He becomes a teacher, 'which was simply a man to whom his book is true, to whom is given a dignity of art that has little to do with his foolishness or weakness or inadequacy as a man'. Towards the end of his life, when he has endured many disappointments, he thinks of academe as 'the only life that had not betrayed him'. And he understands also that there is a continual battle between the academy and the world: the academy must keep the world, and its values, out for as long as possible." Julian Barnes, "Stoner: The Must-Read Novel of 2013," *Guardian*, December 13, 2013.

45. John W. Aldridge, *After the Lost Generation: A Critical Study of the Writers of Two World Wars* (New York: McGraw-Hill, 1951), ix. Aldridge, who taught alongside Williams at Bread Loaf, was himself a World War II combat veteran who had been awarded the Bronze Star. Ciardi had been a machine-gunner on a bomber over Japanese islands.

46. Bain and Duffy, eds., *Whose Woods These Are*, 103.

47. Ibid., 106.

Chapter Sixteen. "Long Life to the Emperor!"

1. Nancy Williams, interview, October 4, 2014.

2. Ibid.

3. Williams to Marie Rodell, April 3, 1970, Collin Papers.

4. Nancy Williams said, "We never insisted that the kids like or see each other. We would have his kids over for dinner a couple times a month, maybe. John didn't discipline his very much—they weren't misbehaving children. But he expected that his and mine would do what he said. Never raised his voice or hand to them." Apparently, John was a sterner and angrier parent when he was married to Lonnie. His son, Jonathan, recalled being punished with a belt a few times. During the holidays, both sets of grandparents—Lonnie's and Nancy's parents—came to the house and socialized.

5. Few of his friends knew the story of how "John Jewell" had become "John Williams."

6. Carol DeBoer-Langworthy, interview, October 3, 2014; Joanne Greenberg, interview, October 8, 2014. None of the many people interviewed, however, believed that Williams' small stature had anything to do with his demeanor. In other words, he didn't try to compensate for it in any obvious way.

7. Robert Pawlowski, email, February 28, 2015.

8. Martha Hume, "John Williams: Artist of Diversity," *Dust* (Winter 1966): 18.

9. Ibid.

10. Williams' typed responses to a questionnaire, undated. Williams Papers.

11. Willard Marsh, "Forwarding Service," in *Beachhead in Bohemia* (Baton Rouge: Louisiana State University Press, 1969), 143.

12. George Rae Williams to Williams, October 25, 1970, Williams Papers.

13. Tony Burton, "Willard 'Butch' Marsh (1922–1970) and His Novel About 1950s Ajijic," Sombrero Books, October 26, 2015, sombrerobooks.com/?p=2682.

14. Miller Williams, September 1970, Williams Papers.

15. Dan Wakefield to Williams, October 1, 1970, Williams Papers.

16. Rodell to Dan Wakefield, October 9, 1970, Collin Papers.

17. Seymour Lawrence to Rodell, September 8, 1970, Collin Papers.

18. Rodell to Lawrence, September 11, 1970, Collin Papers.

19. Rodell to Dan Wakefield, January 27, 1971, Williams Papers.

20. Nancy Williams, interview, October 11, 2015.

21. Ibid.

22. Jerry Murray, "Memories of Mack and Jeannette" (April 2009), www .efanzines.com/EK/eI43/index.htm#murray.

23. David Haward Bain and Mary Smyth Duffy, eds., *Whose Woods These Are: A History of the Bread Loaf Writers' Conference, 1926–1992* (Hopewell, NJ: Ecco Press, 1993), 105.

24. Robert Pack, interview, December 13, 2013.

25. Dan Wakefield, interview, August 3, 2014.

26. Susan Cheever, *Drinking in America: Our Secret History* (New York: Twelve Books, 2015). Cheever, the daughter of the writer John Cheever, wrote, "By the time my father's generation of writers started publishing in the years after World War II, being a writer almost always meant being a drunk" (p. 165).

27. Dan Wakefield, interview, August 3, 2014. The Irish poet Dylan Thomas died of alcoholic poisoning in 1953, a few days after drinking eighteen whiskeys at the White Horse Tavern in Greenwich Village, a favorite waterhole for writers.

28. Michelle Latiolais, interview, December 14, 2013.

29. Williams to Corlies Smith, February 17, 1972, Collin Papers.

30. Smith to Williams, March 1, 1972, Williams Papers.

31. Smith to Williams, April 4, 1972, Collin Papers.

32. Williams to Rodell, June 14, 1972, Collin Papers.

33. Williams to Alan Williams, July 8, 1972, Williams Papers; Rodell to Williams, June 8, 1972, Collin Papers.

34. Dan Wakefield, "John Williams, Plain Writer," *Ploughshares* 7, nos. 3–4 (Fall/Winter 1981): 12.

35. Orville Prescott to Alan D. Williams, July 15, 1972, Williams Papers; J. V. Cunningham to Williams, October 8, 1972, Williams Papers.

PART V. THE SLEEP OF REASON

Chapter Seventeen. "How Can Such a Son of a Bitch Have Such Talent?"

1. Eric Pace, "2 Book Awards Split for the First Time," *New York Times*, April 11, 1973. The National Book Awards are given to one book (and author) annually in each of four major categories: fiction, nonfiction, poetry, and young people's literature. There are other categories, but they generally fall under the main four. Each panel considers hundreds of books.

2. John B. Breslin, "Year of the Big Book: NBA 1973," *Saturday Review*, May 5, 1973, 408–409.

3. Pace, "2 Book Awards Split."

4. Ibid.

5. William Cole, "The Last of the National Book Awards?" The Guest Word, *New York Times*, May 4, 1975, 288.

6. Joanne Greenberg, interview, October 8, 2014.

7. William Zaranka, interview, October 7, 2014. Over the years, Zaranka served as an English professor, program chair of the creative writing program, dean of liberal arts and sciences, and provost of the university. Philip Doe, who also taught in the department, said, "John winning the award wasn't universally greeted with joy" (Philip Doe, interview, October 8, 2014).

8. Carol DeBoer-Rolloff, later DeBoer-Langworthy, became a lecturer in literary biography at Brown. The editor, Martha Rupp, explained to Rolloff why she didn't want to write the article.

9. Carol DeBoer-Langworthy, interview, October 3, 2014.

10. Ibid.

11. Ibid. Williams' remarks about disliking experimental fiction are paraphrased from the interview he gave to Martha Hume for *Dust* in 1966, but he repeated the same sentiments consistently over the years.

12. John F. Baker, "Academe Dominates a Low-Key NBA," *Publishers Weekly*, April 30, 1973, 33.

13. John Barth to Williams, April 18, 1973, Williams Papers.

14. Williams to Durrett Wagner at Swallow Press, May 2, 1973. Williams summarizes Viking's reasons for rejecting his poems in his letter to Wagner. Four partners purchased Swallow Press and moved the business to Chicago following Alan's death in 1966. Suzanne Alaura Klinger, "The Swallow Press Archives: A Finding Guide with Background on the Swallow Press and Its Significance" (master's thesis, University of Chicago, 1984).

15. Robert O. Preyer, Brandeis University English Department chairman, to Williams, April 25, 1973, Williams Papers. The poet Adrienne Rich held the one-year appointment at the time.

16. Philip Doe, interview, October 8, 2014.

17. Robert Pawlowski, email, February 28, 2015.

18. Nancy Williams, interview, October 10, 2014.

19. Marie Rodell to Williams, May 25, 1973, Collin Papers.

20. Baine Kerr, interview, October 8, 2014.

21. Nancy Williams, interview, October 10, 2014.

22. Eric Gould, interview, March 19, 2015; Jonathan Williams, interview, October 9, 2014; David Milofsky, interview, December 13, 2013. Gould taught with Williams for many years. Milofsky was a professor in the department who knew John late in his career.

23. John Ciardi to Williams, June 18, 1971, Williams Papers; Joan Saalfeld, interview, October 7, 2014.

24. Michael White, interview, October 3, 2014.

25. Burton Raffel, interview, June 15, 2015; Miriam Epstein, interview, June 14, 2015.

26. William Zaranka, interview, March 2, 2015.

27. Joanne Greenberg, interview, October 8, 2014.

28. Fred Inglis, interview, June 22, 2014; Steve Heller, interview, March 2, 2015. Heller said the "Anything other than the obvious . . ." remark was directed at the novelist and short story writer Gordon Weaver, who used to tell the story as a joke on himself.

29. Interviews with Williams' former students: Joan Saalfeld, October 7, 2014; Angela Ball, June 14, 2015; Nancy Esterlin, June 27, 2015; Heather McHugh, by email, May 12, 2015; Philip Doe, October 8, 2014; Michelle Latiolais, December 14, 2013; Michael White, October 3, 2014; and William Zaranka, October 7, 2014.

30. Baine Kerr, interview, October 8, 2014.

31. William Zaranka, interview, October 7, 2014.

32. Joseph Nigg, interview, December 12, 2013. Nigg later became the author of popular books for young people about mythical creatures and lost places.

Chapter Eighteen. In Extremis

1. John, almost sixty, had mellowed toward children. The grandchildren were allowed free rein. Jonathan and his wife came to pick up their son, and the little boy "had trashed the apartment," Jonathan later said. "Oh, we're so sorry, we'll pick it up!," he told his father. But Nancy and John replied, "No. Don't bother. We had a wonderful time watching him."

2. Williams to Fred Inglis, Fall 1980, Williams Papers.

3. Nancy Williams to Peggy and Burton Feldman, June 5, 1979, Burton Feldman Papers, University of Denver.

4. Williams to Fred Inglis, Fall 1980, Williams Papers.

5. Ibid.

6. William Cifelli, *John Ciardi: A Biography* (Fayetteville: University of Arkansas Press, 1997), 416. Nancy Williams, interview, October 9, 2014. Windsor Lane, near the top of Solares Hill, the highest point in Key West, is now called the Writer's Compound. It's a private neighborhood of restored shanties, cottages, and bungalows connected by brick walkways and lush gardens. Former residents include Richard Wilbur, John Hersey, Ralph Ellison, and John Ciardi.

7. Dan Wakefield, "John Williams: Plain Writer," *Ploughshares* 7, nos. 3–4 (Fall/Winter 1981).

8. Baine Kerr, interview, December 16, 2013; Cindy Carlisle, interview, December 18, 2013.

9. Baine Kerr, interview, October 8, 2014; Cindy Carlisle, interview, December 18, 2013. Said Inglis, "I've seen him get very aggressively tight once or twice with Nancy and she just wept copiously when it happened. And that was very difficult and embarrassing, about what to do and where to look" (Fred Inglis, interview, September 5, 2014).

10. Williams to Burton Feldman, a colleague at the University of Denver, October 24, 1979, Burton Feldman Papers, University of Denver (Feldman Papers hereafter); William Zaranka, interview, October 7, 2014.

11. His son, Jonathan, believed Williams had an addictive personality: he went at writing, drinking, and smoking with the same ferocious intensity.

12. Nancy Williams, interview, October 9, 2014.

13. Williams to Fred Inglis, Fall 1980, Williams Papers.

14. Dan Wakefield, email, April 11, 2016.

15. Roxie Munro, interview, October 2, 2014.

16. Steve Heller, interview, March 2, 2015. Heller, a first-timer and still in college—technically, too young be there—scheduled himself to read one of his stories to an audience of Pulitzer and National Book Award winners. Touchingly, "it was well-received." David Nemec, interview, February 23, 2015.

17. Jim Clark, letter, February 27, 2015.

18. Bin Ramke, interview, October 7, 2014.

19. John Ciardi to Margaret Mills, National Institute of Arts and Letters, February 20, 1985, Williams Papers.

20. Douglas Woolf, *Hypocritic Days and Other Tales*, edited by Sandra Braman (Santa Barbara, CA: Black Sparrow Press, 1993), 393–399.

21. Gale Woolf, interview, June 7, 2015. Yvonne's partner beginning in 1980 was an Irish American sportsman in Washington State. The relationship that lasted twenty-five years, until his death in 2005.

22. Alan Prendergast, "Sixteen Years After His Death, Not-So-Famous Novelist John Williams Is Finding His Audience," *Westword*, November 3, 2010; Nancy Williams, interview, October 9, 2014.

23. Williams to Fred Inglis, Fall 1980, Williams Papers; Arlo Haskell, "A Day at the Beach, 1984," Key West Literary Seminar, April 29, 2008 (updated September 26, 2016), www.kwls.org/key-wests-life-of-letters/a_day_at_the_beach _in_key_west.

24. Nancy Williams, interview, October 10, 2014.

25. Nancy Williams to Margaret and Burton Feldman, April 29, 1986, Feldman Papers.

26. Williams to Edward Loomis (handwritten draft, circa 1988), Williams Papers. Loomis was a professor of English at the University of California at Santa Barbara.

27. Williams to the Feldmans, April 29, 1986, Feldman Papers; Nancy Williams, interview, October 10, 2014.

28. It must be said that regardless of the friction that existed between Williams and some of the others, the symposium was made possible through grants from the Colorado Endowment for the Humanities; the support of the University of Denver English Department of the Faculty of Arts and Humanities; and the *Denver Quarterly*, which devoted its winter 1986 issue entirely to him and his work, including the first John Williams bibliography. It was an effort that took almost a year to plan.

29. Cifelli, *John Ciardi*, 476.

30. Blake Bailey, *A Tragic Honesty: The Life and Work of Richard Yates* (Reprint, New York: Picador, 2004), 558.

31. Jim Clark, email, February 27, 2015.

32. Clark wrote, in the email of February 27, 2015:

Sadly, Mr. Yates fell completely off the wagon in Denver. He made a bit of a spectacle of himself at the main program at the Denver Public Library, and when I stopped by the hotel to pick him up to take him to the airport, he was nowhere to be found. I asked the desk clerk where I could find Mr. Yates, the writer, as I was supposed to take him to the airport. "You need to speak to the Manager," she replied. I learned that Mr. Yates had collapsed in the lobby a little earlier, suffering delusions and seizures. He ended up staying in the hospital in Denver for about two weeks, drying out.

33. Prendergast, "Sixteen Years After His Death."

34. Audio recording made at the Denver Public Library, March 29, 1986, included in Williams Papers.

35. Nancy Williams, interview, October 10, 2014.

36. *Ozarks at Large: Arkansas Voices*, interview with John Williams broadcast on National Public Radio station KUAF, 1993.

37. George Rae to Williams, March 3, 1987, Williams Papers.

38. The collage of anecdotes comes from a letter from George Rae Marsh to the Williamses, March 21, 1987, Williams Papers; Williams to Frances Collin, May 10, 1989, Collin Papers; Nancy, John, and Kathy Williams to Margaret and Burton Feldman, January 29, 1990, Feldman Papers; Nancy Williams to the Feldmans (the dream), November 14, 1990, Feldman Papers; interviews with Nancy Williams, October 8–10, 2014; and Prendergast, "Sixteen Years After His Death."

Epilogue. John Williams Redux

1. Edwin Frank, interview, October 1, 2015.

2. Colum McCann, "Colum McCann's Top 10 Novels on Poets," *Guardian*, October 2, 2006.

3. Astrid Gagneur, Interview with Anna Gavalda, Myboox, September 19, 2011.

4. Ibid.

5. Oscar Van Gelderen, interview, October 1, 2015.

6. Ibid.

7. Edwin Frank, interview, October 1, 2015; Cristina Marino, interview, October 2, 2015.

8. Edwin Frank, interview, October 1, 2015.

9. John Williams, *Stoner* (New York: New York Review Books, 2006), 277–278.

Works Consulted

Aaron, Daniel. *The Americanist*. Ann Arbor: University of Michigan Press, 2007.

Aldridge, John W. *After the Lost Generation: A Critical Study of the Writers of Two World Wars*. New York: McGraw-Hill, 1951.

Alvarez, A. "Yvor Winters." In *Beyond All This Fiddle: Essays, 1955–1967*. New York: Random House, 1968. Originally published in *The New Statesman*, 1960.

Bailey, Blake. *A Tragic Honesty: The Life and Work of Richard Yates*. Reprint, New York: Picador, 2004.

Bain, David Haward, and Mary Smyth Duffy, eds. *Whose Woods These Are: A History of the Bread Loaf Writers' Conference, 1926–1992*. Hopewell, NJ: Ecco Press, 1993.

Bassing, Eileen. *Where's Annie?* New York: Random House, 1956.

Cheever, Susan. *Drinking in America: Our Secret History*. New York: Twelve Books, 2015.

Cifelli, William. *John Ciardi: A Biography*. Fayetteville: University of Arkansas Press, 1997.

Clemente, Vincente, ed. *John Ciardi: Measure of the Man*. Fayetteville: University of Arkansas Press, 1987.

Creeley, Robert. "Reading Douglas Woolf's Ya! & John-Juan." Dalkey Archive Press website, www.dalkeyarchive.com/reading-douglas-woolfs-ya-john-juan.

Cunningham, J. V. *The Collected Essays of J. V. Cunningham*. Chicago: Swallow Press, 1976.

———."For My Contemporaries." In *The Exclusions of a Rhyme: Poems and Epigrams*. Athens: Ohio University Press / Swallow Press, 1960.

Dickinson, Leon T. *An Historical Sketch of the Department of English, University of Missouri–Columbia*. Columbia: Department of English, University of Missouri, 1986.

Ellman, Richard. "Publisher for Poets." *Saturday Review*, July 22, 1961.

Epstein, Joseph. "Father of History: Herodotus and the Human Dimension in the Past." *Weekly Standard*, October 20, 2014.

Fike, Francis. "Cold Grace: Christian Faith and Stoicism in the Poetry of J. V. Cunningham." In *Renascence: Essays on Values in Literature*. Milwaukee, WI: Marquette University Press, 2007.

Fraser, John. "Leavis, Winters and 'Tradition.'" *Southern Review* (Autumn 1971).

Gruber, Frank. *Zane Grey: A Biography*. New York: Amereon, 1969.

Howard, Gerald. "Jackets Required: Thomas Pynchon's V." Graywolf Press, December 12, 2013, https://www.graywolfpress.org/blogs/jacket-required -thomas-pynchons-v.

———. "Pynchon from A to V: Gerald Howard on *Gravity's Rainbow*." *Bookforum* (Summer 2005), www.bookforum.com/archive/sum_05/pynchon.html.

Hume, Martha. "Artist of Diversity: John Williams." *Dust* (Winter 1966).

Hyman, Stanley Edgar. "Yvor Winters and Evaluation in Criticism." In *The Armed Vision: A Study in the Methods of Modern Literary Criticism*. New York: Alfred A. Knopf, 1955.

Johnson, Richard. "Interview: John Williams." *Empire, Denver Post*, June 9, 1985.

Klinger, Suzanne Alaura. "The Swallow Press Archives: A Finding Guide with Background on the Swallow Press and Its Significance." Master's thesis, University of Chicago, 1984.

Lear, Linda. *Rachel Carson: Witness for Nature*. New York: Houghton-Mifflin, 1997.

Merrill, Flora. "A Short Story Course Can Only Delay, It Cannot Kill an Artist, Says Willa Cather." Reprinted in *Nebraska State Journal*, April 25, 1925.

Milofsky, David. "John Williams Deserves to Be Read Today." *Denver Post*, July 1, 2007.

Mumford, Lewis. *The Golden Day: A Study in American Experience and Culture*. New York: Liverwright, 1926. Online.

Nelson, Dale W. *The Imprint of Alan Swallow: Quality Publishing in the West*. Syracuse, NY: Syracuse University Press, 2010.

Nye, Nelson. "Roundup." *New York Times*, April 4, 1960.

"Our Literary Alumni." *University of Denver Magazine* (September 1964).

Poetry, LII excerpted in Paul. J. Alpers, ed. *Elizabethan Poetry: Modern Essays in Criticism* (Oxford: Oxford University Press, 1967).

Rexroth, Kenneth. *American Poetry in the Twentieth Century*. New York: Seabury Press, 1971.

Seidel, Frederick. "Robert Lowell, The Art of Poetry No. 3." *Paris Review* (Winter- Spring 1961).

Simmons, R. Laurie, and Thomas H. Simmons. "Historic Resources of Downtown Denver." National Register of Historic Places, Multiple Property Documentation Form. US Department of the Interior, National Park Service.

Source Book of Information on Tabard Inn. Columbia, MO: Press of the Crippled Turtle, 1951.

Stanford, Donald E. "Yvor Winters, 1900–1968," *Southern Review* (Summer 1968).

Stone, Edward. *A Certain Morbidness: A View of American Literature.* Carbondale: Southern Illinois University Press, 1969.

Strohminger, Nina, and Shaun Nichols, "The Essential Moral Self." *Cognition* 131 (2014).

Swallow, Alan. *An Editor's Essays of Two Decades.* Seattle: Experiment Press, 1962.

Wakefield, Dan. "John Williams, Plain Writer." *Ploughshares* 7, nos. 3–4 (Fall/ Winter 1981).

White, Theodore. "The Hump: The Historic Airway to China Was Created by US Heroes." *Life*, September 11, 1944.

Williams, John. "Fact in Fiction: Problems for the Historical Novelist." *Denver Quarterly* 7, no. 4 (Winter 1973).

——. "In the American Grain: The Importance of William Carlos Williams." *Colorado Review* (Fall 1997).

——. "The 'Western': Definition of the Myth." *The Nation*, November 18, 1961.

Yvor Winters. "Individual Poets and Modes of Poetry: The 16th Century Lyric in England. A Critical and Historical Reinterpretation." In Paul J. Alpers, ed., *Elizabethan Poetry: Modern Essays in Criticism.* New York: Oxford University Press, 1967. Originally published in *Poetry Magazine* 53 (1939).

Wooley, Brian. "An Interview with John Williams." *Denver Quarterly* (Winter 1986).

Woolf, Douglas. *Hypocritic Days and Other Tales.* Edited by Sandra Braman. Santa Barbara, CA: Black Sparrow Press, 1993.

Yezzi, David. "The Seriousness of Yvor Winters." *New Criterion* (June 1997).

A John Williams Bibliography

NOVELS

Nothing But the Night. Denver: Swallow Press, 1948; Fayetteville: University of
  Arkansas Press, 1990; London: Vintage, 2018. Published in translation in
  Dutch (Lebowski), German (DTV), and Italian (Fazi), and forthcoming in
  Catalan from Ediciones 62.
Butcher's Crossing. New York: Macmillan, 1960; London: Victor Gollancz, 1960;
  London: Odham's Press, 1961; New York: Dolphin Books, 1962; London:
  Panther Books, 1963; Boston: Gregg Press, 1978; Fayetteville: University of
  Arkansas Press, 1987; New York: New York Review Books, 2007; London:
  Vintage, December 2013. Published in translation in Bulgarian (Labyrinth),
  Chinese (Horizon Media), Danish (Lindhardt & Ringhof), Dutch (Lebowski),
  Finnish (Bazar), French (Piranha), German (DTV), Hebrew (Yedioth),
  Italian (Fazi), Korean (Opus), Norwegian (CappelenDamm), Portuguese
  (Brazil) (Absurdaventura), Serbian (Plato), Spanish (Lumen/Random House
  Mondadori), Swedish (Natur & Kultur), and Turkish (Koton Kitap).
Stoner. New York: Viking, 1965; New York: Lancer Books, 1966; New York: Pocket
  Books, 1972; London: Allen Lane, 1973; Fayetteville: University of Arkansas
  Press, 1987; New York: New York Review Books, 2006; New York: New York
  Review Books, 2015 (50th Anniversary Hardcover edition); London: Vintage
  Classics, 2012 (American Greats series). Published in translation in Albanian
  (IDK), Arabic (Dar Athar), Bulgarian (Labyrinth), Catalan (Ediciones 62),
  Chinese (CM Publishing, Horizon Media), Croatian (Fraktura), Czech (Kniha
  Zlin), Danish (Lindhardt and Ringhof), Dutch (Lebowski, best seller), Finnish

(Bazar), German (DTV, best seller on the *Der Spiegel* list for over a year), Greek (Gutenberg), Hebrew (Yedioth), Icelandic (Draumsyn), Italian (Fazi), Korean (Random House), Latvian (Zvaigzne ABC), Lithuanian (Baltos Lankos), Norwegian (Cappelen Damm), Polish (Sonia Draga), Portuguese (Brazil) (Editora Absurdaventura), Portuguese (Portugal) (Dom Quixote), Romanian (Polirom), Russian (Astrel), Slovak (Artforum), Slovene (Mladinska), Spanish (Argentina) (Fiordo Editorial via Ediciones Baile del Sol), Spanish (Spain) (Ediciones Baile del Sol), Swedish (Natur & Kultur), Turkish (Koton Kitap), and Ukrainian (Ranok).

Augustus. New York: Viking, 1972; London: Allen Lane, 1973; New York: Dell Press, 1973; New York: Penguin Books, 1979; Fayetteville: University of Arkansas Press, 1993; New York: New York Review Books, 2014; London: Vintage, 2013. Published in translation in Bulgarian (Labyrinth), Catalan (Ediciones 62), Chinese (Horizon and Chi Ming), Croatian (Fraktura), Danish (Lindhardt and Ringhof), Finnish (Bazar), French (Piranha), German (DTV), Greek (Dardanos), Hebrew (Yedioth), Italian (Fazi, Frasinelli, Sperling and Kupfer), Japanese (Sakuhin Sha), Korean (GU-Fic), Latin (Lebowski), Norwegian (CappelenDamm), Portuguese (Brazil) (Editora Radio Londres), Spanish (Ediciones Pamies), Swedish (Natur & Kultur), and Ukrainian (Ranok).

BOOKS OF POETRY

The Broken Landscape. Denver: Swallow Press, 1949.
The Necessary Lie. Denver: Verb Publications, 1965.

FICTION APPEARING IN PERIODICALS

"Short Story 2." *Story* 33, no. 130 (Spring 1960).
"The Sleep of Reason." *Ploughshares* 7, nos. 3–4 (October 1981): 23–60.

POETRY APPEARING IN PERIODICALS

"Love Poem." *New Mexico Quarterly* 16, no. 3 (Autumn 1946): 359.
"Time, Place and Circumstance." *Interim* 2, nos. 3–4 (1946): 34–37.
"Variation on a Theme by Donne." *Yale Poetry Review* 5 (Autumn 1946): 12.
"The Waiting Man." *Matrix* 9, nos. 3–4 (Winter 1946–1947), 37.
"The Harbinger of Sunstroke." *Experiment* 3, no. 1 (Spring 1947): 191–192.
"Statement." *University of Kansas City Review* 13, no. 4 (Summer 1947): 327.
"Weapon." *Experiment* 3, no. 1 (Spring 1947): 192.
"The Braggart Mind." *Experiment* 4, no. 2 (1948): 148.
"The Fishes." *Berkeley: A Journal of Modern Culture* 5 (1948): 5.
"The Forest Is All Blown." *The Tiger's Eye: On Arts and Letters* 5 (October 1948): 16.
"The Land." *Experiment* 4, no. 1 (1948): 239.
"Ode." *Arizona Quarterly* 4, no. 2 (1948): 148.

"The Pocketing Season." *Experiment* 4, no. 1 (1948): 240.

"Casualty." *Poetry Book Magazine* 13 (1949): 5.

"The Wall." *Poetry* 74, no. 6 (Summer 1949): 319.

"The Dancer." *Poetry Book Magazine* 4, no. 4 (Summer 1952): 10.

"Song of the Arctic Explorers." *Talisman* 2 (1952): 44.

"Act Five, Scene Two." *Prairie Schooner* 1 (1953): 17.

"The Affliction." *Prairie Schooner* 1 (1953): 20.

"The Demons." *Talisman* 4 (Winter 1953): 22–27.

"The Lovers." *Western Review* 17, no. 2 (Winter 1953): 101–102.

"The Steps of Love." *Prairie Schooner* 1 (1953): 18.

"Voyage." *Prairie Schooner* 1 (1953): 19.

"On the Key to My Bookcase." *Western Review* 18, no. 3 (Spring 1954): 198.

"A Summer Day." *Between Worlds* 1, no. 1 (Summer 1960): 46–47.

"The Name of Death." *Colorado Quarterly* 9 (Winter 1961): 224.

"Passage." *Colorado Quarterly* 9 (Winter 1961): 225.

"The Sparrow." *Western Humanities Review* 15 (Winter 1961): 32.

"A Return." *Voices: A Journal of Poetry* 178 (May–August 1962): 26.

"Cold Coffee." *South Dakota Review* 1, no. 1 (December 1963): 35.

"The Progress of the Soul." *South Dakota Review* 1, no. 1 (December 1963): 33–34.

"Seascape with Figure." *Verb: A Broadsheet in the Flat Style* 2, nos. 3–4
  (November–December 1964): 6–7.

"A Winter Garden." *South Dakota Review* 1, no. 1 (December 1963): 36.

"Letters from Rome." *Poetry Northwest* 7, no. 3 (Autumn 1966): 27–28.

"At Bernini's Fountains." *Southern Review* 3, no. 2 (Spring 1967): 406.

"Letter to a Friend." *Denver Quarterly* 3, no. 2 (Summer 1968): 74–78.

POEMS APPEARING IN ANTHOLOGIES

"Six Poems: The Dead; The Meaning of Violence; For My Students, Returning
  to College; A History; The Skaters; The Leaf." In *New Poems by American
  Poets #2*, ed. Rolfe Humphries. New York: Ballantine Books, 1957, 169–172.

"An Airman, Falling, Addresses His Sweetheart." In *The Sound of Wings*, ed.
  Joseph B. Roberts and Paul L. Brand. New York: Henry Holt, 1957.

"Nightmare." In *One of the Family*, ed. Fred Inglis. London: Ginn, 1971.

"Four Poems: Letter from the Atlantic; At the Theater; The Skaters; Cold Coffee."
  In *Contemporary Poetry in America*, ed. Miller Williams. New York: Random
  House, 1972, 64–65.

"The Skaters." In *Hosannah the Home Run!*, ed. Alice Fleming. Boston: Little,
  Brown, 1972.

"Letter from Oxford." In *The Scene*, ed. Fred Inglis. Cambridge: Cambridge
  University Press, 1972.

"The Skaters." In *Direction*, ed. Theodore Clymer, Leo P. Ruth, Peter Evanechko,
  and Julia Higgs. New York: Random House, 1974.

"On Reading Aloud My Early Poems." In *Western Wind: An Introduction to Poetry*,
  ed. John Frederick Nims. New York: Random House, 1974, 359.

"Two Poems." In *Poets of Western America*, ed. Clinton F. Larson and William Stafford. Provo: Brigham Young University Press, 1975.

EDITORIAL

Twentieth Century Literature: A Scholarly and Critical Journal, 1954–1956.
University of Denver Quarterly: A Journal of Modern Culture, 1966–1970.
English Renaissance Poetry. Garden City: Doubleday, 1963. New York: Anchor Books, 1973. New York: W. W. Norton, 1974.

ESSAYS APPEARING IN PERIODICALS

"J. V. Cunningham: The Major and the Minor." *Arizona Quarterly* 6, no. 2 (Summer 1950): 132–146.
"The 'Western': Definition of Myth." *The Nation* 43, no. 17 (November 18, 1961): 401–406.
"Concerning Little Magazines: Something Like a Symposium" (editorial statement). *Carleton Miscellany* 7, no. 2 (Spring 1966): 1974–1976.
"Editorial Statement." *Denver Quarterly* 1, no. 1 (Spring 1966).
"Henry Miller: The Success of Failure." *Virginia Quarterly Review* 44, no. 2 (Spring 1968): 225–245. (Also anthologized twice; see below.)
"Fact in Fiction: Problems for the Historical Novelist." *Denver Quarterly* 7, no. 4 (Winter 1973): 13–36.
"Fulke Greville: The World and God." *Denver Quarterly* (Summer 1975).

ESSAYS APPEARING IN ANTHOLOGIES

"The Western: Definition of the Myth." In *The Popular Arts: A Critical Reader*, ed. Irving Deer and Harriet A. Deer. New York: Charles Scribner's Sons, 1967.
"Henry Miller: The Success of Failure." In *American Literary Anthology #3*, ed. George Plimpton and Peter Ardery. New York: Viking Press, 1970. Reprinted in *Contemporary Literary Criticism*, ed. Carolyn Riley. Detroit: Gale Research Co., 1973.
"The Future of the Novel." In *Contemporary Literary Experience*, ed. David Madden. Pasadena, CA: Salem Press, 1974.

WORKS ABOUT JOHN WILLIAMS
Selected Reviews

Nothing But the Night

Sewanee Review 57, no. 1 (Winter 1949): 127–135 (F. Cudworth Flint).
Sewanee Review 56, no. 4 (Autumn 1964): 671–684 (Robert B. Heilman).

Butcher's Crossing

Bignardi, Irene. "Che cosa si impara leggendo un western." *La Repubblica*, March 20, 2013.

Blackburn, Virginia. "How the West Was Slaughtered: *Butcher's Crossing* Review." *The Express*, January 5, 2014.

Brenner, Jack. "Butcher's Crossing: The Husks and Shells of Exploitation." *Western American Literature* 8, no. 4 (Winter 1973).

Foulds, Alan. "Butcher's Crossing Is Not at All Like Stoner—But Just as Superbly Written." *The Spectator* (January 18, 2014).

Heilman, Robert B. "The Western Theme: Exploiters and Explorers." *Partisan Review* (March 1961).

Kemp, Peter. "Shock and Gore: *Butcher's Crossing*." *Sunday Times*, January 5, 2014.

Lezard, Nicholas. "Is John Williams' Wild West Novel Better Than the Hit *Stoner*?" *Guardian*, January 7, 2014.

Malvaldi, Marco. "Verso la grande frontiera: Un viaggio di formazione che anticipa Cormac McCarthy." *La Stampa*, March 23, 2013.

Partisan Review 28, no. 2 (March-April 1961): 286–297 (Robert B. Heilman).

Van Essen, Rob. "Moby Dick in the Wild Western." *Boeken* (November 22, 2013).

Stoner

Akbar, Arifa. "The Quiet Professor Who Finally Became a Bestseller." *The Independent*, June 4, 2013.

Almond, Steve. "Lost & Found: Stoner." *Tin House* (June 2009).

Barnes, Julian. "Stoner: The Must-Read Novel of 2013." *Guardian*, December 13, 2013.

Best Sellers 32 (May 1, 1972): 71.

Bigsby, Christopher. "Stoner: A Classic Tale of a 'Small' Academic Life." *Times Higher Education UK* (September 12, 2013).

Bland, Archie. "John Williams' Stoner Has Achieved Late Popular Acclaim But Is the Dead Author's Second Novel Another Forgotten Work of Brilliance?" *The Independent*, December 6, 2013.

Booklist 61 (June 1, 1965): 953.

Books & Bookmen 18 (July 1973): 134.

Chevilley, Philippe. "Romain Américain: *Stoner* de John Williams." *Les Echos*, September 5, 2011.

Cripps, Ed. "*Stoner*: The Literary Rediscovery of the Year." *Huffington Post*, July 28, 2013.

Daily Mail (London). "Stone Me, It's a Truly Great Read." August 17, 2013.

Deats, Sara Munson, and Lagretta Tallent Lenker, eds. *Aging and Identity: A Humanities Perspective*. Westport, CT: Praeger, 1999.

Dickstein, Morris. "The Inner Lives of Men." *New York Times Book Review*, June 17, 2007.

"Gavalda, son coup de *Stoner.*" *Elle* (September 9, 2011).

Guardian Weekly 108 (May 5, 1973): 25.

Guerrera, Antonello. "Stoner Mania." *La Repubblica,* August 8, 2013.

Habash, Gabe. "A 'Perfect' American Novel Strikes Gold Overseas." *Publishers Weekly* (April 27, 2013).

Heathcock, Alan. "Three Books to Take to a Fistfight." NPR, April 28, 2011.

Kirkus Reviews 33 (March 1, 1965): 264.

Kreider, Tim. "The Greatest American Novel You've Never Heard Of." *The New Yorker,* "Page-Turner" (blog), October 21, 2013.

Library Journal 90 (April 1, 1965): 1749.

Listener 89 (June 21, 1973): 840.

McCann, Colum. "Book of a Lifetime: *Stoner* by John Williams." *The Independent,* June 15, 2013.

———. "Stoner by John Williams." *The Independent,* June 15, 2013.

Montague, Sarah. "Ian McEwan: Stoner di Williams tocca la verita: Come la grande letteratura." *La Repubblica,* August 10, 2013.

Neuhoff, Eric. "Un homme ordinaire qui ne ressemble a personne." *Le Figaro* (September 1, 2011).

New Yorker 41 (June 12, 1965): 155.

Nivet, Jean-François. "Révélation Américaine: *Stoner* de John Williams, traduit de l'Anglais par Anna Gavalda." *L'Humanité Supplement* (January 5, 2012).

Nucci, Matteo. "Da *Stoner* a *Augusto*, la vita anonima di un genio letterario perduto e ritrovato." *Il Venerdi* (November 1, 2013).

Observer, April 22, 1973, 33.

Snow, C. P. "Good Man and Foes." *Financial Times,* May 24, 1973.

Southern Review (Winter 1967): 186–196.

Stark, John. "The Novels of John Williams." *Hollins Critic* 17, no. 4 (1980): 12–13.

Sunday Mirror (London). "Books," August 4, 2013.

Sutherland, John. "Literature Needs More Lazarus Miracles Like *Stoner.*" *The Telegraph,* July 13, 2103.

Times Literary Supplement, May 18, 1973, 545.

Virginia Quarterly Review 41 (Autumn 1965): cxx.

Augustus

America 128 (May 5, 1973): 408.

Book World 6 (October 29, 1972): 15.

Economist Survey 249 (November 10, 1973): 16.

Kirkus Reviews 40 (August 15, 1972): 975.

Library Journal 97 (September 1, 1972): 2756.

Listener 90 (October 4, 1973): 459.

National Observer 11 (December 9, 1972): 25.

New Yorker 48 (November 25, 1972): 199.

New York Times 122 (October 28, 172): 29.

New York Times Book Review (April 8, 1973): 30 (John Leo).
New York Times Book Review (August 26, 1979): 31.
Publishers Weekly 202 (September 18, 1972): 71.
Saturday Review 1 (January 13, 1973): 66.
Time 100 (December 18, 1972): 107.
Times Literary Supplement (January 11, 1974): 25.
Wall Street Journal 181 (January 24, 1973): 18.

The Broken Landscape

Arizona Quarterly 6, no. 3 (1950): 269.
Partisan Review 17, no. 2 (February 1950): [189]–193 (Randall Jarrell).

Necessary Lie

Southern Review (Winter 1967): 197–228 (G. Lensing).

Critical Studies

Brenner, Jack. "Butcher's Crossing: The Husks and Shells of Exploitation." *Western American Literature* (February 1973): 243–259.

Hartt, Julian. "Two Historical Novels." *Virginia Quarterly Review* (Summer 1973): 450–458.

Heilman, Robert B. "Butcher's Crossing." *Partisan Review* 28, no. 2 (March–April 1961): 286–297.

———. "The Western Theme: Exploiters and Explorer." *Partisan Review* (March–April 1962): 286–297.

Hobson, Geary. "Reassessing John Williams' *Stoner*: Twelve Years After." *New America* 3, no. 2 (1977).

Howe, Irving. "The Virtues of Failure." *New Republic* (February 12, 1966): 19–20.

Leo, John. "A Portrait Shaded toward the Stoic." (Review/discussion of *Augustus*.) *New York Times Book Review* (April 8, 1973): 30.

Nelson, Robert J. "Accounts of Mutual Acquaintances to a Group of Friends: The Fiction of John Williams." *Denver Quarterly* (Winter 1973): 13–36.

Snow, C. P. "Good Man and Foes." *Financial Times* (London), May 24, 1973.

Stamper, Major Rex. "John Williams: An Introduction to the Major Novels." *Mississippi Review* 3, no. 1 (1974): 89–98.

Stark, John. "The Novels of John Williams." *Hollins Critic* 17, no. 4 (October 1980). (List of books by Williams, 12–13, is inaccurate.)

Walsh, George. "John Williams." In *Twentieth Century Western Writers*, ed. James Vinson. Detroit: Gale Research, 1982, 815–816.

Werner, Craig. "John Williams." *Dictionary of Literary Biography*. Detroit: Gale Research Co., 1980), 371–377.

Of Additional Interest

Book World (January 27, 1974): 4.

Book World 9 (September 16, 1973): 13.

Breslin, John B. "Year of the Big Book—NBA 1973." *America* 128 (May 5, 1973): 408–409.

Pace, Eric. "The National Book Award in Fiction: A Curious Case." *New York Times Book Review* (May 6, 1972): 16–17.

———. "Two Book Awards Split for the First Time." *New York Times*, April 11, 1973, 38.

Interviews

"Artist of Diversity." *Dust* (Winter 1966).

"John Williams." *Denver Quarterly* 20, no. 3 (Winter 1986).

Wakefield, Dan. "John Williams, Plain Writer." *Ploughshares* 7, nos. 3–4 (Fall/ Winter 1981): 9–22.

Index

Page numbers in italics refer to photographs.

Aaron, Daniel: *The Americanist*, 140
Aiken, Conrad, 23, 36, 41
Ajijic, Mexico, 93, 98, 105–107, 114–115, 138, 161–162, 186, 212–215
alcoholism, 216–218, 241, 243, 281n27
Aldridge, John, *132*
Algren, Nelson, 101
Als, Hilton, 170
American Scholar, 62, 119
Ammaniti, Niccolò, 252
Anchor Books, 147–149, 154–155, 158
Appleyard, Bryan, 254
Antioch Review, 93, 211
Arendt, Hannah, 166
Aristotle, 89
Arizona Quarterly, 93
Asimov, Isaac, 106
Association of Writers & Writing Programs (AWP), 101
Aswell, Edward, 45, 48 262n9

Augustus (Williams): inspiration for, 151–152; National Book Award for, viii, 223–224, 226–227, 229, 232–233, 242, 249, 281n1; submission and publication of, 217–219, 228; synopsis of, 193–194; writing of, 159–160, 192–197, 200, 211, 214

Baldwin, James: *Going to Meet the Man*, 249
Barnes, Julian, 254, 279n44
Barth, John, 229; *Chimera*, 223–224, 226; Williams' first meeting with, 226–227
Bassing, Ellen, 107–108; *Where's Annie?*, 107, 269n20
Bellow, Saul, 166; *Herzog*, 249
Berger, Thomas: *Little Big Man*, 105
Berryman, John, 145
Bertinetti, Roberto, 252
Bignardi, Irene, 252
Bishop, Elizabeth, 41, 145
Blake, Eunice, *132*

Borges, Jorge Luis, 229
Bourjaily, Vance, 114
Bowers, Edgar, 78
Brague, Harry, 92, 116, 267n11
Brandeis University, 119, 227–229
Bread Loaf Writers Conference, *132*,
    187–190, 192, 198, 200–203, 207,
    213–214, 216, 235, 242, 247
Brecht, Bertolt, 91
Brogan, Louise, 65
Brooks, Cleanth, 52, 156
Brooks, Gwendolyn, 145
Brower, Brock, *132*, 201; *The Late
    Great Creature*, 227
Browne, Thomas: *Hydriotaphia,
    Urn Burial*, 90
"Buffalo Bill" Cody, 102–103
Buffalo Bill's Wild West, 102–103,
    269n9
buffalo hunting, viii, 13, 66, 104,
    109–110, 117, 120–121, *131*, 195, 249
Burroughs, Edgar Rice, 10
Burroughs, William S., 166, 263n10
Butcher's Crossing (Williams), viii, 10,
    13, 66, *130*, *131*, 141, 143, 193, 195;
    final title decision about, 117–120;
    New York Times review of, as a
    western, 120–122, 142, 145, 159,
    213, 232; reprintings of, 218–219,
    243; submission and publication
    of, 112–120; synopsis of, 109–110;
    writing of (working title *The Naked
    World*), 104–105, 108, 110, 113–120
Butler, Frank, 102

Candido, Anne Marie, vii–viii
Carruth, Hayden, 82–83
Carson, Rachel: *Silent Spring*, 112, 150
Cather, Willa, 18, 89; *My Antonia*, 108;
    O, Pioneers!, 108; "Paul's Case," 23;
    The Professor's House, 157
Cefelli, Edward M., 244
Chapman, Gerald, 101–103, 139–140,
    148, 194, 228

Charles Scribner's and Sons, 92, 116,
    146
Chiang Kai-shek, 30
Ciardi, John, ix, *132*, 188–190, 200,
    201–202, 207, 216, 230, 235, 239,
    241, 244
Clark, James, 245
Clark, Walter van Tilburg, 101, 105
Clarksville, Texas, 4–7, 47, 120, *124*
Cody, William Frederick "Buffalo Bill,"
    102–103
Cogswell, Theodore, 106, 214–215, 246,
    270n20
Coleman, Marjorie, 21, 22
Collin, Frances, 232, 246, 270n4
Colman, Ronald: in *Lost Horizon*, 19;
    in *Prisoner of Zenda*, 19; in *A Tale of
    Two Cities*, 16–18; Williams' emula-
    tion of, 19, 36, *125*, 142, 173, 209
Connell, Evan S., 223
Coover, Robert, 166
Crane, Stephen: "The Blue Hotel," 7;
    Williams' admiration for, 108, 119
Crawford, Judith, 250–251
Crawford Doyle Booksellers (New York
    City), 250–251
Creeley, Robert, 63, 143
Crews, Harry, 201
Cunningham, James Vincent (J. V.),
    78, 119, *131*, 206, 219, 228; "For
    My Contemporaries," 81; marriage
    of, 168; Williams' essay on, 82–83;
    Winters Circle and, 79–83; *Woe
    or Wonder: The Emotional Effect
    of Shakespearean Tragedy*, 83–84
Curtis Publishing, 218
Custer, George Armstrong, 103

Davis, Catherine, 78
DeBoer-Rolloff, Carol, 225, 281n8
Denver Quarterly, 186, 192, 206, 227,
    231, 274n5, 284n28
Dickstein, Morris, 250, 251
Doe, Philip, 281n7

Donne, John, 77, 145
Doubleday, 118, 147, 154–155
Doyle, John, 250–251
Drayton, Michael, 95
du Maurier, Daphne: *The Glass Blowers*, 150

Eakins, Thomas, 251
Eliot, T. S., 78, 229
Elizabethans, 87, 94–96, 117, 146–148
Ellis, Bret Easton, 254
Ellison, Harlan, 106, 263n10, 273n6
Emerson, Ralph Waldo, 77, 108, 206; *Butcher's Crossing* and, 10, *131*; on *Hydriotaphia, Urn Burial* (Browne), 90; "Threnody," 90
Empson, William, 78
Engle, Paul, 114, 122
Epstein, Seymour, *132*, 189, 192–193, 203, 231–233; *Leah*, 189
Esquire, 117, 211, 244
Expósito, Tito, 252

Fagles, Robert, 218
Fairchild, A. H. R., 86, 87–90, 173, 175
Farrell, James T., 101
Faulkner, William, 18, 44, 89, 103, 217
Fazi, Elido, 252
Fazi Editore, 252, 255
Fielder, Leslie A., 223
Fields, Kenneth, 73, 74
First World War. *See* World War I
Fles, Barthold, 91–93
Fortunato, Mario, 252
Frank, Edwin, 251, 254–255
Friedan, Betty: *The Feminine Mystique*, 113
Frost, Robert, 41, 188, 190, 201

Gage, Phineas, 275n38
Gascoigne, George, 77
Gass, William, 223
Gavalda, Anna, 251–252

Gibbs, Barbara: "Accusatory Poem," 82, 168, 274n15
Ginzburg, Harold, 167
Ginzburg, Thomas, 167, 218, 226
Gold, Herbert, 65
Googe, Barnabe, 77
Gordon, Caroline, 65
Goya, Francisco, 235
G. P. Putnam, 93
Grass, Günter, 206; *The Tin Drum*, 150
Gray, Thomas, 76
Great Depression, 13–14, 22–23, 194, 203
Greenberg, Joanne, *134*, 197, 210, 224, 230; *I Never Promised You a Rose Garden*, 165
Greville, Fulke (1st Baron Brooke), 77; *The Life of the Renowned Philip Sidney*, 95; Williams' dissertation on, 94–95, 98, 117, 119, 146, 157
Grey, Zane: *Riders of the Purple Sage*, 10; Williams' childhood reading of, 10
Gunn, Thom, 78
Guthrie, A. B., Jr.: *The Big Sky*, 105, 122

Haldeman-Julius, Emanuel, 52, 263n10
Haley, Alex: *The Autobiography of Malcolm X*, 249
Hall, Donald, 78
Halls, Oakley: *Warlock*, 105
Hamlin, Florence, 98, 99
Hamlin, William, 98
Harcourt Brace, 54, 146
Hardin, John G., 3
Hardin Junior College, 3, 20–21, 55, *125*
Harris, Mark, 73–74, 79; *Bang the Drum Slowly*, 73
Harrison, John, vii
Hart, Al, 153–154
Heller, Steve, 282n28, 283n16

Hemingway, Ernest, 34, 41, 217, 267n11; *Death in the Afternoon*, 98–99

Herodotus, 76

Hilton, James: *Lost Horizon*, 19, 120

Holmes, John Clellon, 243; *Go*, 243

Homer: *Iliad*, 218

Homer: *Odyssey*, 105, 218

Hope, Anthony: *Prisoner of Zenda*, 19

Howe, Irving, 80, 168, 178, 192

Hudson Review, 82

Hunt, Morton M., 110–111, 113, 115, 270n27

Hurston, Zora Neale, 103

Hyman, Stanley Edgar, 74, 77

Ibsen, Henrik: *Pillars of Society*, 24

Inglis, Fred, 139, 234–235, 238

Iowa Writers' Workshop, 114, 122

James, Henry, 176

Jewell, Amelia (née Walker; Williams' mother), 4–5, 8–10, 14, 23, 47, *123*

Jewell, J. E. (Williams' father), 5–8, 11, *124*

Johnson, Pyke, 147, 149, 154, 156, 158, 163, 273n13

Jonson, Ben, 77, 95

Jordan, Satyavati C., 37

Joyce, James, 167; *Ulysses*, 41, 160

Justice, Donald, 78

Kazin, Alfred, 145

Kees, Weldon, 65

Kennedy, X. J., *132*

Kent, Rockwell, 166

Kernan, Alvin B., 276n41

Kerr, Baine, 231, 236–237, 245, 275n20

Kesey, Ken, 166; *One Flew over the Cuckoo's Nest*, 206

Key West, Florida, 40–46, 233–238, 240, 241–242, 245, 246; Writer's Compound (Windsor Lane), 235, 283n6

Kumin, Maxine, 201

Lawrence, D. H., 78, 100; *Lady Chatterley's Lover*, 20; *The Plumed Serpent*, 106

Lawrence, Seymour, 214

Leavenworth, James, 141–142

Leavis, F. R., 78

Lebowski Publishers, 253–254

Lederer, William, *132*

Le Dilettante, 252

Levine, Philip, 78

Lewis, C. S., 95

Lewis, Janet, ix, 65, 73–75, 96, 108, 118–119, 147, 236; *The Ghost of Monsieur Scarron*, 118; marriage of, to Winters, ix, 74–75, 266n5; *The Wife of Martin Guerre*, 73

Lewis, Sinclair, 217

Liberty, 23

Little, Brown and Company, 118, 154

Little Blue Books, 52, 263n10

Lomax, Hollis N., 90, 172–176

London, Jack: *Call of the Wild*, 108

Lowell, Robert, 78, 265–266n4

Lukács, György, 229

MacLeish, Archibald, 65

Macmillan, 115–118, 120–122, 145–147, 154, 271n19

Mademoiselle, 65–66, 67

Mailer, Norman, 106, 206

male chauvinism, 140

Manfred, Frederick, 191

Mann, Heinrich, 91

Marsh, George Rae (née Williams; Williams' half-sister), 60, 67, *128*, 214–215, 246; acting career of, 40; birth and childhood of, 9, 11, 15, 21, 23; and death of brother, 247; marriage of, to "Butch" Marsh, 68–69, 93, 98, 106–107, 114, 137–138, 161–162, 186, 211–213; marriage of, to Ted Cogswell, 215–216; writing career of, 269–270n20

Marsh, Willard "Butch," *128*; *Beachhead in Bohemia*, 199, 212; education of, 114, 137; grave of, 213; illness and death of, 211–213; marriage of, to George Rae, 68–70, 79, 93, 98–99, 105–108, 114, 137–138, 161–162, 186, 211–212; teaching career of, 161, 198–199, 211–212; *A Week with No Friday*, 108, 162, 178, 186, 198

Martin, Edward Alexander, *132*

Maugham, Somerset: *The Razor's Edge*, 106

McCann, Colum, 251–252

McCarthy, Cormac, 105

McEwan, Ian, 254

McGinley, Phyllis, 166

McGrath, Thomas, 65

McHugh, Heather, 156

McIntosh, Peggy, 204–205

McMahon, J. D., 6–7

McMurty, Larry: *Horseman, Pass By*, 105

Melville, Herman: *The Confidence Man*, 143

Middlebury College, 188, 202, 207, 216

Miller, Henry, 65

Milton, John, 82, 88

Missouri Writers' Workshop, 96, 106

Mitford, Jessica, 91, 251

Moore, Marianne, 166

moral identity, 176, 275n38

Mumford, Lewis: *The Golden Day*, 103

Munro, Roxie, 239

Munroe, Harriet, 75–76

Naked World, The (Williams). See *Butcher's Crossing* (Williams)

Nashe, Thomas, 77

National Book Award, viii, 223–224, 226–227, 229, 232–233, 242, 244, 249, 281n1

National Book Committee, 224

Nelson, Clara, 254

New Criticism, 52, 76, 145, 202, 263n11, 268n3

New Directions, 146

New Republic, 91, 178–179, 192

Newsom, Jack, 21, 22, 26, 38, 40, 46, 260n16

New Yorker, 206

New York Review of Books, 251, 254–255

Nims, John Frederick, *132*

Nin, Anaïs, 65, 93

Nothing But the Night (Williams), 91, 95, 116, 170, 219, 227; Butch's critique of, 60–62; submission and publication of, 45, 48–50, 54, 59–61; synopsis of, 41–44; writing of, 41

Nye, Nelson C., 121–122

Oakley, Annie, 102

O'Neill, Eugene, 217; *Long Day's Journey into Night*, 217

Pack, Robert, *132*, 201, 216

Pawlowski, Robert, 179

Peden, William, 146

Percy, Walker, 223

Peterson, Margaret, 78

Petrarchan School of poetry, 76–77, 149

Pinkerton, Helen, 78

Pinsky, Robert, 78

Ploughshares, 235, 250

Poetry, 75–76, 82, 97, 147

Poirier, Richard, 229

Popular Books, 219

Porter, Katherine Anne, 101, 103

Proust, Marcel, 23, 36, 41, 196

Pynchon, Thomas, 166–167, 229

Raleigh, Walter, 77

Ramsay, Robert L., 86–89, 96, 173, 175

Rexroth, Kenneth, 77

Richards, I. A., 78
Richardson, Elizabeth, 138
Richardson, Robert D., 138–139, 203–205
Robbe-Grillet, Alain, 229
Rodell, Marie (Williams' agent), 111–121, 195, 209, 213–214, 217–219, 226, 228; death of, 232; *Stoner*'s publication and, 144–145, 147–150, 153–154, 160, 163–164, 168, 177
Roethke, Theodore, 145
Romanticism, 77–78, 103, 109, 173
Romantic poetry, 65–66, 75, 90, 94, 174–175
Roosevelt, Franklin Delano, 13–14; and the New Deal, 14, 22

Salinger, J. D.: *Raise High the Roof Beam, Carpenters and Seymour: An Introduction*, 150
Sandoz, Marie: *Old Jules*, 53
Sassoon, Siegfried, 166
Saturday Evening Post, 23, 114–115, 211
Saturday Evening Post Stories 1954, 114
Scott, Cecil, 115–120, 122, 145–147, 153–154
Scribner's. *See* Charles Scribner's and Sons
Second World War. *See* World War II
Sevareid, Eric, 31
Sewanee Review, 97
Sheckley, Robert, 106
Shepard, Harwell V. "Shep," 25, 29
Sidney, Philip, 77, 95
Silverberg, Robert, 106
Sinclair, Upton, 94
Sitting Bull, 269n9
Sloane, William M., *132*, 183, 187, 201
Smart, George K. "Ken," 44–45, 46, 48–49, 54–55, 59, 78, 234, 262nn6–7
Smith, Annie Laurie (Williams' eighth-grade English teacher), 18

Smith, Avalon "Lonnie" (Williams' third wife), 59, 70, *129*
Smith, Corlies M. "Cork," 167–168, 177–179, 195, 213, 217–219, 226, 239
Smith College, 192, 199–200
Snow, C. P., 250
Solomon, Barbara Probst: *The Beat of Life*, 167
Sontag, Susan, 206
Southern Review, 52
Spenser, Edmund, 77
Spicy Adventure, 20
Spicy Detective, 20, 94
Spicy Mystery, 20
Spillane, Mickey: *I, the Jury*, 95
Stanford University, 74, 80–81, 206, 231, 236; Merry Pranksters and, 206
Stapleton, Benjamin F., 56
Stegner, Wallace, ix, 206
Steinbeck, John, 18, 89, 167, 217
Stephens, Alan, 56, 78, 96–98
Stevens, Wallace, 41, 65
Stewart, Mary: *The Moon-Spinners*, 150
stoicism, 78, 83, 96
Stoner (Williams), xiii, 9, 57, 66, 85–86, 89–91, *129*, *131*; autographing party for, 177–178; Dutch edition of, 253–254; existentialism of, 255; French edition of, 252; as *New York Review of Books* Classics imprint, 251; as "the perfect novel," 250, 251; reprintings of, 214, 243, 251; review of, by Irving Howe, 178–179, 192; similarities between Williams and title character of, 279n44; submission and publication of, 163–164, 177–178; synopsis of, 168–177; translations and international editions of, 252–254; as Waterstones Book of the Year, 254; working title, *A Matter of Light*, for, 144, 149–150, 153–154, 163–164;

working title, *A Matter of Love*,
for, 163, 168, 177; writing of, 144,
149–150, 153–154, 160
Strode, Hudson, 45, 234
Swallow, Alan, 47, 50–54, 98, 100–103,
149, 156, 177, 183–184; death of,
191; early years of, 51–52; education
of, 52; first published book of, 53;
influence of Little Blue Books on,
52; marriage of, to Mae, 52; publishing principles of, 53–54
Swallow, Mae (née Elder), 52–54, 79,
183, 191
Swallow Press, 49, 53–54, 58–59,
64–65, 69–70, 73–74, 79, 84, 90–91,
94, 96–97, 183–184, 191, 265n1,
282n14

Tale of Two Cities, A (film), 16–18, *125*
Tate, Allen, 52, 65, 78, 268n3; *On the
Limits of Poetry*, 73
Tiger's Eye, The, 45
Trilling, Lionel, 78, 166, 229
Tuchman, Barbara, 166
Turberville, George, 77

University of Denver: *Denver Quarterly*, 186, 192, 206, 227, 231,
274n5, 284n28; Williams as
professor at, 98–101, 119, 130, 133,
138–139, 183–184, 190, 202–206,
228–234; Williams as student at,
ix, 55–59
University of Missouri: Missouri
Writers' Workshop, 96, 106; and
Ramsay-Fairchild feud, 86–90, 96,
173, 175
Upson, William Hazlett, *132*

van Doren, Mark, 65
van Gelderen, Oscar, 253
Viking Press, 116, 146, 166–167, 177,
214, 218, 226, 227, 239, 251,
274n10, 282n14

Vonnegut, Kurt, 106, 206, 267n11; *God
Bless You, Mr. Rosewater*, 269n18

Wakefield, Dan, *132*, 189–190, 200–
201, 213–214, 216–217, 228, 235,
238, 250; *Revolt in the South*, 189
Walker, Amelia (Williams' mother).
See Jewell, Amelia (née Walker;
Williams' mother)
Walker, Elbert G. (Williams' grand-
father), 4
Walker, Laura Belle (née Lee; Williams'
grandmother), 4
Walter, Bruno, 91
Warren, Robert Penn, 52; *All the King's
Men*, 107
Webster, Donovan, 261n12
West, Morris L.: *The Shoes of the
Fisherman*, 150
West, Ray B., 96, 97
Western Review, 96, 97
Westward Movement, 103–105
Whole Earth Catalog, 223–224
Wichita Falls, 5–24, 65, 194, 229;
"The Corner," *124*; Hardin Junior
College, 3, 20–21, 55, *125*; Newby-
McMahon Building, 6–7; Texas oil
boom, 5–6; Wichita Players, 24
Wilder, Thornton: *The Ides of March*,
219; *Our Town*, 22
Williams, Alyeene Rosida (née Bryan;
Williams' first wife): divorce of,
from Williams, 35, 40; marriage of,
to Williams, 26–30
Williams, Avalon "Lonnie" (née Smith;
Williams' third wife): *Broken
Landscape* dedicated to, 70; divorce
of, from Williams, 199–200, 208;
education of, 83, 90; first meeting
of, with Williams, 59; marriage of,
to Williams, 84, 85, 93, 98–99, 105,
119, 140–141, 143, 148–149, 153, 161,
185–186, 195, 274n25, 280n4
Williams, George Clinton, 8

Williams, George Rae. *See* Marsh, George Rae (née Williams; Williams' half-sister)

Williams, John: birth of, 5; at Brandeis (visiting professor), 227–229; at Bread Loaf, *132*, 198, 200–203, 207, 213–214, 216, 235, 242, 247; and "Celebration of John Williams," 244–245; composition notebooks of, 36–37, 40; courses taught at Brandeis by, 229; death of, 247; dissertation of, on Greville, 94–95, 98, 117, 119, 146, 157; as editor at *Denver Quarterly*, 186, 192, 206, 227, 231, 274n5; as editor at Swallow Press, 64–65; emulation of Ronald Colman by, 19, 36, 125, 142, 173, 209; endowed chair of, 233; enlistment of, in Army Air Corps, 28–30; European trip of, 195–198; final illness of, 237–240, 245, 247; Guggenheim Foundation application of, 118–119, 122; Guggenheim Foundation Fellowship of, 239–240; at Hardin Junior College, 20–21, 55, *125*; in high school, 18–20; and hog butchering with grandfather, 12–13; in India, 30–36; influence of *A Tale of Two Cities* (film) on, 16–18; in junior high school, 15–18; in Key West, 40–46, 233–246; as lecturer at Berkeley, 64; Lovelace Bookstore after-school job of, 3, 20, 23; marriage of, to Alyeene, 26–27, 29–30, 35, 40; marriage of, to Lonnie, 84, 85, 93, 98–99, 105, 119, 140–141, 143, 148–149, 153, 161, 185–186, 195, 274n25, 280n4; marriage of, to Nancy, 209, 211, 214–215, 228–229, 233–238, 242–244, 247; marriage of, to Yvonne, 55–56, 58–59, 62–64, 67–70; military service of, 28–38; with mother, *123*; and mother's

death and illness, 45–48; and Oxford University summer session, 148–162; as parent and grandparent, 161, 280n4, 283n1; personal identity of, 10–12, 15–16; portraits of, 35–36, *125*, *126*; as radio announcer at KRRV and KDNT (as "Jon Williams"), 24–27, 39, 125; as radio announcer at WKWF, 38, 40–46; relationship of, with George Rae, 215; as Smith College writer-in-residence, 192, 199–201; and staging of *Our Town* on KWFT, 22; and Texas Institute of Letters award for fiction, 229; at University of Arkansas (guest lecturer), 242; at University of Denver (professor), 98–101, 119, *130*, *133*, 138–139, 183–184, 190, 202–206, 228–234; at University of Denver (student), ix, 55–56; and Wichita Players performance, 24; *Wichita Times Record* student feature piece on, 18–19; "Winters affair" and, 153, 154–159, 236, 273n10, 273n13

—works of: *The Broken Landscape* (poetry collection), 70; *Dr. Cooper Speaking* (radio drama), 21, 24; "Drouth" (poem), 62; *English Renaissance Poetry* (edited anthology), 146–149, 154, 159, 177, 246; "J. V. Cunningham: The Major and the Minor" (critical essay), 82–83; "The Lovers" (poem), 70; "Memories: Texas, 1932" (poem), 48; *The Necessary Life* (poetry collection), 177; "An Old Actor to His Audience" (poem), 221–222; *The Shape of the Air* (poetry collection), 144, 164; *The Sleep of Reason* (unfinished novel), 33, 235–236, 239–240, 245–246; *Splendid in Ashes* (unpublished novel), 90–92, 95, 168; "The Summer" (short story),

65–67. See also *Augustus*; *Butcher's Crossing*; *Nothing But the Night*; *Stoner*

Williams, Jonathan (Williams' son), 140, 161, 195, 199–201, 280n4, 283n1

Williams, Katherine (Williams' daughter), 93, 98, 161, 194–195, 209, 246, 277n10

Williams, Miller, 201, 213, 242, 247

Williams, Nancy Ann Leavenworth (née Gardner; Williams' fourth wife), ix, *133*, 158–159, 161, 166, 183, 185, 187, 200, 251; education of, 141–144; first meeting of, with Williams, 141–144; marriage of, to Williams, 209, 211, 214–215, 228–229, 233–238, 242–244, 247

Williams, Pamela (Williams' daughter), 105, 161, 195, 209

Williams, Tennessee, 41, 103; *A Streetcar Named Desire*, 106

Williams, William Carlos, 145

Williams, Yvonne Elyce. *See* Woolf, Yvonne Stone (née Williams)

Willis, T. G., 20

Wills, Garry, 223

Wimsatt, William Kurtz, 156

Winters, Yvor, ix, 51, 168, 177, 275–276n41; "The Anatomy of Nonsense," 94; *Collected Poems*, 96–98; *In Defense of Reason*, 65, 77, 94–95, 149; *Forms of Discovery*, 158; *The Immobile Wind*, 75; influence of, on Williams, 94–98, 145–147; *The Magpie's Shadow*, 75; marriage of, to Janet Lewis, ix, 74–75, 266n5; as moral figure for students, 266n14; "On a View of Pasadena from the Hills," 76; Williams and ("Winters affair"), 153, 154–159, 236, 273n10, 273n13

Winters Circle, 74–84, 95, 147

Wister, Owen: *The Virginian*, 53–54

Wolfe, Thomas, 45; influence of, on Williams, 18–19, 23, 41; *Look Homeward, Angel*, 18, 19

Wolfe, Tom: *The Electric Kool-Aid Acid Test*, 206

Woolf, Douglas, 62–64; marriage of, to Yvonne, *127*, 240; *Wall to Wall*, 63, 64, 241, 264n10

Woolf, Leonard, 62

Woolf, Virginia, 62; *Mrs. Dalloway*, 160

Woolf, Yvonne Stone (née Williams), 50, *127*, 240–241; divorce from Williams, 69–70; marriage to Williams, 55–56, 58–59, 62–64

Wordsworth, William, 76, 145

World War I, 28–29, 86; George Williams and, 8, 29; *Stoner* and, 168

World War II, 56, 262n23; and attack on Pearl Harbor, 28; and Bread Loaf, 203; and Hump-fliers, 31–34, *126*, 261n12; and John Williams, 29–38, 151–152, 239; and Leonard Woolf, 62–63; and *The Sleep of Reason*, 235; and Ted Cogswell, 106

W. W. Norton, 116

Wyatt, Thomas, 77, 94, 149, 157, 158; "They Flee from Me," 94

Yacht, Marc, 262n6

Yale Review, 115, 211

Yardley, Jonathan, 223–224

Yates, Richard, 244–245, 278n25, 284n32; *The Easter Parade*, 244; *Revolutionary Road*, 244

Yourcenar, Marguerite: *Memoirs of Hadrian*, 196

Zaranka, William, 281n7

Charles J. Shields is the author of *Mockingbird: A Portrait of Harper Lee*, a *New York Times* best seller. His young adult biography of Harper Lee, *I Am Scout*, was chosen an ALA Best Book for Young Adults. In 2011, Shields published *And So It Goes: Kurt Vonnegut, A Life*, a *New York Times* and *Washington Post* Notable Nonfiction Book of the Year.

CPSIA information can be obtained
at www.ICGtesting.com
Printed in the USA
FSHW020631190620

9 781477 320105